OXFORD TEXTUAL PERSPECTIVES

Turn-Taking in Shakespeare

T0369582

GENERAL EDITORS

Elaine Treharne   Greg Walker

Turn-Taking in Shakespeare

OLIVER MORGAN

OXFORD

UNIVERSITY PRESS

OXFORD

UNIVERSITY PRESS

Great Clarendon Street, Oxford, OX2 6DP,
United Kingdom

Oxford University Press is a department of the University of Oxford.
It furthers the University's objective of excellence in research, scholarship,
and education by publishing worldwide. Oxford is a registered trade mark of
Oxford University Press in the UK and in certain other countries

First Edition published in 2019

Impression: 1

Published in the United States of America by Oxford University Press
198 Madison Avenue, New York, NY 10016, United States of America

British Library Cataloguing in Publication Data

Data available

Library of Congress Control Number: 2019937222

ISBN 978–0–19–883635–3 (Hbk.)
ISBN 978–0–19–883636–0 (Pbk.)

Printed and bound by
CPI Group (UK) Ltd, Croydon, CR0 4YY

SERIES EDITORS' PREFACE

Oxford Textual Perspectives is a new series of informative and provocative studies focused upon texts (conceived of in the broadest sense of that term) and the technologies, cultures, and communities that produce, inform, and receive them. It provides fresh interpretations of fundamental works, images, and artefacts and of the vital and challenging issues emerging in English literary studies. By engaging with the contexts and materiality of the text—its production, transmission, and reception history—and by frequently testing and exploring the boundaries of the notions of text and meaning themselves, the volumes in the series question conventional frameworks and provide innovative interpretations of both canonical and less well-known works. These books will offer new perspectives, and challenge familiar ones, both on and through texts and textual communities. While they focus on specific authors, periods, and issues, they nonetheless scan wider horizons, addressing themes and provoking questions that have a more general application to literary studies and cultural history as a whole. Each is designed to be as accessible to the non-specialist reader as it is fresh and rewarding for the specialist, combining an informative orientation in a landscape with detailed analysis of the territory and suggestions for further travel.

Elaine Treharne and *Greg Walker*

For my wife

ACKNOWLEDGEMENTS

Like me, this book has taken the scenic route. Many kind strangers have helped it on its way, only a few of whom can be acknowledged here. For all, our thanks.

More specifically, I am grateful to two schools—St Bede's Senior School in Upper Dicker and the International School of Geneva at La Grande Boissière—for letting me be part-time when they would rather I had been full-. Without their flexibility I would probably still be teaching, full-time, at one or other of them. I am also grateful to two universities—the University of Sussex, where my work on turn-taking began, and the University of Geneva, where it came to fruition. I arrived in Switzerland as an academic refugee. I will leave as the author of this monograph.

For advice, encouragement, proofreading, forbearance, and distraction, I am grateful to Maggie Andrews, Guillemette Bolens, Naomi Booth, Sophia Booth, Sarah Brazil, David Cheshire, Brian Cummings, Mark D'Arcy, Matthew Dimmock, Raphael Lyne, Lynne Magnusson, Roberta Piazza, Sameer Rahim, and Margaret Tudeau-Clayton. For persuading Oxford University Press to publish my work, I am grateful to the series editors, Elaine Treharne and Greg Walker, and to three anonymous reviewers. For giving ear to their persuasions, I am grateful to Oxford University Press. For guiding me through the process, I am grateful to Catherine Owen and Aimee Wright. For his patient copy-editing, to Wade Guyitt.

Special thanks are due to Lukas Erne, my doctoral supervisor, without whom I would never have had a monograph to publish. Likewise to my family, whose inability to take turns in conversation remains a rich source of inspiration and example. My six niblings (Lucia, Erin, Edu, Florence, Stanley, and Remi) were no help at all but will enjoy seeing their names in a book.

My greatest debt is to Eric Griffiths, who taught me to hear the printed voice.

CONTENTS

LIST OF ILLUSTRATIONS

ABBREVIATIONS

ESTC   *English Short Title Catalogue* (British Library), http://estc.bl.uk/.

Folio, F   *Mr. VVilliam Shakespeares Comedies, Histories, & Tragedies* (London: Isaac Iaggard and Ed. Blount, 1623).

NOS   *The Complete Works: Modern Critical Edition*, ed. by Gary Taylor, Gabriel Egan, John Jowett, and Terri Bourus, The New Oxford Shakespeare (Oxford: Oxford University Press, 2017). All quotations from Shakespeare are from this edition unless otherwise stated.

ODNB   *Oxford Dictionary of National Biography* (Oxford University Press), http://www.oxforddnb.com/.

OED   *Oxford English Dictionary Online* (Oxford University Press), http://www.oed.com/.

OLD   *Oxford Latin Dictionary*, ed. by P. G. W. Glare, 2nd edn, 2 vols (Oxford: Oxford University Press, 2012).

Q1, Q2   First quarto, second quarto.

TLN   Through-line numbers as given in *The First Folio of Shakespeare: The Norton Facsimile*, ed. by Charlton Hinman, 2nd edn (New York: Norton, 1996).

Introduction

Charles Dickens had a genius for conversational abstraction. Take Mr and Mrs Tibbs, for example, proprietors of 'The Boarding-House' in one of his earliest stories:

> Mrs. Tibbs was always talking. Mr. Tibbs rarely spoke; but if it were at any time possible to put in a word, just when he should have said nothing at all, he did it. Mrs. Tibbs detested long stories, and Mr. Tibbs had one, the conclusion of which had never been heard by his most intimate friends. It always began, 'I recollect when I was in the volunteer corps, in eighteen hundred and six,'—but as he spoke very slowly and softly, and his better half very quickly and loudly, he rarely got beyond the introductory sentence.[1]

It tells us something about this couple that Mr Tibbs served in the volunteer corps—an early forerunner of the Territorial Army. It tells us something that he did so in 1806—some thirty years before 'The Boarding-House' was published, when the Napoleonic threat was at its height. It tells us something, too, that he is keen to mention these facts in company. But the particular story that Mr Tibbs is unable to finish tells us little in comparison with the fact that he is unable to finish it. More important than the content of the Tibbses' conversation is the pattern into which it habitually falls. Rather than provide us with a specimen of their talk, Dickens begins by sketching it in the abstract.

He is able to do so because whenever people talk to one another there are at least two things going on at once. First, and most obviously, there

---

[1] Charles Dickens, *Sketches by 'Boz': Illustrative of Every-Day Life and Every-Day People*, 2 vols (London: John Macrone, 1836), I, pp. 148–9.

is an exchange of speech. Second, and slightly less obviously, there is a negotiation about how that exchange is organized—about whose turn it is to talk at any given moment. These two things are not separate—it is largely through speech that opportunities to speak are apportioned—but they are separable, as the example from 'The Boarding-House' shows. What I am calling the 'shape' of a conversation is the outcome of this negotiation. It is a record of who spoke when, for how long, and to whom. It matters because it tells us how the parties conducted themselves in the joint task of managing the conversational floor, what sort of etiquette seems to have been in operation when they did so, the social role taken by each of them, and where, if at all, negotiations may have heated up or broken down. Dickens is extremely alert to the significance of this second, organizational, level of conversational activity. His dialogue is accompanied by a running commentary on how the characters manage the exchange of turns at talk. He often introduces a character, as he introduces the Tibbses, with a brief sketch of their interactional habits—by providing the reader with a map, as it were, with which to navigate their contributions to the dialogue.

The reader of Shakespeare gets no such assistance. Shakespearean drama has no narrator and very few stage directions. If the Tibbses were minor characters in *Hamlet*, we would simply have to notice that Mr Tibbs always manages to speak 'just when he should have said nothing at all' and that Mrs Tibbs always cuts him off. In the case of the Tibbses, this would not be difficult. Their mode of interacting has all the clarity of caricature—together they form a kind of conversational grotesque, like a pigmy married to a giant. But the principle holds for Shakespeare's own characters, in ways that are often more subtle. When and how much they speak, what prompts or prevents them from doing so, to whom, in what circumstances, and why—how they conduct themselves, that is, in the ongoing negotiation that structures any exchange of speech—these are things that we are shown but not told. They are just as important, however, to an understanding of Hamlet's relationship with Gertrude, or of Lear's relationships with his daughters, as they are to an understanding of the relationship between Mr and Mrs Tibbs. The difference is that Dickens' dialogue is self-interpreting in this respect, while Shakespeare's awaits interpretation.

What we might expect, then, given the abundance of writing on Shakespeare, is a rich history of critical engagement with the patterning of his dialogue. No such history exists. Shakespeare's brilliance as a poet and a playwright has long overshadowed his brilliance as a writer of dialogue—his extraordinary grasp of what Erving Goffman has called the 'traffic rules' of interaction.[2] As Lynne Magnusson has pointed out, 'it seems odd that we have so few shared terms or concepts to help us, as theatre-goers, readers or actors, to understand and talk about dialogue as opposed to single-voiced poems or speeches'.[3] This is true of dialogue in general, and it is true, in particular, of dialogical form. Most students of literature encounter the term 'stichomythia' at school, but this is the only such term they encounter. It is as if our ability to describe poetic form were restricted to recognizing the presence or absence of heroic couplets.

The aim of this book is to put that right—to do for Shakespeare's dialogue what Dickens does for his own: to pay attention, that is, to its patterns and shapes and contours, and to map and abstract and explain them. At the heart of the project lies a simple act of redescription. That part of the dramatic text which has traditionally been referred to as a 'speech'—the string of words which follows a character's name and which we therefore understand to be spoken by that character—I propose to rechristen a 'turn at talk'. Implicit in this minor terminological shift is a major shift of perspective. Instead of reading Shakespearean dialogue as a series of rhetorical set-pieces—lengthy, poetic, persuasive, a treasure-trove for auditioning actors and aspiring anthologists—it encourages us to read it *as* dialogue. Adopting the turn as the basic unit of dialogical analysis foregrounds the negotiated, interactive quality of dramatic language. It makes visible that second, less obvious, level of communicative activity that gives shape to the first. Literary criticism, William Empson has suggested, is largely a matter of being able to identify 'the right handle to take hold of the bundle'.[4] My central claim is this: when the bundle is Shakespearean dialogue, the right handle is the turn at talk.

[2] Erving Goffman, *Interaction Ritual: Essays on Face-to-Face Behaviour* (New York: Anchor, 1967), p. 12.

[3] Lynne Magnusson, 'Dialogue', in *Reading Shakespeare's Dramatic Language*, ed. by Sylvia Adamson, et al. (London: Thomson Learning, 2001), pp. 130–43 (p. 131). See also the same author's *Shakespeare and Social Dialogue: Dramatic Language and Elizabethan Letters* (Cambridge: Cambridge University Press, 1999), pp. 4, 183–4n.

[4] William Empson, 'The Structure of Complex Words', *The Sewanee Review*, 56 (1948), 230–50 (p. 239).

The term itself is not new. It has a long history of popular usage that stretches back at least as far as Shakespeare.[5] In the last forty years—since the publication of Sacks, Schegloff, and Jefferson's ground-breaking study, 'A Simplest Systematics for the Organization of Turn-Taking for Conversation'—the turn-taking model has become a standard tool of interactional linguistics.[6] Rather than simply adopt this model, however, I will be using it to develop a distinctively literary critical approach to turn-taking—an approach that owes as much to Emrys Jones as it does to Erving Goffman or Harvey Sacks. But before we start staking out academic territory and splitting theoretical hairs, it is worth looking at a couple of examples. If attention to turn-taking can help us to notice things in Shakespeare's dialogue that we might not otherwise have noticed, what are they?

My first example comes from 5.1 of *Measure for Measure*, in which Vincentio, Duke of Vienna, is petitioned by a young woman, Isabella.

> DUKE [...]   What would you say?
> ISABELLA   I am the sister of one Claudio,
> 70   Condemned upon the act of fornication
> To lose his head, condemned by Angelo.
> I, in probation of a sisterhood,

---

[5] According to the OED, the root of the English verb 'turn' is the Latin verb *tornare* ('to turn in a lathe, round off'), which survives in English, as in many other European languages, in the more inclusive sense of 'rotate' (without the need for a lathe). The noun is derived partly from the verb and partly from the French noun *tour*. By the thirteenth century it was being used to refer to a 'movement, device, or trick, by which a wrestler attempts to throw his antagonist' (*turn*, n. 20), presumably because throwing someone to the ground involves a violent act of rotation. This usage then seems to have expanded: first to cover everything that happens from the start of a bout of wrestling to the moment at which one of the wrestlers is thrown, then to cover a spell or bout of any other activity—a 'go' at doing something (*turn*, n. 25a). These two strands of meaning—that of rotation and that of a 'go'—combined in the late fourteenth century to produce the sense relevant here, a sense clumsily defined by the OED as 'the time for action or proceeding of any kind which comes round to each individual of a series in succession' (*turn*, n. 28a). The word began to be applied to acts of speech at some point between Chaucer and Shakespeare, who uses it in this way only once (*Titus Andronicus*, 5.3.118), although examples are increasingly common during his lifetime.

[6] Harvey Sacks, Emanuel A. Schegloff, and Gail Jefferson, 'A Simplest Systematics for the Organization of Turn-Taking for Conversation', *Language*, 50 (1974), 696–735.

Was sent to by my brother, one Lucio
As then the messenger.

LUCIO   That's I, an't like your grace.

75   I came to her from Claudio, and desired her
To try her gracious fortune with Lord Angelo
For her poor brother's pardon.

ISABELLA   That's he indeed.

DUKE [to Lucio]   You were not bid to speak.

LUCIO   No, my good lord,
Nor wished to hold my peace.

80   DUKE   I wish you now, then. Pray you take note of it;
And when you have a business for yourself,
Pray God you then be perfect.

LUCIO   I warrant your honour.

DUKE   The warrant's for yourself; take heed to't.

ISABELLA   This gentleman told somewhat of my tale—

85   LUCIO   Right.

DUKE   It may be right, but you are i'the wrong
To speak before your time.—Proceed.

ISABELLA   I went
To this pernicious caitiff deputy [...]

                                        (5.1.68–88)

What Shakespeare could have written here is a single extended speech
in which Isabella complains to the duke of her treatment at the hands of
his deputy. All the plot requires at this point is that Angelo be publicly
accused. A less gifted dramatist, or even a younger Shakespeare, might
have left it at that. Mature Shakespeare crafts an intricate three-way
scuffle over who speaks when. Notice how Isabella—ostensibly the
protagonist of the scene—quickly becomes sidelined by the two men,
both of whom appear to think they are helping her. Lucio interrupts her
story to supply a detail that she is perfectly capable of supplying herself.
Vincentio steps in to silence Lucio but only succeeds in amplifying and
extending the disruption. Notice, too, how his intervention at line 78,
'You were not bid to speak', is spoken, as it were, 'across' Isabella,
ignoring her turn to reply directly to Lucio. Rather than cutting the
interloper out of the exchange, Vincentio puts him squarely at its
centre. There is a contradiction, in other words, between the meaning

of his speech as a speech and its implications as a conversational move. 'You were not bid to speak' functions something like 'Will you please be quiet?'—seeming both to forbid a response and to demand one. The response it demands is an apology. Lucio need only say 'Sorry, I'll shut up now' and we can get back to the business at hand. Only a fool could misunderstand this, but Lucio *is* a fool (or, at least, a 'fantastic'). So he responds to the slight contradiction in the duke's behaviour by behaving in an even more contradictory manner himself. On the one hand, he is entirely acquiescent, offering assurances and agreeing with whatever the duke says. On the other hand, he keeps answering back, no matter how clear it is made that the correct response is silence. Lucio is the conversational equivalent of a screwed-up ball of Sellotape—every attempt to remove him from one finger ends with him stuck to another.

The punchline comes with his shortest, and most apparently acquiescent, turn: 'Right'. Timing, we are told, is the secret of comedy. The script may provide the words, but the comedian provides the performance. The kind of timing possessed by Morecambe and Wise or Tony Hancock is not something that can be written down. And perhaps this is so. But look again at the timing of Lucio's 'Right':

> LUCIO   I warrant your honour.
> DUKE   The warrant's for yourself; take heed to't.
> ISABELLA   This gentleman told somewhat of my tale—
> 85 LUCIO   Right.
> DUKE   It may be right, but you are i'the wrong [...]

At line 83 the duke tells him, for a third time, to shut up. And for one turn Lucio seems to have done so. Then, just as the dialogue appears to have moved on, up he pops to reignite the whole tedious argument. And sandwiched between the duke's exasperated imperative and Lucio's infuriating reply is Isabella's observation that 'This gentleman told somewhat of my tale'—another remark to which 'Right' could plausibly be a response. It is as if Lucio is deliberately exploiting this ambiguity—appearing to reply to Isabella in order to have the last word over Vincentio. He uses her words as cover, peeping out from behind her turn to fire one last dart at the duke. It's a tiny, tiny effect—a little patch of yellow at the corner of the canvas—but it is characteristic of the skill and subtlety with which Shakespearean dialogue is crafted.

I want to contrast this with something a little larger, an effect that resonates across two plays and upon which hangs the fate of a kingdom. In each of the two parts of *Henry IV* there is a reconciliation scene between the king and the Prince of Wales. The first comes in 3.2 of *1 Henry IV*, with the crown facing a major rebellion in the north of England. Dismayed by Hal's licentiousness, the king summons him for 'some private conference' (3.2.2). Alone together for the first and only time in the play, the two men exchange long and, for the most part, perfectly formed speeches—the father rebuking his wayward son, the son apologizing and promising to reform. In contrast to the undignified squabbling of the example from *Measure for Measure*, this is high and serious drama. In place of the rapid and chaotic exchange of turns, we have a stately and dignified alternation. There is just one crack in this otherwise smooth interactional surface:

> KING [...]
> 85 And in that very line, Harry, standest thou;
>   For thou hast lost thy princely privilege
>   With vile participation. Not an eye
>   But is a-weary of thy common sight,
>   Save mine, which hath desired to see thee more,
> 90 Which now doth that I would not have it do—
>   Make blind itself with foolish tenderness.
>   PRINCE   I shall hereafter, my thrice-gracious lord,
>   Be more myself.
>   KING   For all the world,
>   As thou art to this hour was Richard then,
> 95 When I from France set foot at Ravenspurgh,
>   And even as I was then is Percy now.
>   (3.2.85–96)

Henry has been developing a double analogy—between Hal and Richard II on the one hand, and himself and Hotspur on the other—for fifty lines before Hal speaks and will continue to do so for thirty lines afterwards. At the height of his tirade, he suddenly grinds to a halt. One explanation for the rhetorical glitch is that his voice fails him— the same foolish tenderness that 'make[s] blind' his eye makes dumb his tongue, and Hal takes advantage of the pause to offer a response.

Another explanation is that the sight of his father so moved is too much for the prince. He interrupts the old man because he simply can't bear to hear any more. Either way, the promise to reform is premature. The king ignores it and picks up in his next turn exactly where he left off in his last. The two turns constitute a single speech, and Hal must listen to the whole of it before any promises or apologies will be heard.

Compare this to their second reconciliation, in 4.3 of *2 Henry IV*, as Henry lies dying. Dazed by insomnia, harassed by rebels, and despairing of his son, the king suffers an 'apoplexy' (4.3.130). Recovered slightly but nearing his end, he is carried into a side room, where his crown is set on a pillow. Hal arrives late (as usual) and, left alone with the sleeping king, begins to soliloquize. Within twelve lines he has concluded that his father is dead, within twenty he has crowned himself, and within thirty he has walked out of the room with the crown still on his head. But Henry is not dead, and he wakes up as soon as Hal has left. So the second reconciliation begins with another lengthy tirade, this time on the theme of the young man's impatience for his father's death. Once again it stops short:

> KING HENRY [...]
> O my poor kingdom, sick with civil blows!
> When that my care could not withhold thy riots,
> 265   What wilt thou do when riot is thy care?
> O, thou wilt be a wilderness again,
> Peopled with wolves, thy old inhabitants.
> PRINCE HARRY   O pardon me, my liege! But for my tears,
> The moist impediments unto my speech,
> 270   I had forestalled this dear and deep rebuke
> Ere you with grief had spoke and I had heard
> The course of it so far. There is your crown;
>   *[He returns the crown]*
> And He that wears the crown immortally
> Long guard it yours!
>
>   (13[4.3].263–76)

For the first five words of his speech, it sounds as though Hal is apologizing for interrupting his father. It turns out, however, that he is apologizing for not having interrupted him sooner. He was unable to do so because, in a reversal of what happened in the previous play, it is now the son that is choked with grief. Never having thought to hear his father speak again, Hal cuts short the next thing his father says. As Emrys Jones has pointed out, the prince's unluckily timed entry and exit—coming in just after his father has dropped off, finding him 'dead', and then leaving just before he wakes up—'are a means of re-enacting their whole relationship [. . .] They have, so to speak, been missing each other all their lives'.[7] And this habit of somehow mistiming things, of first walking past and then awkwardly bumping into each other, is re-enacted again in the shape of the dialogue. There is a form of dramatic synecdoche at work here, in which the fumbled transitions between two speakers are made to stand for the larger transition between two kings. And not only does this resonate back to the earlier play: it also resonates outwards into Elizabethan society. Anxiety over the succession dominated the last years of Elizabeth's reign, as it had dominated the reign of her father before her.[8] The 1534 Act of Succession outlines the various treasonable activities 'whereby your highness [Henry VIII] might be disturbed or interrupted of the crown of this realm'.[9] Interrupting his father 'of the crown' is precisely what Hal has just done, by placing it, prematurely, on his own head. And he apologizes for this interruption by interrupting his father's speech. The metaphor works because hereditary monarchy, like dialogue, is a form of turn-taking. Hal is the next speaker in the great conversation of state, waiting—with an awkward mixture of dread and impatience—for his father to fall silent.

Taken together, these two examples show just how sensitively Shakespearean dialogue is shaped to meet the demands of the dramatic moment. Either scene could have been written straight (as it were) without the extra layer of complexity that the wrangling over speaking rights provides. But Shakespeare, like any good dramatist, intuitively thinks in turn-taking terms. He understands the mechanics of conversation and exploits them dramatically, for small effects as well as large.

[7] Emrys Jones, *Scenic Form in Shakespeare* (Oxford: Clarendon Press, 1971), p. 38.
[8] For a useful summary of the issues involved, see E. W. Ives, 'Tudor Dynastic Problems Revisited', *Historical Research*, 81 (2008), 255–79.
[9] *The Tudor Constitution: Documents and Commentary*, ed. by G. R. Elton (Cambridge: Cambridge University Press, 1960), p. 10.

There is a constant counterpoint in his work between dialogical form and linguistic content, between what is said and when. What the two examples also show is the kind of analysis that attention to such details can yield, even without the benefit of a precise technical vocabulary or an elegant theoretical apparatus. One aim of this book is to provide such a vocabulary and propose such an apparatus. But these are a boon rather than a necessity. As soon as the basic point is grasped—that as well as scripting the words the characters say to each other, Shakespeare also scripts an ongoing negotiation between them about whose turn it is to talk—then the kind of analysis I have provided in this chapter becomes possible. More than that, it becomes natural. Any socialized human being has a lifetime's experience of how turn-taking functions. They may not be able to articulate it clearly, but that experience is nonetheless central to the way in which they read drama. All that is lacking is a name to call it by.

*   *   *

If the claims I am making on behalf of this approach are justified then it would seem odd that critics have not already adopted it. More than forty years has passed since the publication of Sacks, Schegloff, and Jefferson's 'Simplest Systematics'. This study, which inadvertently founded the branch of linguistics now known as 'conversation analysis', has become the most frequently cited article in the history of *Language* (the official journal of the Linguistic Society of America), and the model of conversation it proposes has been adopted by researchers in a variety of other fields.[10] In spite of its obvious relevance to the study of dramatic dialogue, however, it has had little impact on critics and editors of Shakespeare. The phrases 'turn-taking' and 'turn at talk' appear only twice in 123,000 annotated entries to the World Shakespeare Bibliography Online.[11] Full-text searches of *Shakespeare Survey*, *Shakespeare Quarterly*, and *Shakespeare* yield a

[10] Brian D. Joseph, 'The Editor's Department: Reviewing Our Contents', *Language*, 79 (2003), 461–3.
[11] Magdalena Adamczyk, 'Shakespeare's Wordplay Gender-Wise: Punning as a Marker of Male-Female Relationships', in *Topics in Shakespeare's English*, ed. by Piotr Kakietek and Joanna Nykiel (Czestochowa: Wydawnictwo Wyzszej Szkoly Lingwistycznej, 2010), pp. 185–200; and John Haddon, 'Talk in Life and *Othello*', *Use of English*, 56 (2005), 202–21.

combined total of three further articles, one of which is a review.[12] These facts need explaining.

Most scholars who work on language in Shakespeare are more interested in classical rhetoric than contemporary linguistics—in the analytical tools available to Shakespeare rather than those available to us. Above all, they are interested in what he is likely to have learned at school.[13] This makes sense, of course, and such work is extremely valuable for understanding how Shakespeare came to write in the way he did and how his contemporaries might have understood his writing. It is no doubt true that 'critical sophistication in this period comes in the form of rhetorical analysis' and that the study of rhetoric can help us to 'think [ourselves] back into a Renaissance frame of mind'.[14] But it does not follow from this that rhetorical analysis is able to account for everything that happens in a Shakespeare play. What rhetoric theorizes is oratory, not conversation. It can help us to understand how individual speeches perform acts of persuasion but not how a group of characters exchanges turns at talk or why this particular character is the one making a speech in the first place. I will return, in some detail, to the question of exactly what rhetoric does and does not tell us about dramatic dialogue. All that matters here is to recognize the shortfall. Literary sophistication often exceeds—or at least precedes—our ability as critics to describe it. Which is not to suggest that we should abandon historicist approaches to Shakespeare's language, only that we should recognize their limitations. As well as trying to recover Renaissance ways of thinking, we should be taking advantage of the fact that we are no longer bound by them.

There are critics, of course, who seek to do just that—to bring the insights of contemporary linguistics to bear upon early modern

[12] Lynne Magnusson, '"Voice Potential": Language and Symbolic Capital in *Othello*', *Shakespeare Survey*, 50 (1997), 91–9; William Dodd, review of *Shakespeare and Social Dialogue: Dramatic Language and Elizabethan Letters* by Lynne Magnusson, *Shakespeare Quarterly*, 52 (2001), 154–7; Roderick Hugh McKeown, '"I Will Stop Your Mouth": The Regulation of Jesting in *Much Ado About Nothing*', *Shakespeare*, 11 (2015), 1–22.
[13] See, for example, Colin Burrow, 'Shakespeare and Humanistic Culture', in *Shakespeare and the Classics*, ed. by Charles Martindale and A. B. Taylor (Cambridge: Cambridge University Press, 2004), pp. 9–27.
[14] Neil Rhodes, *The Power of Eloquence and English Renaissance Literature* (London: Harvester Wheatsheaf, 1991), p. vii; Brian Vickers, *In Defence of Rhetoric* (Oxford: Clarendon Press, 1988), p. 283.

texts—but few such critics work on dialogue. Literary linguistics remains a minority sport, especially among Shakespeareans, and linguistic approaches to literature still tend to focus, like linguistics itself, on the sentence as the fundamental unit of analysis—on the syntactical and lexical choices that constitute style. This tendency is embodied in the term 'stylistics', often used as a shorthand for linguistically informed literary analysis. Shakespeare is studied as a stylist rather than a dramatist, with the emphasis on linguistic texture rather than dialogical form. Critics who make use of less-traditional approaches, such as conversation analysis or pragmatics, are a minority within a minority. They do exist, however, and it will be necessary to position my own work in relation to theirs.

This book differs from previous accounts of turn-taking in dramatic dialogue in two main ways. It is simultaneously narrower in focus and more broadly inclusive—narrower in focus because it does not present the turn-taking model as part of a larger theoretical apparatus, more broadly inclusive because it is addressed to a general Shakespearean audience. Most literary linguists, if they mention turn-taking at all, do so only in passing. It tends to be offered as part of a package deal of pragmatic tools—thrown in for free when one makes a more substantial purchase, such as speech act theory, politeness theory, or Gricean implicature.[15] The two most comprehensive accounts currently available are those provided by Keir Elam (fifteen pages in a book of over three hundred) and Vimala Herman (a single article, later republished as part of a monograph).[16] In purely quantitative terms, this is not enough space to do the subject justice. Turn-taking is as fundamental to dialogue as rhythm is to verse, and Shakespeare's handling of it is virtuosic. Dialogical form is the undiscovered country of Shakespearean

---

[15] See, for example, Mick Short, *Exploring the Language of Poems, Plays, and Prose*, Learning about Language (London: Longman, 1996); Jonathan Culpeper, *Language and Characterisation in Plays and Texts: People in Plays and Other Texts*, Textual Explorations (Harlow: Longman, 2001).

[16] Keir Elam, *Shakespeare's Universe of Discourse: Language-Games in the Comedies* (Cambridge: Cambridge University Press, 1984), pp. 185–99; Vimala Herman, 'Dramatic Dialogue and the Systematics of Turn-Taking', *Semiotica*, 83 (1991), 97–122. This became the second chapter of a monograph, *Dramatic Discourse: Dialogue as Interaction in Plays* (London: Routledge, 1995), pp. 76–121.

criticism, and it will take more than a handful of articles and half-chapters to map it with any sort of precision.

The package-deal approach to literary pragmatics also creates a second problem. By embedding the turn-taking model within a larger theoretical framework, these writers imply that there is a necessary connection between the two—that adopting one means adopting the other. This is not the case. The recognition that dialogue is best understood as a series of turns at talk need not commit us to any further theoretical assumptions. We can adopt the turn as the unit of dialogical analysis without needing to import the entire apparatus of conversation analysis, or pragmatics, or signing ourselves up as card-carrying discourse analysts. Which is not to say that such approaches have nothing to contribute to the study of literary dialogue—only that there is something to be gained from considering turn-taking as a subject in its own right. One weakness of much work in this area, I want to suggest, is its ambition. Like a teenager bringing in the shopping, the stylistician tries to carry across too many linguistic tools in one trip. The instinct is understandable, but its effect can be counterproductive. By trying to do too much at once, we make it hard to do anything properly. The reader interested in speech act theory, politeness, the cooperative principle, repair, or forms of address will find these subjects amply and ably discussed elsewhere.[17]

The second way in which this book differs from earlier work on turn-taking in dramatic dialogue is the extent to which it is prepared to adapt—rather than simply adopt—the standard linguistic model. This is partly a question of translation. Conversation analysts speak a highly specialized academic dialect, and I want to make it possible for the reader to benefit from their insights without having to learn their language. The problem seems to get worse, rather than better, when

---

[17] See, for starters, Stanley E. Fish, 'How to Do Things with Austin and Searle: Speech Act Theory and Literary Criticism', *MLN*, 91 (1976), 983–1025; Roger Brown and Albert Gilman, 'Politeness Theory and Shakespeare's Four Major Tragedies', *Language in Society*, 18 (1989), 159–212; Marilyn M. Cooper, 'Implicature, Convention, and *The Taming of the Shrew*', *Poetics*, 10 (1981), 1–14; Clara Calvo, 'Pronouns of Address and Social Negotiation in *As You Like It*', *Language and Literature*, 1 (1992), 5–27; A. J. Gilbert, *Shakespeare's Dramatic Speech: Studies in Renaissance Literature* (Lewiston, NY: Edwin Mellen Press, 1997); Beatrix Busse, *Vocative Constructions in the Language of Shakespeare* (Amsterdam: John Benjamins, 2006).

conversation analysis comes into contact with literary linguistics. This is Vimala Herman's description of turn-taking:

> The joint management of the alternating issue of speech amongst participants in an episode or scene, unfolding in time, creates the trajectory of development, in its specificity, of situation and event that channels the course of the dramatic action, within the immediacies of its making, amongst the *dramatis personae* involved.[18]

The article from which I have just quoted, 'Dramatic Dialogue and the Systematics of Turn-Taking', could not be more relevant to the subject of this monograph. In so far as I understand what Herman is saying here, I agree with it. A failure to recognize that the exchange of turns is jointly managed 'within the immediacies of its own making'—subject, that is, to an ongoing negotiation about who speaks when—is a major failing in critical work on dialogue. But in order to correct that failing, we need to arrive at a way of discussing it that is accessible to the very wide range of scholars who work on Shakespeare. By writing as she does, Herman restricts her audience to a small circle of discourse analysts, literary linguists, and stylisticians. Her influence is felt at the periphery of the field, not at its centre.

Nor is this merely a question of how best to sell a product in the academic marketplace. The linguistic model also needs adapting to take account of the profound differences between real conversation and dramatic dialogue. Real conversation, when written down, is messy, fragmentary, and recalcitrant. It is not, of course, mere chaos—it does have structure—but this structure has no responsibility to make itself known on the page. The structure of dramatic dialogue, on the other hand, has a responsibility to do just that. It is turn-taking crafted for the sake of a reader or an audience, and it operates within a recognizable set of parameters. Some sense of what this distinction might mean in practice can be gained by comparing the study of turn-taking to the study of prosody.

The linguist studies prosody either by recording speech acoustically or by monitoring 'the spatiotemporal behaviour of different articulators'— that is, the physical movements of the vocal tract during the act of

---

[18] Herman, 'Dramatic Dialogue and the Systematics of Turn-Taking', p. 97.

speaking.[19] These data are then converted into graphic representations and analysed using sophisticated computer software. Linguistic prosodists investigate such phenomena as 'vowel duration differences due to vowel height', 'vowel lengthening before voiced obstruents', and 'durational contrasts between phonologically short and long vowels'.[20] They have the following sorts of conclusions to offer:

> Syllable structure can also affect segment duration (e.g., segments tend to be shorter in complex versus simple syllables) and the length of a word can influence syllable duration (i.e., medial syllables tend to be shorter in polysyllabic words). All things being equal, segments or syllables at the beginning or end of a prosodic phrase or larger discourse segment are longer than medial syllables, speeding up and slowing down tempo tends to shorten and lengthen syllables respectively, and finally, speaking style in general can also influence speech segment duration.[21]

In short, linguistic prosody is a rigorously empirical scientific endeavour, practised in a laboratory using specialist equipment by men in white coats (metaphorically speaking).

The literary critical approach to prosody, on the other hand, requires no more than a pencil. Rather than making a sound-recording and running it through a spectrograph, the literary critic can scan a poem without even reading it aloud. She can do so because her aim is not complete description but analytically useful description. Traditional scansion treats the syllable as a stable and discrete acoustic unit into which language can be reliably segmented, and it makes a binary distinction between stressed and unstressed syllables. Both of these assumptions are naïve by the standards of contemporary linguistics.[22] But the value of the literary approach is precisely its simplicity. The approximations are worth making because they allow us to draw

---

[19] Janet Fletcher, 'The Prosody of Speech: Timing and Rhythm', in *The Handbook of Phonetic Sciences*, ed. by William J. Hardcastle, John Laver, and Fiona E. Gibbon, Blackwell Handbooks in Linguistics, 2nd edn (Chichester: Wiley-Blackwell, 2010), pp. 523–602 (525).
[20] Fletcher, p. 525.   [21] Fletcher, p. 525.
[22] Anders Löfqvist, for example, objects that 'the movements associated with different production units blend seamlessly with each other' in such a way that 'in the articulatory record there are no boundaries between units'. See his 'Theories and Models of Speech Production', in *The Handbook of Phonetic Sciences*, pp. 353–77 (354).

comparisons at the right level of detail—a level of detail roughly in keeping with the prosodic parameters of the writing. Familiar with the conventions of English poetry, with the genre and period in which the poem was written, and with the habits of the poet in question, the critic knows in advance what kind of patterns she is likely to find. Even when a poet chooses to break with convention, or to exploit the imprecision of the model expressively, scanning the poem will usually alert us to this fact. By attempting to put all the pegs into square holes, we quickly discover which of them are round.

My point is not that either of these two approaches is superior to the other but that each is adapted to a specific form of enquiry and a specific type of material, and that the differences between them are instructive when it comes to thinking about the difference between dramatic dialogue and real conversation. What is appropriate in the analysis of one is not necessarily appropriate in the analysis of the other. Dramatic dialogue is a stylized form of turn-taking, in which the patterns of real conversation are heightened and made obvious—just as the rhythms of ordinary language are heightened into verse. People no more speak in stichomythia than they do in heroic couplets. Previous attempts to employ the turn-taking model in the service of literary analysis have not been sufficiently aware of these differences—either that, or they have been too timid to act on them. This book is bolder. Rather than import the linguistic model, it attempts to devise a literary critical equivalent for it.

The book itself is divided into two parts, each containing a series of four connected chapters, the first of which provides a theoretical framework for the three that follow. Part One deals with the question of conversational sequence—how a group of speakers works out whose turn it is to speak next and what it means for a character to speak in or out of turn. This is what was at issue in the example from *Measure for Measure*. It proposes a simple set of terms with which to analyse sequence in dramatic dialogue and attempts to demonstrate both their usefulness and their limitations. Part Two looks at the more complicated question of transitions between turns—how one speaker can know when another has finished and what it means for a character to speak either too early or too late. This is what was at issue in the scenes between Hal and his father. There are no neat answers to this second set of questions—the dramatic text is profoundly ambiguous with regard to timing—but Shakespeare's writing is characteristically inventive when it comes to escaping such limitations. These chapters consider some of the ways in which syntax, punctuation, and metre can be used to suggest abandoned, interrupted, or overlapping speech. A final, concluding, chapter examines the implications of the turn-taking approach for our understanding of early modern performance practices.

|PART ONE|

Sequence

| 1 |

Speaking When You're Spoken To

No sooner have Chaucer's pilgrims reached the 'Wateryng of Seint Thomas', on what is now the Old Kent Road, than they are faced with a problem—'who shal telle the firste tale'?[1] Their solution is to draw 'cut', an apparently random process that selects the Knight to go first. But this solution is only temporary. When the Knight's tale ends, the pilgrims are back where they started—facing the same problem again but with one candidate fewer. Rather than draw cut for a second time, the Host invites the Monk to go next. A second solution, it would seem, is for the Host to take charge—doling out opportunities to speak like the pots of ale he doles out at The Tabard. But the second solution is even less successful than the first. Before the Monk can begin, the Miller interrupts and drunkenly insists on telling his own tale immediately. So a third solution, if we can call it that, is to take the path of least resistance—to abandon any attempt to structure the contest systematically and allow the pilgrims to fight it out between them. Who shouteth loudest, speaketh first. The Miller's tale turns out to be a thinly veiled attack on the Reeve, and the Reeve's tale follows it—not because he insists but because the other pilgrims recognize his right of reply. And so on. Each time a tale reaches its conclusion, it is followed

---

[1] 'The Canterbury Tales', in *The Riverside Chaucer*, ed. Larry D. Benson, 3rd edn (Oxford: Oxford University Press, 1987), I.826–9 (p. 36).

by a prologue in which the characters negotiate the question of who goes next. Much of the fun of the poem derives from the jostling that occurs at these moments of transition and from the unpredictability they give to the ordering of the tales.

The problem faced by the pilgrims on the road to Canterbury is not unique. It is common, in fact, to all spoken interaction. Harvey Sacks has called it 'the speaker sequencing problem':

> And by the 'speaker sequencing problem' I mean this: If the society happens to have, as one basic rule for conversation in it, that not more than one party should talk at a time, then there needs to be techniques whereby speakers, potential speakers, etc., go about order-ing their speech relative to each other. And one wants to find those techniques, see how they work, etc.[2]

The example of the pilgrims is useful because it allows us to examine such techniques in slow motion, as it were, like tennis being played with a beach ball. Turn-taking is the basic structural principle on which *The Canterbury Tales* is built—a principle it shares with Boccaccio's *Decameron,* Castiglione's *Book of the Courtier*, and book four of Ovid's *Metamorphoses*. The poem is a kind of dialogue, albeit on a massive scale, in which we can read the mechanics of conversation writ large. Somehow, between them, the pilgrims build a collaborative structure, a sequence of tales. And for every tale the reader can do as I have done here—can ask, that is, why this tale comes next. And for every tale there is a prologue that provides the answer. At least, there probably would be if the text of the poem were not incomplete.

Exactly the same is true of Shakespearean dialogue, only on a much smaller scale. In every scene the characters take turns to speak. Between them they build a collaborative structure, not of tales but of turns at talk. And for every turn the reader can ask, as she can ask of Chaucer's pilgrims, why this speaker comes next. The question is more difficult to answer because the decisions are being made more quickly and there is no clear separation between the two levels of communicative activity. There are moments in Shakespeare at which the sequencing of speakers

---

[2] Harvey Sacks, *Lectures on Conversation*, ed. by Gail Jefferson, 2 vols (Oxford: Blackwell, 1992), I, p. 624.

becomes the subject of the dialogue—as when Vincentio tells Lucio that he was not 'bid to speak'—but these are rare. Ordinarily the characters exchange turns at talk without reference to the order in which they are doing so or how that order is determined. But that does not invalidate the question. It can still be asked, and it still has an answer. Just like Chaucer's pilgrims, Shakespeare's characters are continually having to find ways of solving the speaker sequencing problem. The order in which they speak is a record of how they do so.

This chapter will look at some of the ways in which linguists—and linguistically minded sociologists—have gone about answering the same question in relation to real conversation, and will ask how useful such answers are for the analysis of dramatic dialogue. It is one of two primarily theoretical chapters (the other being Chapter 5), which serve as introductions to the two parts of the book. Having explained what I think is wrong—from a literary critical point of view—with linguistic approaches to the problem, I will conclude by proposing a simplified model of turn-sequencing, more suited to the needs of editors and critics of Shakespeare. The next chapter will explore how this model can be used to build a basic vocabulary of terms with which to describe dialogical form, and the final two chapters of Part One will use those tools to investigate two specific issues in Shakespearean dialogue: the turn-taking etiquette that surrounds Shakespeare's kings, and the curiously ambiguous status of the aside as an utterance that both is and is not a turn at talk.

Before getting started, however, it is worth making a distinction. I am using the word 'sequence' here (and throughout this book) to refer to the order in which a group of characters speaks. The sequence of speakers in any scene can be read off from the speech-headings. The opening scene of *King Lear*, for example, begins KENT, GLOUCESTER, KENT, GLOUCESTER, KENT, GLOUCESTER, KENT, GLOUCESTER, BASTARD. When Sacks first formulated 'the speaker sequencing problem', this was the sense in which he was using the word. It has subsequently acquired a second, more technical, meaning in conversation analysis which needs to be distinguished from the first. As Emanuel Schegloff puts it,

> turns do not follow one another like identical beads on a string. They have some organization and 'shape' to them, aside from their organiz- ation as single turns and as series-of-turns (that is, as turns starting

with a backconnection and ending with a forward one). One might say that they seem to be grouped in batches or clumps, one bunch seeming to 'hang together' or cohere, and then another, and another, etc.[3]

These clumps or runs of turns are known in the literature as 'sequences'. A question and its answer are thus considered a sequence (of a type called an 'adjacency pair') because the question calls forth the answer and the answer responds to the question.[4] The same 'sequence' of turns (in the first sense) that constitutes 1.1 of *King Lear* could thus be broken down into a series of smaller 'sequences' (in the second sense). Clearly there is potential for confusion here—enough potential to justify jettisoning one use of the term. But this is not simply a question of whether we choose to draw an arbitrary boundary around a smaller or a larger chunk of data. The two senses of the word are qualitatively different. One is formal—it refers to the order in which things happen. The other is functional—it refers to *what* happens. The order in which the characters speak is something that the play tells us. It is built into the structure of the text. How we choose to group these turns into sequences of actions is not. That is something the conversation analyst must decide for himself, using a typology of possible sequence-types gleaned from a textbook on conversation analysis. The distinction is important and will become more important at a later stage in my argument. All the reader need do for the moment is be aware of it and keep in mind which side of the fence we are on.

* * *

The speaker sequencing problem is not one that arises in traditional approaches to the study of language—including those, such as grammar and rhetoric, that Shakespeare is likely to have encountered at school. It was not until the twentieth century that linguistic theory began to pay serious attention to conversation, and, even then, it did so using a two-person model. Saussure's famous diagram of the *circuit de*

---

[3] Emanuel A. Schegloff, *A Primer in Conversation Analysis, Volume 1: Sequence Organization in Interaction* (Cambridge: Cambridge University Press, 2007), p. 1.

[4] For a full account of this second type of sequence, see Emanuel A. Schegloff, 'On the Organization of Sequences as a Source of "Coherence" in Talk-in-Interaction', in *Conversational Organization and Its Development*, ed. by Bruce Dorval (Norwood, NJ: Ablex, 1990), pp. 51–77.

la parole shows a speaker and a hearer, not a group of potential speakers listening out for an opportunity to take their own turn at talk.[5] The rise of ordinary language philosophy and its linguistic off-shoot, pragmatics, did little to alter this. Wittgenstein, Austin, Searle, Grice, and Sperber and Wilson are all concerned with how A understands B, not with how A, B, and C manage, between them, to organize a conversation.

The first hints of an interest in the problem—and in turn-taking more generally—are to be found not in grammatical or rhetorical handbooks but in the Italian conduct manuals that began to flood England in the late sixteenth century.[6] The most comprehensive of these, in its handling of conversational etiquette, is Giovanni Della Casa's *Galateo*, first printed in English in 1576. The book contains a wealth of advice for the socially aspirational young gentleman, on everything from how to dress appropriately to the importance of not looking into your handkerchief after you have blown your nose. As a conversational rulebook it is primarily concerned with how to speak and what to say, but there are also some tips on when to open your mouth. According to Della Casa, '[i]t is good maner for a man to speake, and likewise to hold his peace, as it comes to his turne, and occasion requires'.[7] This is both difficult to argue with and difficult to put into practice. Della Casa is aware that an exchange of speech can be mistimed or lopsided and that there are social rules governing when and when not to talk, but he does not go so far as to spell those rules

[5] Ferdinand de Saussure, *Saussure's Third Course of Lectures on General Linguistics (1910–11): From the Notebooks of Emile Constantin*, ed. by Eisuke Komatsu, trans. by Roy Harris (Oxford: Pergamon Press, 1993), p. 67. On the ubiquity and persistence of this model, see Roy Harris, 'The Speech-Communication Model in Twentieth Century Linguistics and its Sources' in *The Foundations of Linguistic Theory, Selected Writings of Roy Harris*, ed. by Nigel Love (London: Routledge, 1990), pp. 151–7.

[6] On which, see Anna Bryson, *From Civility to Courtesy: Changing Codes of Conduct in Early Modern England*, Oxford Studies in Social History (Oxford: Clarendon Press, 1998).

[7] *Galateo of Maister Iohn Della Casa*, trans. by Robert Peterson (London: Henry Middleton, 1576), sig. N3v. In Peterson's translation this becomes the first interactionally self-conscious use of the word 'turn' in English. In Della Casa's Italian the phrase is 'quando la volta viene a-llui' in which the word 'volta' can mean 'time' as well as 'turn'. See *Galateo*, ed. by Claudio Milanini (Milan: BUR, 2008) p. 145. Italian conversation analysts prefer the less ambiguous 'turno'. See, for example, 'L'organizzazione della presa di turno nella conversazione', in *Linguaggio e contesto sociale*, ed. by R. Giglioli and G. Fele (Bologna: Il Mulino, 2000), pp. 97–135.

out. We are told not to speak out of turn but not how to tell whose turn it is to speak. His advice is the equivalent of saying 'drive safely' or 'don't crash'—a useful reminder, in its way, but only practicable if you already know that red means stop and green means go, that in Britain we drive on the left, how roundabouts work, and so on. To put it more sharply, Della Casa recognizes that there *is* a speaker sequencing problem, but he does not tell us how to solve it. The reader in search of more detailed guidance would have to wait another four centuries.

Like its early modern ancestor, twentieth-century interest in turn-taking originates outside the traditional boundaries of linguistic study—in the work of Erving Goffman, a Canadian sociologist. Goffman was the first person to theorize conversation as an exchange of 'turns at talk' and the first to theorize turn-taking as a form of social organization.[8] Curiously, however, he never quite managed to synthesize his work in these two areas. Or rather, by the time he got round to doing so, two of his former pupils—Harvey Sacks and Emanuel Schegloff—had beaten him to the punch.[9] The originality of Goffman's approach lies in his rejection of what he calls the 'correlational drive' in sociology—the attempt to establish statistically significant relationships between human behaviour and social variables (also characteristic, we might add, of much sociolinguistics).[10] What he advocates instead is a form of micro-analysis dedicated to the study of the 'social situation'. A social situation arises 'whenever two or more individuals find themselves in

[8] See, respectively, 'The Neglected Situation', *American Anthropologist*, 66 (1964), 133–6 (p. 136); and 'The Territories of the Self', in *Relations in Public: Microstudies of the Social Order* (New York: Basic Books, 1971), pp. 28–61. As early as 1955 Goffman had arrived at a view of interaction along roughly the same lines: 'In any society, whenever the physical possibility of spoken interaction arises, it seems that a system of practices, conventions, and procedural rules comes into play which functions as a means of guiding and organizing the flow of messages' ('On Face-Work: An Analysis of Ritual Elements in Social Interaction', *Psychiatry: Journal for the Study of Interpersonal Processes*, 18 (1955), 213–31 (p. 226)). The key development in 1964 is the reconceptualization of the 'flow of messages' as an exchange of turns at talk.

[9] Goffman's response to 'A Simplest Systematics' is *Forms of Talk* (Oxford: Blackwell, 1981). On the 'Oedipal' relationship between the three men, see Emanuel A. Schegloff, 'Goffman and the Analysis of Conversation', in *Erving Goffman: Exploring the Interaction Order*, ed. by Paul Drew and Anthony J. Wootton (Cambridge: Polity Press, 1988), pp. 89–135. The third author of 'A Simplest Systematics', Gail Jefferson, was a student of Harvey Sacks.

[10] Goffman, 'The Neglected Situation', p. 135.

one another's immediate presence' and lasts 'until the next-to-last person leaves'.[11] Despite being 'the natural home of speech', the social situation has been badly neglected. Goffman's concern is 'to promote acceptance of this face-to-face domain as an analytically viable one'—to uncover the 'traffic rules' of interaction by paying attention to 'the syntactical relations among the acts of different persons mutually present to one another'.[12] Rather than standing on a bridge with a clipboard, counting and categorizing the cars as they pass, he wants to work out how they avoid crashing into each other.

Goffman's fullest analysis of what it means to take a turn at something is given in the context of a discussion of service encounters, without reference to language. A turn, he suggests, is a type of social claim—more specifically, it is a claim to a special kind of 'territory'.

> This concept from ethology seems apt, because the claim is not so much to a discrete and particular matter but rather to a field of things—to a preserve—and because the boundaries of the field are ordinarily patrolled and defended by the claimant.[13]

The kind of turn-taking he has in mind is a means of determining 'the order in which a claimant receives a good of some kind relative to other claimants in the situation'.[14] The territory 'patrolled and defended' by the claimant is their place in a sequence—their ownership, as it were, of a particular time slot, even if it is not possible to predict exactly when that slot will arrive. The shape of the sequence itself is determined by what Goffman calls a 'decision rule':

> [A] decision rule is involved, ordering participants categorically ('women and children first,' or 'whites before blacks'), or individually ('smallest first, then next smallest'), or some mixture of both. [...] In our Western society, perhaps the most important principle in turn organization is 'first come, first served,' establishing the claim of an individual to come right after the person 'ahead' and right before the person 'behind.'[15]

---

[11] Goffman, 'The Neglected Situation', p. 135.
[12] Goffman, 'The Interaction Order', *American Sociological Review*, 48 (1983), 1–17 (p. 2); and *Interaction Ritual*, p. 2.
[13] Goffman, 'The Territories of the Self', p. 28.
[14] Goffman, 'The Territories of the Self', p. 28.
[15] Goffman, 'The Territories of the Self', p. 35.

Although he does not himself make the connection, the same can apply in spoken interaction. One way of solving the speaker sequencing problem is to follow a decision rule. The Speaker's List in a parliamentary debate, for example, is established on a 'first come, first served' basis. In an academic seminar, the participants will often introduce themselves in a sequence determined by the order in which they are sitting ('clockwise round the table'), a principle that we also find at work in the *Decameron*.[16] The first solution tried by Chaucer's pilgrims on their way to Canterbury is a Goffmanian decision rule (whoever draws the short straw goes first), and some critics have suspected that the Host may be intending to structure the entire contest by secretly following a rule of this type—it seems a little too convenient that the highest-status character should be chosen to go first by a supposedly random process. When the next highest is nominated to go second, it looks as though we may be about to proceed, in orderly fashion, from the top of the social scale to the bottom.[17] For an example from Shakespeare we need look no further than King Lear, who is following a decision rule when he requires his daughters to profess their love for him in order of their seniority ('eldest first'). Such examples, whilst interesting, are relatively unusual. The kind of turn-taking described by Erving Goffman is common at the post office but rare in spoken interaction. For a more comprehensive explanation, we must turn to the work of Sacks, Schegloff, and Jefferson.

More than forty years after its first publication, 'A Simplest Systematics for the Organization of Turn-Taking for Conversation' remains

[16] As, for example, at the conclusion of Philomena's tale on the first day: 'when *Dioneus* sitting next vnto her, (without tarrying for any other command from the Queene, knowing by the order formerly begunne, that he was to follow in the same course) spake in this manner', *The Decameron, Containing an Hundred Pleasant Nouels* (London: Isaac Jaggard, 1620), sig. D5r. For further examples, see sigs E5v, G1r, G3v, H1v. This translation was printed anonymously but is sometimes attributed to John Florio.

[17] According to Ethel M. Albert, this is how speech is organized amongst the Burundi, for whom 'the order in which individuals speak in a group is strictly determined by seniority of rank' and there are 'no recorded instances of confusion or conflict in the matter of determining order of precedence even in very large groups'. See her '"Rhetoric," "Logic," and "Poetics" in Burundi: Culture Patterning of Speech Behavior', *American Anthropologist*, 66 (1964), 35–54.

the standard account of how people take turns at talk.[18] In place of the Goffmanian decision rule, Sacks, Schegloff, and Jefferson propose what they call a 'turn allocation mechanism'. They distinguish two basic types. The first is 'pre-allocation'—so-called because the order in which people speak is determined, or could have been worked out, beforehand. The second is 'local allocation'. This means that turns are allocated one at a time, with no way of knowing, in advance, what the sequence will be. Armed with this distinction, Sacks, Schegloff, and Jefferson propose a more general model for understanding the different ways in which the speaker sequencing problem can be solved:

> The foregoing suffices to suggest a structural possibility: that turn-taking systems, or at least the class of them whose members each preserve 'one party talks at a time', are, with respect to their allocational arrangements, linearly arrayed. The linear array is one in which one polar type (exemplified by conversation) involves 'one-turn-at-a-time' allocation, i.e. the use of local allocational means; the other pole (exemplified by debate) involves pre-allocation of all turns; and medial types (exemplified by meetings) involve various mixes of pre-allocational and local allocational means.[19]

It is not helpful to think in terms of discrete 'systems'—things are rarely this neat, either in reality or in Shakespearean drama—but the two basic poles of this linear array are more or less as Sacks, Schegloff, and Jefferson describe them. Pre-allocation is characteristic of turn-taking in formal and institutional settings and amongst large groups of people—of ceremony and ritual, legal proceedings, and state occasions. Local allocation is characteristic of relaxed, intimate, and informal situations—of conversation in the everyday sense of that word.

---

[18] Objections to 'A Simplest Systematics' tend to take the form of objections to turn-taking itself rather than to this particular turn-taking model. See, for example, Daniel C. O'Connell, Sabine Kowal, and Erika Kaltenbacher, 'Turn-Taking: A Critical Analysis of the Research Tradition', *Journal of Psycholinguistic Research*, 19 (1990), 345–73; and Stephen J. Cowley, 'Of Timing, Turn-Taking, and Conversations', *Journal of Psycholinguistic Research*, 27 (1998), 541–71. Talbot J. Taylor and Deborah Cameron go a step further and object to any example of what they call a 'rules and units' approach to the study of conversation. See their *Analysing Conversation: Rules and Units in the Structure of Talk*, Language & Communication Library (Oxford: Pergamon, 1987).

[19] Sacks, Schegloff, and Jefferson, p. 729.

The distinction is useful, and literary criticism would do well to adopt it. To what extent turns at talk have been pre-allocated, how far the characters (as well as the actors) are following a sequential script, where (if at all) they depart from or return to it—these are crucial questions when it comes to understanding the structure of dramatic dialogue. Shakespeare is a master of the disrupted formal occasion—of the scene in which a ceremony or a trial or a dramatic performance descends into chaos—but we, as critics, lack a vocabulary with which to describe such disruptions. Take, for example, the aborted wedding of Hero to Claudio in *Much Ado about Nothing*:

> FRIAR *[to Claudio]* You come hither, my lord, to marry this lady?
> CLAUDIO No.
> 5 LEONATO To be married to her. Friar, you come to marry her.
> FRIAR *[to Hero]* Lady, you come hither to be married to this Count?
> HERO I do.
> FRIAR If either of you know any inward impediment why you
>   should not be conjoined, I charge you on your souls to utter it.
>
> $(4.1.3-9)$

It is not just Claudio's disavowal of the intention to get married that is a problem here. A wedding ceremony is, amongst other things, an interactional pattern. Part of what gives it its power is that the right people speak in the right order, and that order is FRIAR, GROOM, FRIAR, BRIDE not FRIAR, GROOM, FATHER-OF-THE-BRIDE, FRIAR, BRIDE. Leonato's intervention is not part of the sequential script. He intervenes, of course, to clear up what he thinks is a misunderstanding between Claudio and the Friar over two senses of the verb 'marry'. But by clarifying the meaning of the service, Leonato disrupts its shape. The scene as a whole plays out a beautiful counterpoint between pre-allocated turn-taking and a desperately improvised series of interventions. Shakespeare manages to script a ceremony that is being patched up even as it falls apart, and the distinction between pre- and local allocation can help us to chart exactly how he does so.

One further point about pre-allocation before we move on to the more difficult question of how turns can be locally allocated. It is in the study of the pre-allocated patterns of formal interaction that the analysis of turn-taking becomes historically grounded. In order to be able to recognize when a wedding, or a trial, or a meeting of ambassadors goes wrong, we need to know what an early modern audience would have expected it to look like had it gone right. The order in which the characters speak is crucial to such expectations. A comprehensive analysis of the wedding scene from *Much Ado about Nothing* would need to take account of the history of the marriage service in England— including (but not limited to) its multiple iterations in the *Book of Common Prayer*. The literary-critical study of turn-taking needs to be accompanied, in other words, by an equally rigorous attempt to recover the interactional patterns of the past—a kind of turn-taking archaeology, if you will. I address a problem of this nature in Chapter 3, 'Apostrophizing the King', which seeks to put the ugly altercation between Bolingbroke and Mowbray at the start of *Richard II* into the context of early modern expectations about trial proceedings and royal etiquette.

*   *   *

More difficult to explain is how turns are locally allocated—how the speaker sequencing problem is solved in the absence of a clear decision rule or an institutionalized script. This, after all, is how most conversation occurs—not within the straitjacket of a pre-determined structure but in apparently free play. It is not enough to assume that each person simply speaks when he or she wants to, because there are times at which everyone wants to speak and times at which no one does. Somehow, between them, the participants improvise a solution to this problem, in real time, on a turn-by-turn basis. But how?

Central to the explanation provided by Sacks, Schegloff, and Jefferson is the concept of 'selection'. Person A can allocate a turn to person B by employing what they pithily call a '"current speaker selects next" technique'.[20] One way in which conversational sequences are constructed, then, is like a game of 'tag' in which the speaker is 'it' and anoints his or her successor through an act of linguistic touching. Alternatively, we might think of the speakership as an invisible ball (or conch) that the interlocutors pass between them—having it in your possession enables you to choose who has it next. There are potentially

---

[20] Sacks, Schegloff, and Jefferson, p. 704.

many different ways in which one speaker can select another, and Sacks, Schegloff, and Jefferson make no attempt to provide a typology. For the model to function, all that matters is that selection is possible. The archetypal current-speaker-selects-next technique is an addressed question. In conversation analytic terms, a question is understood as the 'first pair part' of a two-part sequence called an 'adjacency pair', with the answer as the 'second pair part'.

> Thus an important general technique whereby current speaker selects next—perhaps the central one—involves the affiliation of an address term (or some other device for achieving 'addressing', e.g. gaze direction) to a first pair-part. But addressing a party will not necessarily, in itself, select him as next speaker.[21]

Later conversation analysts are less cautious. What is claimed here for the addressed question has come to be generalized to all forms of selection. They all have the same two components—an act of address and a 'sequence-initiating action'.[22] Both must be present for selection to take place. When the Host invites the Monk to tell a tale, for example, it qualifies as 'selection' because he both addresses him and initiates a request–compliance sequence.

The option available to the current speaker, of selecting who speaks next, logically entails a second possibility—that this option is not exercised. By choosing not to employ a current-speaker-selects-next technique, the speaker leaves the floor open. So long as no one has been selected, anyone can volunteer. Sacks, Schegloff, and Jefferson call this 'self-selection', in contrast to 'other selection', which is their term for what happens when one speaker selects another. If other-selection is a game of tag, self-selection is a game of 'snap'—it is speed of response that wins the turn. Any locally allocated transition between two speakers is necessarily of one of these two types. Thus:

> (a) If the turn-so-far is so constructed as to involve the use of a 'current speaker selects next' technique, then the party so selected has

---

[21] Sacks, Schegloff, and Jefferson, p. 717.

[22] For a summary of more recent research, see Makoto Hayashi, 'Turn Allocation and Turn Sharing', in *The Handbook of Conversation Analysis*, ed. by Jack Sidnell and Tanya Stivers (Chichester: Wiley-Blackwell, 2013), pp. 167–90.

the right and is obliged to take [the] next turn to speak; no others have such rights or obligations, and transfer occurs at that place.

(b) If the turn-so-far is so constructed as not to involve the use of a 'current speaker selects next' technique, then self-selection for next speakership may, but need not, be instituted; first starter acquires rights to a turn, and transfer occurs at that place.[23]

Later research has investigated what happens when two or more potential next speakers self-select simultaneously. Generally, after a brief period of overlap, all but one of them will withdraw. How they determine which of them this should be is complex and need not concern us here.[24]

Sacks, Schegloff, and Jefferson's model has obvious implications for the study of dramatic dialogue. The distinction between 'self-selection' and 'other-selection' is particularly useful. Which characters select which other characters to speak, who tends to self-select (or to speak only when selected), which characters break these rules to speak when someone else has been selected, why and when they do so—a range of applications comes immediately to mind. It is tempting, then, simply to adopt the model in its original form and apply it to Shakespeare's plays. I think that would be a mistake, however, for two reasons.

The first is that the criteria for identifying selection combine two things which, as literary critics, we might want to keep separate—the act of addressing someone (at whom the turn points) and the performance of a 'sequence-initiating action' (what the turn does). They confound, that is, the distinction I have already drawn between the two senses of the word 'sequence'—between dialogical form and dialogical function. To analyse dramatic dialogue using this model, we would need to be able to distinguish between those turns which initiate sequences and those which do not. It is by no means clear that such a distinction is tenable. Sacks and Schegloff have claimed of the adjacency pair, for example, that 'the component utterances of such sequences have an achieved relatedness beyond that which may

---

[23] Sacks, Schegloff, and Jefferson, p. 704.
[24] For a detailed account of how this works, see Emanuel A. Schegloff, 'Overlapping Talk and the Organization of Turn-Taking for Conversation', *Language in Society*, 29 (2000), 1–63.

otherwise obtain between adjacent utterances'.[25] But how far beyond? And how is this distance to be measured? Without answers to these questions, the analyst has no way of deciding whether an act of selection has, or has not, taken place. Even the apparently obvious case of an addressed question is not quite so straightforward as it looks. It is possible to ask someone a question rhetorically, in such a way as to make it clear that an answer is not required. Does this count as a 'sequence-initiating action'? And, if not, on what grounds are we to make the distinction? By restricting ourselves to a formal analysis of dialogical sequence we can side-step these problems. Which is not to say that functional relationships between turns are something that we can ignore—only that it is possible (and, for the literary critic, advantageous) to describe the turn-taking structure of a scene without putting turns into functional categories.

The second problem relates to self-selection. The conversation analytic model assumes that when no 'current speaker selects next technique' has been used, the listening parties are all equally unselected and all have an equal right to self-select—that when nobody has been chosen, anyone can volunteer. Intuitively this seems wrong, and Sacks, Schegloff, and Jefferson recognize that it is not always the case. They identify the operation of what they call the '"last as next" bias', whereby the speaker of the previous turn seems to have an increased chance of speaking next.[26]

> [The bias] remains invariant over increases in the number of parties—and, with each additional increment in number of parties, tends progressively to concentrate the distribution of turns among a sub-set of potential next speakers. With three parties, one might be 'left out' were the bias to operate stringently; with four parties, two would be 'left out', etc.[27]

The bias is caused, they claim, by a specific type of question—one which requests an expansion, clarification, or repetition of the previous turn—such as these, from *Twelfth Night*:

---

[25] Emanuel A. Schegloff and Harvey Sacks, 'Opening up Closings', *Semiotica*, 8 (2009), 289–327 (pp. 295–6).
[26] Sacks, Schegloff, and Jefferson, p. 712.
[27] Sacks, Schegloff, and Jefferson, p. 712.

MALVOLIO 'Remember who commended thy yellow stockings'—
OLIVIA Thy yellow stockings?
MALVOLIO 'And wished to see thee cross-gartered.'
OLIVIA Cross-gartered?

(3.4.43–6)

According to Sacks, Schegloff, and Jefferson, 'this question-type may be used without any affiliated technique for selecting a particular other, and thereby selects the just prior speaker as next speaker'.[28] It is a unique feature of such questions that they can select someone to speak without being explicitly addressed to that person. The bias exists because it is only the previous speaker who can be selected in this way. What Sacks, Schegloff, and Jefferson do not explain is why it is only this particular type of turn that can do this. Nor do they explain whether the absence of a 'technique' for identifying the addressee of the question means that it is, in fact, unaddressed—or whether it is *because* the question is so obviously addressed to the previous speaker that no such technique is necessary. Sacks, Schegloff, and Jefferson do not answer these questions because they do not see them as important. The sources of the last-as-next bias, they insist, are 'external to the turn-taking system's basic organization'.[29] This may be so. But, once again, they do not explain why. And, in the absence of such an explanation, it is legitimate to consider an alternative possibility—that what Sacks, Schegloff, and Jefferson call the last-as-next bias is not a unique feature of a specific type of question but a generalized feature of all conversational turns.

* * *

In the introduction to this book I promised the reader that I would be 'bold' in reducing the complex apparatus of interactional linguistics to a set of manageable literary critical tools. In fulfilment of that promise I now propose the following—that we can radically simplify the standard turn-taking model by replacing Sacks, Schegloff, and Jefferson's awkwardly phrased sequencing rules with a single neat aphorism

---

[28] Sacks, Schegloff, and Jefferson, p. 717.
[29] Sacks, Schegloff, and Jefferson, p. 709.

I learnt from my grandmother. The first rule of conversational sequencing is not 'if the turn-so-far is so constructed as to involve the use of a "current speaker selects next" technique, then the party so selected has the right and is obliged to take [the] next turn to speak; no others have such rights or obligations'. It is, instead, 'speak when you're spoken to'. There is a deep folk-wisdom, I want to suggest, in this apparently simple formulation, and by adopting it we can solve—or dissolve—the two problems I identified with Sacks, Schegloff, and Jefferson's model.[30]

We might start by considering what work the phrase does. One reason it is so frequently in the mouths of people like my grandmother is that it can be used to check at least three forms of behaviour. Most commonly it serves to reprimand a child for speaking out of turn. What it means in this context is 'speak *only* when you are spoken to—do not butt in, wait to be addressed'. But it is equally useful for reprimanding a child who is stubbornly silent. In this context it means 'do not ignore someone who speaks to you—acknowledge what they have said with a reply'. And implicit in this second usage is a third, less obvious, imperative. A child who waited dutifully to be spoken to but then directed what she said to another child—rather than to the adult who had just addressed her—could certainly claim to have spoken *when* she was spoken to, but she would not get far with my grandmother. Pragmatically, the phrase means both 'speak when you're spoken to' and 'speak to the person who spoke to you'.

This, I suggest, is the real source of the last-as-next bias—a bias which operates universally, across all turn-types, not just in a single special case. Sacks, Schegloff, and Jefferson are wrong to claim that when no 'current speaker selects next technique' has been used, the listening parties are all equally unselected and all have an equal right to self-select. Having been singled out by the previous turn, the addressee is on a slightly different footing. As Erving Goffman puts it, 'among official hearers one must distinguish the addressed recipient from

---

[30] The reader not satisfied with my grandmother's credentials as an authority on interpersonal behaviour might wish to compare Erasmus: 'A chylde syttynge with his betters shulde neuer speke but necessyte compell or el he be bydden', *De Civilitate Morun* [sic] *Puerilium* [*Lytell Booke of Good Maners for Chyldren*], trans. by Robert Whittington (London: Wynkyn de Worde, 1532), sig. C4r.

"unaddressed" ones'. It is to the addressed recipient, he suggests, that the speaker 'addresses his visual attention and to whom, incidentally, he expects to turn over the speaking role'.[31] When there is competition for turns, the addressee has an advantage—has the backing, as it were, of the previous incumbent. When no one wants to speak, it is to the addressee that the others will instinctively look. To put it another way, the basic assumption which underpins all conversational sequencing is that the addressee of the current turn will become the speaker of the next. Things do not always turn out this way, and that is not necessarily a problem, but the expectation is normative—it provides what we might think of as a default solution to the speaker sequencing problem.

In effect, I am proposing both to loosen the requirements of the existing model and to tighten them: to loosen them by removing one of the two criteria necessary for an act of selection, and to tighten them by heaping a further obligation on the person so selected. A new speaker can be nominated without the need for a sequence initiating action, but, as well as being required to speak, they are required to reply—to speak, that is, specifically to the person by whom they were nominated. The difficulty, of course, is in establishing that any such expectation exists. Were I a linguist I would set out to prove it empirically (and I do not think it would be difficult to prove). As a literary critic, however, I ask the reader to accept the claim on a slightly different basis. First, because their own understanding of conversation, based on a lifetime of daily experience, will confirm it. Second, because what little we know about the cognitive processes that underlie turn-taking suggests that I am right. Third, because the assumption is analytically useful when it comes to understanding dramatic dialogue. The second and third of these reasons will require some elaboration.

Recent work in cognitive linguistics suggests that the ability to take turns is both phylogenetically and ontogenetically older than language—that it developed earlier in the life of the species and that it develops earlier in the life of a child. The second of these claims is beyond dispute. As one study puts it, 'mothers and infants start to

---

[31] Goffman, 'Footing', in *Forms of Talk* (Oxford: Blackwell, 1981), pp. 124–59 (pp. 132–3).

adopt a more turn-taking like pattern in vocal exchanges from around 5 months onward as evidenced by the decrease in the percentage of overlap that infants produce'.[32] Within the first year the child has developed what we might think of as a turn-taking reflex (in the everyday rather than the medical sense of that word), without which they would not be able to learn language. Crucially, however, this line of research focuses exclusively on two-party, parent–child interaction. There is, so far as I am aware, no research yet available on the development of multiparty turn-taking, but it seems unlikely that this too develops in the first year of life. Learning to speak is not the same thing as learning how to solve the speaker sequencing problem. One requires the ability to react, the other requires the ability to know when action is appropriate. The prefrontal cortex—the part of the brain 'especially important for many of the cognitive processes that underlie reasoning, decision making, self-control, planning, and memory'— undergoes dramatic changes between the ages of four and six. It is only at this age that the child develops the ability to follow a rule—to resolve an 'object dispute' with another child, for example, by taking turns with a toy.[33] Taken together, what these two strands of research suggest is that, cognitively speaking, duologue is more basic than dialogue. One relies on the fundamental cognitive equipment that first makes turn-taking possible, the other on the rule-following ability acquired later.

That the speak-when-you're-spoken-to assumption is analytically useful in the study of dialogue is something that, I hope, the next three chapters will show. All I want to do here is point out that there are good reasons for thinking that it ought to be. Like the prosodic assumptions that make it possible for us to scan verse, this assumption makes it possible for us to abstract and analyse dialogical form. It allows us to sidestep the problem of identifying 'sequence-initiating actions' in dialogue because all that is required to explain why one speaker follows

[32] Elma E. Hilbrink, Merideth Gattis, and Stephen C. Levinson, 'Early Developmental Changes in the Timing of Turn-Taking: A Longitudinal Study of Mother–infant Inter-action', *Frontiers in Psychology*, 6 (2015), art. no. 1492. See also Maya Gratier, et al., 'Early Development of Turn-Taking in Vocal Interaction between Mothers and Infants', *Language Sciences*, 6 (2015), art. no. 1167.

[33] *Handbook of Child Psychology and Developmental Science*, 7th edn, 4 vols, ed. by Richard M. Lerner (Chichester: Wiley, 2015), III, p. 467.

another is the fact that they have just been addressed. By asking a question, or performing any other 'sequence-initiating action', the speaker increases the pressure on the addressee to provide a response, but that pressure exists even if no question is asked. An act of address is always an act of nomination, regardless of what is said. Rather than making a binary distinction between 'selection' and 'non-selection', we should think in terms of a continuum—with the bare fact of having been addressed at one end and torture by the Inquisition at the other.

A couple of examples may help here. Consider, once again, the opening of *King Lear*. Much of the drama of this scene derives from the tension between Cordelia's resolution to 'Love, and be silent' and her father's desire to hear her 'speak'.

> LEAR [...]   (*To Cordelia*) Now our joy,
>   Although our last and least, to whose young love
>   The vines of France and milk of Burgundy
> 85   Strive to be interested: what can you say to draw
>   A third more opulent than your sisters? Speak.
> CORDELIA   Nothing, my lord.[34]

$$(1.1.82–7)$$

This is an act of selection in the full conversation analytic sense. We have both address and a sequence initiating action. But even the stronger word 'selection' is inadequate here. The basic fact of Cordelia being addressed by her father is overlaid with a series of other actions and circumstances, both verbal and non-verbal, that massively intensify the force of the nomination. Lear both asks her a question and adds the redundant imperative 'speak', recasting what she is about to say as an act of obedience as well as a reply. Further pressure is built by the shape of the dialogue. With the narrative clarity of a folk tale, the king addresses each of his daughters in turn, in accordance, as I have suggested, with a Goffmanian decision rule. The point in the sequence at which Cordelia will be required to speak can thus be identified four

---

[34] I quote here from 'The Tragedy of King Lear' in *The Complete Works*, ed. by Stanley Wells and Gary Taylor, The Oxford Shakespeare, 2nd edn (Oxford: Oxford University Press, 2005)—a text based on the Folio. The New Oxford Shakespeare contains a single text of *King Lear*, based on the 1608 Quarto, in which this speech is shorter.

turns in advance, by the audience as well as the character. We watch its approach, as she does, with a mounting sense of dread. Add to this what we know about the plot and about the social roles of the participants. Cordelia's inheritance, and the fate of the kingdom, are at stake in her reply. Lear is the king as well as her father, and this is an ostentatiously public spectacle. To do anything other than comply with his wishes is to offer him an affront. All of which contributes to the force of the nomination. In a little over fifty lines the scene has built an unstoppable sequential momentum. Cordelia is placed under excruciating pressure to speak—and to speak in a particular way. Her response, however, is defiant. She refuses to participate in Lear's absurd game, to flatter his vanity, or to compete with her sisters. She flouts his authority and exposes the folly of his actions. She privately hurts and publicly humiliates him. Every plan Lear had for this moment is frustrated and defeated. But, crucially, Cordelia does not keep silent. To refuse to speak at all would be a step too far. Rather than say nothing, she says 'Nothing'.

At the other end of the spectrum is the passage we have already examined, in which Vincentio fails to silence Lucio. The two exchanges could not be more different, but they both rely on the operation of the same basic principle. Lear addresses Cordelia, and, by addressing her, he nominates her to speak. He does everything he can to intensify the pressure exerted by this nomination, and, even though she defies him in every other respect, she still fulfils the obligation to reply. She speaks because she is spoken to. Vincentio addresses Lucio simply in order to shut him up. He does everything he can to cancel the force of this nomination—to make it clear that what he requires is silence rather than a response. Only a fool, I have suggested, could misunderstand him. But Lucio is a fool, and what allows him to misunderstand the duke is the one basic assumption that underpins all conversational sequencing. He too speaks because he is spoken to.[35]

One final point, specific to dialogue as it appears on the page. The speak-when-you're-spoken-to assumption is as fundamental to the way

---

[35] An infuriating tendency to keep replying—even to direct imperatives to shut up—is characteristic of Shakespeare's fools. Compare, for example, Costard during the reading of Armado's letter (Love's Labour's Lost, 1.1.210–17).

in which we read as it is to the way in which we talk. Consider the following exchange, in which Elizabeth Bennet is quizzed about her upbringing by Lady Catherine de Bourgh:

> 'Your father's estate is entailed on Mr. Collins, I think. For your sake,' turning to Charlotte, 'I am glad of it; but otherwise I see no occasion for entailing estates from the female line.—It was not thought necessary in Sir Lewis de Bourgh's family.—Do you play and sing, Miss Bennet?'
>
> 'A little.'
>
> 'Oh! then—some time or other we shall be happy to hear you. Our instrument is a capital one, probably superior to—You shall try it some day.—Do your sisters play and sing?'
>
> 'One of them does.'
>
> 'Why did not you all learn?—You ought all to have learned. The Miss Webbs all play, and their father has not so good an income as your's.—Do you draw?'
>
> 'No, not at all.'
>
> 'What, none of you?'
>
> 'Not one.'
>
> 'That is very strange. But I suppose you had no opportunity. Your mother should have taken you to town every spring for the benefit of masters.'
>
> 'My mother would have had no objection, but my father hates London.'
>
> 'Has your governess left you?'
>
> 'We never had any governess.'
>
> 'No governess! How was that possible? Five daughters brought up at home without a governess!—I never heard of such a thing. Your mother must have been quite a slave to your education.'[36]

Discounting servants, there are eight characters present at this interview. The narrator sees fit to disambiguate 'for your sake' in the first turn quoted, to make it clear that Lady Catherine has turned to address Charlotte. When she addresses Miss Bennet by name at the end of the same turn, it is clear that she has turned back. But the twelve turns that follow contain no unambiguous terms of address (none of them employs, that is, an 'affiliated technique for selecting a particular

---

[36] Jane Austen, *Pride and Prejudice*, ed. by Pat Rogers, The Cambridge Edition of the Works of Jane Austen (Cambridge: Cambridge University Press, 2006), pp. 185–6.

other'), and they are presented to the reader without a single narratorial intervention. Yet at no point is there any reasonable cause to doubt who is speaking or to whom. This is partly due to the reader's grasp of the characters and situation, to the use of pronouns, and to the way in which each question seems to grow naturally from the last. But it would not be implausible, on these grounds, for Miss de Bourgh to join her mother in questioning their new acquaintance, or for Charlotte to assist her friend in answering. The phrase 'not one', for example, could just as easily be a contraction of 'not one of them' as 'not one of us'—with Charlotte intervening to attest to the extraordinary fact that none of the Miss Bennets can draw. Austen is able to rely on the reader not to make this mistake because speak-when-you're-spoken-to is the Occam's razor of dialogical interpretation. Unless we have reason to think otherwise, we assume that the character speaking is the one who was last addressed and that the character to whom they are speaking is the one who last addressed them. The assumption is natural, but it can also be misleading—as the next chapter will show. What matters is to recognize that the same set of expectations that enables us to participate in conversation also enables us to interpret dialogue—that the rules of turn-taking are as crucial to the way we read as they are to the way in which we talk. If we want to read well, we need to pay attention to them.

| 2 |

Figures of Dialogue

In the preceding chapter I argued that we could radically simplify the standard turn-taking model by making a single, very reasonable, assumption. This chapter will look at the implications of that assumption for the analysis of Shakespearean dialogue. It argues that such an approach makes two things easier—the development of a stable vocabulary for the description of dialogical form, and the development of a system of dialogical scansion with which to abstract and describe the turn-taking structure of a scene. The basis of both claims is the same. If we accept the speak-when-you're-spoken-to rule as normative—as the default solution to the speaker sequencing problem—then deviations from that rule become meaningful. There is only a limited number of ways in which these can occur, and it is possible to describe them in purely formal terms. By analysing the distribution of such deviations across larger stretches of talk, we can begin to characterize the turn-taking structure of scenes, to make comparisons between them, and to locate moments at which something out of the ordinary might be happening. The first half of this chapter will explain how I think this can be done, and the second half will practise it on a series of examples culled from the work of other critics. This should enable the reader to decide for him- or herself whether my approach has anything new to offer.

Strictly observed, the speak-when-you're-spoken-to rule would make conversation impossible. It must be broken in order for a conversation to begin (someone will have to speak first, without having been addressed), and it must be broken again for a conversation to end (someone will have to speak last, without receiving a reply). In a two-party conversation, or duologue, these are the only occasions on which it is broken. Since there are only two speakers, the only possible sequence is ABAB. The only questions at issue are when—and sometimes whether—the sequence will start, and where it will end. Multi-party conversation, on the other hand, requires frequent deviations from the speak-when-you're-spoken-to rule in order to function. Allowed to operate unhindered, the twin pressures which underpin the last-as-next bias—the pressure to supply a response and the pressure to address that response to the previous speaker—will produce a simple alternation between A and B, regardless of how many people are present. Dialogue tends as naturally towards duologue as a river to the sea. In order to prevent it from getting there, the cycle of reciprocal obligations between speaker and addressee must be broken: the parties must swim upstream, as it were, against the current of the bias. There are only three ways in which they can do this—three ways, that is, in which someone outside the central axis of speaker and addressee can acquire a turn at talk.

The first is for someone to speak without having been spoken to. A addresses B, but, for whatever reason, it is C who speaks next. This I call 'intervention'. It is not the same thing that conversation analysts call 'self-selection', although most examples of one will also be examples of the other. First, because what conversation analysis considers to be merely an act of volunteering I consider to be acting against the sequential pressure produced by the address of the previous turn. C intervenes *between* A's remark and a projected reply from B. Second, because when no one has been addressed, no intervention can occur. Opening a conversation in a lift, for example, is self-selection but not intervention. Nor is intervention the same thing as interruption. To intervene is not necessarily to speak out of turn—it only becomes so in a context in which it is socially inappropriate. There are other contexts in which it might be regarded with indifference or welcomed as an act of mercy. To intervene is to take a turn at talk, like another slice of cake, without having been offered it—not rude necessarily but risky amongst people you don't know well. A few examples should help to make this clear.

This is Falstaff, in *1 Henry IV*, intervening between the king and the rebel Worcester:

```
       WORCESTER    Hear me, my liege.
          For mine own part, I could be well content
          To entertain the lag-end of my life
25        With quiet hours; for I protest,
          I have not sought the day of this dislike.
       KING    You have not sought it? How comes it, then?
       FALSTAFF    Rebellion lay in his way, and he found it.
       PRINCE    Peace, chewet, peace!
30     WORCESTER  [to the King]
          It pleased your majesty to turn your looks
          Of favour from myself and all our house [ ... ]
                              (5.1.22–31)
```

This is a clear case of intervention as interruption. Rather than cutting Worcester off before he has finished, Falstaff cuts him off before he has started. What makes it so clear is that the king both addresses Worcester and asks him a question—specifies who should speak, and specifies the kind of thing he should say—combining an act of address with a 'sequence initiating action'. He is also the king. His interactional wishes, like his wishes more generally, should be respected. The sequential pressure on Worcester to speak next—and on everyone else to let him speak next—is strong. The comedy of Falstaff's answer lies partly in his sarcastic dismissal of any explanation Worcester might give and partly in the audaciousness of his speaking so flagrantly out of turn.

Compare Gertrude, intervening—equally publicly—between her husband and her son:

```
       KING [ ... ]                    For your intent
          In going back to school in Wittenberg,
          It is most retrograde to our desire,
115       And we beseech you bend you to remain
          Here in the cheer and comfort of our eye,
          Our chiefest courtier, cousin, and our son.
       QUEEN    Let not thy mother lose her prayers, Hamlet.
          I pray thee stay with us, go not to Wittenberg.
120    HAMLET    I shall in all my best obey you, madam.
       KING    Why, 'tis a loving and a fair reply.
                              (2[1.2].112–21)
```

By intervening in this way, Gertrude simultaneously relieves Hamlet of the obligation to reply to Claudius and nullifies the risk that he will do so impertinently. Both men are able to save face—Hamlet because he is obeying his mother rather than his uncle, Claudius because Hamlet does as he is told. Gertrude steps between them in the dialogue like a barman stepping between two drunks in a pub. Her intervention functions as a kind of conversational buffer, preventing the two men from coming to blows.

Notice too how the two examples differ. Falstaff replies to the previous speaker, albeit sarcastically, in place of the person who has just been addressed. Gertrude continues where the previous speaker left off, directing what she says to the same addressee. Falstaff's intervention substitutes for a reply, Gertrude's for a continuation. In both cases A addresses B and C speaks next, but in one case C addresses A, and in the other B. Other permutations are possible, but you get the idea. An intervention is a formal structure with no inherent meaning. It can be an act of rescue or an act of aggression, ostentatious or tactful, momentous or trivial. It can relieve someone of the obligation to speak, make it easier for them to do so, or deny them the opportunity altogether.

The second way in which multiparty conversation can deviate from duologue is for the addressee to take the turn they have been offered— to accept the nomination, as it were—but not to address what they say back to the previous speaker. Since this is essentially a failure of acknowledgement (the very specific form of acknowledgement that comes from addressing someone), I'm going to call it 'blanking'. It is not the same thing as ignoring someone, although the two may coincide. It is possible, for example, for B to 'blank' A in such a way that what he says is still clearly a response to A. As with 'intervention', the name is intended to be suggestive but not (I hope) misleading. A useful example is Richard's treatment of Buckingham in 4.2 of *Richard III*:

> BUCKINGHAM   My lord, I claim the gift, my due by promise,
>   For which your honour and your faith is pawned,
>   Th'earldom of Hereford and the movables
>   Which you have promisèd I shall possess.
> 90 KING RICHARD   Stanley, look to your wife. If she convey
>   Letters to Richmond, you shall answer it.
>
> (4.2.86–91)

Richard blanks Buckingham to address Stanley on an unrelated matter, cutting his accomplice out of the conversation. This is a raw display of power at the conversational level. Richard is annoyed at Buckingham for his reluctance to arrange the murder of the princes in the tower. His interactional conduct is a way of making it clear that any promises he may formerly have made to his accomplice will only be honoured if it suits him now, as king, to honour them. He puts the duke into a turn-taking limbo. Having knocked once, and received no answer, Buckingham is caught between the need to knock again and the consciousness that it is rude, or even dangerous, to insist. Excluded from a duologue with the king, he is a supplicant for a chance to speak as well as for an earldom. Compare Claudius' treatment of Polonius in 1.2 of *Hamlet*:

> KING   Have you your father's leave? What says Polonius?
> POLONIUS   He hath, my lord, wrung from me my slow leave
>   By laboursome petition, and at last
> 60   Upon his will I sealed my hard consent.
>   I do beseech you give him leave to go.
> KING   Take thy fair hour, Laertes. Time be thine,
>   And thy best graces spend it at thy will.
>
> (2[1.2].57–63)

Two points are of interest here. First, Polonius intervenes by answering a question addressed to Laertes—standing in, as it were, for his son, to provide information on a subject that more nearly concerns himself. Secondly, what the king says next is simultaneously addressed to Laertes and a response to Polonius. He blanks the counsellor but does not ignore him. The move is decisive, regal even, but it has none of the menace of Richard blanking Buckingham.

The third way in which the parties to a conversation can avoid lapsing into duologue is through a form of apostrophe—a 'turning away' of the voice from one addressee to another. This occurs when A addresses B, and B begins his own turn by replying to A. He then pivots, mid-turn, from addressing A to addressing C and thus nominates C, rather than A, to speak next. An apostrophe of this kind is a way of moving from one conversational dyad to another—of closing off a duologue with the person who just addressed you and opening one with someone else. This is how Lear extracts expressions of love (or tries to) from each of his daughters in turn.

LEAR *[to Gonoril]*   Of all these bounds, even from this line to this,
   With shady forests and wide-skirted meads,
   We make thee lady. To thine and Alban's issue
   Be this perpetual.—What says our second daughter?
55 Our dearest Regan, wife to Cornwall, speak.

           (1[1.1].51–5)

The turn begins with Lear responding to Goneril and ends with him calling on Regan. Goneril is given no opportunity to react, verbally, to what her father has said—no opportunity to thank him, even, for her portion of the kingdom. To do so she would have to intervene between Lear's question to Regan and Regan's response. In this way the king decisively ends his interaction with one daughter and moves on to the next. The difference between apostrophizing someone and blanking them is that the previous speaker receives at least some acknowledgement before the pivot takes place. Not always much, however. Compare Coriolanus (still known simply as Caius Martius at this point in the play) arriving at a scene of public disorder that his friend Menenius has been doing his best to contain:

    Enter Caius Martius
MENENIUS [. . .]   Hail, noble Martius.
CAIUS MARTIUS
  Thanks. What's the matter, you dissentious rogues,
  That, rubbing the poor itch of your opinion,
  Make yourselves scabs?
SECOND CITIZEN   We have ever your good word.
          (1.1.145–8)

Coriolanus gives the older man the barest of recognition—the single word 'thanks'—before turning his ire on the citizens. He waits for no explanation as to what is happening and makes no real attempt to gauge the situation himself. Instead he jumps straight to the conclusion that the citizens are behaving disgracefully and that he, rather than Menenius, is the man to deal with them. This is the first time that Coriolanus speaks in the play. His very first word is followed by a brutal act of apostrophe that neatly encapsulates both the bluntness of his character—he does not stand on ceremony—and his ideological position—there can be no doubt who is at fault. It's a brilliantly concise piece of characterization, and it is rooted in the shape of the dialogue.

In these three ways, then—intervention, blanking, and apostrophe—turns at talk can be shared out, snatched at, or thrust upon the unsuspecting bystander. The three terms provide a basic vocabulary for discussing conversational sequencing and the ways in which a group of characters can be seen to negotiate access to the floor. They do not offer a complete description of everything that can happen in dialogue, nor are they intended to do so. What they do offer, I hope, is a way of bringing the right sort of issues into focus. I propose to call them 'figures of dialogue', in analogy to the 'figures of speech' familiar from classical rhetoric. What distinguishes the two types of figure is that figures of dialogue can only occur in situations involving more than one potential speaker. They occur, that is, across and between the speech of several characters, rather than within the speech of one. Consider the difference between a dialogical apostrophe and a rhetorical one. When Lear turns away from his unkind daughters to call on the gods, he is doing something very different from what he does when he turns from one daughter to another. A rhetorical apostrophe is one to which we cannot or do not expect an answer (it is analogous in this sense to a rhetorical question)—usually because the person addressed is absent or because what is addressed is not a person. A dialogical apostrophe, however, has interactional consequences—what is addressed is not just a person but a potential next speaker. The implications of this distinction will form one of the central subjects of the next chapter.

It is important to stress, once again, that none of these figures is rare, either in conversation or in Shakespearean dialogue. Rather, they are fundamental to the way in which multiparty interaction works. It is not the case that every example of intervention is dramatically significant, nor is it the case that they can all be interpreted in the same sort of way. One conclusion we can come to when looking at the turn-taking structure of a scene is that it dramatizes precisely the kind of conversation in which interventions are commonplace. But that still tells us something about the scene. Looking at how frequently such figures occur, and where, can help us to locate moments at which something out of the ordinary is occurring. It can help us to characterize the type of interaction taking place, the social rules by which it is shaped, and the different roles that each of the characters takes. This form of analysis—which steps back from individual examples of dialogical figures to look at a larger turn-taking pattern—I want to call 'dialogical scansion'. How best to go about practising it is now my concern.

* * *

A useful hint in this direction is provided by Emrys Jones in his classic study *Scenic Form in Shakespeare*. 'Scenic form' encompasses more than just dialogical form, but suffers similar neglect and for much the same reason. Whenever we read Shakespeare, Jones suggests, 'so much significance of a verbal and poetic nature claims attention that it is possible, perhaps even natural, to overlook or not to notice its basic structural shaping'.[1] Scenic form is whatever is left when we remove the distraction of Shakespeare's language.

> What Shakespeare has invented is something—a structure, an *occa-sion*—which may be said to be (however dangerous the phrase) independent of the words which are usually thought to give the scene its realization. This 'something' we may call 'scenic form'.[2]

Anything that carries over in the translation of a scene from one language to another—plot, stage action, entrances and exits, the speech acts each character performs (as distinct from the words they use to perform them)—is part of its scenic form. This includes turn-taking, although the phrase is not one Jones is likely to have known. Here, for example, is his analysis of the funeral procession in 1.1 of *1 Henry VI*:

> There are four speakers: Bedford, Gloucester, Exeter, and Winchester. If we designate these speakers as A, B, C, and D, the order of their speeches in the first part of the scene (1–56) is as follows: A, B, C, D, B, D, B, A. That is to say, Bedford is the 'leader', who opens and closes this exchange. Gloucester and Winchester are the fractious members of the group whose quarrelling threatens to disrupt the formality of the occasion. Exeter, in accordance with his role as the loyal watch-dog of the commonweal, has only one speech: he knows his place and keeps it. Thus, even in this short passage, each of the four speakers is given a clear role: the chief spokesman or leader, the two qua[r]rellers, and the honest man—just as in any closed social group different social 'roles' will tend to be distributed among its members.[3]

---

[1] Jones, *Scenic Form*, p. 3.   [2] Jones, *Scenic Form*, p. 3.
[3] Jones, *Scenic Form*, pp. 16–17.

I set aside the very interesting questions of whether or not Shakespeare wrote this scene and how far I agree with the analysis Jones provides. The point of interest is not his conclusion but his method. Notice, first, that he abstracts a pattern from the dialogue and finds meaning in it. Secondly, that he does so using a convention borrowed from prosody—assigning each character a letter, like the rhymes in a rhyme scheme. Notice, thirdly, that he recognizes the sociological implications of the pattern he describes—that the sequence of speakers is at least partly a product of the characters' social roles. What Jones is practising here is a simple form of dialogical scansion.

I believe this practice is worth reviving, with one minor modification. As well as a letter to denote the speaker of each turn, we need one to denote the addressee. The advantage of this change is that it enables us to identify deviations from the speak-when-you're-spoken-to rule from a formal description of the dialogue. It makes them visible in the sequence of letters generated by the process of scansion. Here, for example, are the eight turns analysed by Jones with the extra letters added:

1	2	3	4	5	6	7	8
A→All,	B→All,	C→All,	D→All,	B→D,	D→B,	B→D,	A→BD

Even without us knowing who these characters are or what they are saying to each other, this pattern gives us a sense of the shape of the dialogue—in precisely the same way that a rhyme scheme and syllable count (ABAB, 8.6.8.6) gives us a sense of the shape of a stanza or that a sequence of stressed and unstressed syllables (x / x / x / x /) gives us a sense of the shape of a line. We can spot an intervention or an apostrophe in the same way we might spot a trochaic substitution—as a deviation from a normative pattern.

The first thing to notice about this particular stretch of dialogue is that for the first four turns the characters appear to be speaking in a round—once each until everyone has had a go—and addressing themselves not to one another but to everyone at once. While it is possible to improvise such a pattern in conversation, it suggests that what is happening is some sort of ceremony—that these turns may have been pre-allocated in accordance with a decision rule. And, as Jones points out, the order in which the characters speak implies an order of precedence. The pattern is broken in turn 5 when B addresses

D directly, presumably in response to something D has just said. We can say the pattern is 'broken' because there are still two characters on stage (E and F) who have not yet spoken. If what is happening in turns 1–4 is a round of ceremonial speech, that round is not yet complete. Turns 5–7 are a duologue between B and D, which is brought to a close in turn 8 when A intervenes to address both of them together. The fact that A does this reinforces the impression that he is the highest-status character and that the duologue between B and D is not part of the ceremonial script. C neither contributes to the squabble between B and D nor considers himself responsible for putting it to an end. He speaks once, at the appropriate point in the round, and otherwise keeps his mouth shut. The two lowest-ranking characters, E and F, remain silent. They do not complain about the round being abandoned before it reaches them.

The analysis I have just given could have been written by someone who had never read the scene in question and had no idea which play it was from. All they would have needed is the dialogical skeleton of the first eight turns and a list of the characters onstage. My point is not that we should practise dramatic criticism in this way (except perhaps as a parlour game or a pedagogical tool) but that it is possible to do so. And the fact that it is possible is proof, if proof were needed, of the central importance of dialogical form to the way in which drama functions. There is much, of course, that such an analysis leaves out. We cannot know, simply from the shape of the scene, that the characters are engaged in a formal lament, that Bedford (as the dead king's eldest living brother) is indeed the highest-ranking character, that what Gloucester objects to is Winchester's claim that Henry V owed his successes to the prayers of the church, that the two men are squabbling in front of the late king's corpse, and so on. But these are the kind of things that readers and critics are unlikely to miss. What the process of scanning the dialogue does is help us to notice things we might not otherwise have noticed and to be precise where we might otherwise have been vague. A full analysis of the scene would require careful attention to both its dialogical form and its linguistic texture (and to the potential for counterpoint between the two). Scanning dialogue is like scanning verse—it is a step on the way to an informed critical reading, not a substitute for one.

These, then, are the basic tools of the approach I am recommending. The rest of the chapter will be dedicated to a practical demonstration of what they can do. Before proceeding, however, it is worth adding a caveat. It is not the case that we always can identify the addressee of a turn, or at all points during a turn, nor (as we have seen) that the addressee is always singular. Nor is it the case that every character onstage can always hear what every other character says, or that every string of words which follows a character's name is straightforwardly a turn at talk. Ambiguities with regard to address or the clusivity of pronouns, asides, soliloquy, and many other more subtle dialogical effects all pose problems for the model I have proposed. What the model does is to provide a way of facing those problems with a clearer understanding of what is at stake. Much of this book—most of it perhaps—is concerned with the moments at which the model breaks down. But it is the model that enables us to identify such moments as potentially significant (the square-pegs-in-round-holes principle). Above all, what I am arguing for is the vital importance of paying attention to the addressivity of turns at talk—not in the Bakhtinian sense of how each turn is shaped for a particular hearer but in the far more mundane sense of whom the turn is pointing at. It is not possible to act or direct a play without having to resolve this question—the actor must know at whom to look, how loudly to speak, where to stand, and so on. For the reader, or the critic, or the editor, on the other hand, it is possible to read a play not just without deciding such questions but without even asking them. Every utterance in a dramatic text is accompanied by a paratextual marker to identify the speaker. Very few of them are accompanied by a corresponding marker to identify the addressee. It is assumed that a competent reader will be able to work this out for herself—a second set of names down the right-hand side of the page would only be unnecessary clutter. This may well be true, but it has consequences for the way in which we read. The typographical form of the dramatic text encourages us to disattend to addressivity and thus to the shape of the dialogue. Or rather, it relies on our grasp of the speak-when-you're-spoken-to rule to obviate the need for explicit information.

*   *   *

It is now time to look at some practical applications of this approach—to field-test it, as it were, in the crowded and often bad-tempered arena of Shakespeare criticism. I have not gone out of my way to find examples of either good or bad dialogical analysis. My aim has rather been to give a cross-sectional view of the different kinds of criticism that touch on these issues. My first example is taken from a handbook on stylistics, my second from a monograph on Shakespearean dialogue, and my third from an essay which attempts to define character. All three are written by critics of repute, and all three, it seems to me, are valuable. In all three cases, however, I think a greater attention to the mechanics of turn-taking has something to add.

My first example is taken from Mick Short's *Exploring the Language of Poems, Plays, and Prose*—a standard introductory textbook for students of stylistics. Short devotes two chapters to drama, which he describes as 'the conversational genre'.[4] He does not give a detailed account of any specific turn-taking model, but he does provide a checklist that can be used to assess whether a speaker is 'powerful' or 'powerless'.

	Powerful speakers	Powerless speakers
Who has most turns?	x	
Who has the least?		x
Who has the longest turns?	x	
Who has the shortest?		x
Who initiates conversational exchanges?	x	
Who responds?		x
Who allocates turns to others?[5]	x	

Short demonstrates the usefulness of his checklist by applying it to an extract from *Richard III*—the same moment at which we have already glanced, when Buckingham attempts to claim the earldom of Hereford only to be told that Richard is 'not in the giving vein today'.[6] Short quotes the scene at considerable length:

---

[4] Short, *Exploring the Language of Poems, Plays, and Prose*, p. 68.

[5] Short, p. 206. I have omitted four further questions relating to topic control and address-terms.

[6] Short's work is still considered exemplary. His checklist was reprinted in 2014 by Marina Lambrou in a chapter on 'Stylistics, conversation analysis and the cooperative principle' for *The Routledge Handbook of Stylistics*, ed. by Michael Burke, Routledge Handbooks in English Language Studies (London: Routledge, 2014), pp. 137–54. Lambrou promises to show how the tools of conversation analysis 'can be applied for the analysis of spoken interaction in literary texts beyond the mechanics of turn-taking' (p. 137). What follows is a brief sketch of 'A Simplest Systematics' and Grice's maxims, followed by the checklist. She then commends Short for his 'subtle' analysis of *Richard III*.

BUCKINGHAM   A→B
   My lord, I have considered in my mind
   The late request that you did sound me in.
KING RICHARD   B→A
   Well, let that rest. Dorset is fled to Richmond.
BUCKINGHAM   I hear the news, my lord.   A→B
KING RICHARD   B→C
90   Stanley, he is your wife's son. Well, look to it.
BUCKINGHAM   A→B
   My lord, I claim the gift, my due by promise,
   For which your honour and your faith is pawned:
   Th'earldom of Hereford, and the movables
   Which you have promisèd I shall possess.
KING RICHARD   B→C
95   Stanley, look to your wife. If she convey
   Letters to Richmond, you shall answer it.
BUCKINGHAM   A→B
   What says your highness to my just request?
KING RICHARD   B→B
   I do remember me, Henry the Sixth
   Did prophesy that Richmond should be king,
100   When Richmond was a little peevish boy.
   A king...perhaps...perhaps.
BUCKINGHAM   My lord?   A→B
KING RICHARD   B→B
   How chance the prophet could not at that time
   Have told me, I being by, that I should kill him?
BUCKINGHAM   A→B
   My lord, your promise for the earldom.
KING RICHARD   B→B
105   Richmond? When last I was at Exeter,
   The Mayor in courtesy showed me the castle,
   And called it 'Ruge-mount'—at which name I started,
   Because a bard of Ireland told me once
   I should not live long after I saw 'Richmond'.
110 BUCKINGHAM   My lord?   A→B
   KING RICHARD   Ay? What's o'clock?   B→A

BUCKINGHAM		A→B
I am thus bold to put your grace in mind		
Of what you promised me.		
KING RICHARD	But what's o'clock?	B→A
BUCKINGHAM	Upon the stroke of ten.	A→B
115 KING RICHARD	Well, let it strike!	B→A
BUCKINGHAM	Why 'let it strike'?	A→B
KING RICHARD		B→A
Because that, like a jack, thou keep'st the stroke		
Betwixt thy begging and my meditation.		
I am not in the giving vein today.		
BUCKINGHAM		A→B
120 Why then resolve me, whe'er you will or no?		
KING RICHARD		B→A
Thou troublest me. I am not in the vein.[7]		

$$(4.2.86\text{--}121)$$

The aim of Short's analysis is to show that Richard is more powerful than Buckingham—as indeed he is. It begins by pointing out that 'as there are only two characters talking, the number of turns each has is equal' but that Richard 'dominates the word count' (164 to 107).[8] Both of these statements are potentially misleading—the first because it implies that what we have here is a duologue, the second because it is too crude a statistic to tell us much about such a short exchange. What matters is not the number of characters who speak but the number of potential speakers, not how much or how often a character speaks but why and when. The problem with the quantitative approach to dialogue is that it assumes all turn-taking is competitive, that all characters are equally competitive, and that they are all equally competitive at all moments—like Hungry Hungry Hippos gobbling up marbles, which can then be counted to see who has the most 'power'.[9] It ignores the

---

[7] I quote here from *The Complete Works*, ed. by Stanley Wells and Gary Taylor, The Oxford Shakespeare, 2nd edn (Oxford: Oxford University Press, 2005). The NOS contains a truncated form of this exchange based on the Folio (rather than the 1598 Quarto) text of the play.

[8] Short, p. 208.

[9] The reader unfamiliar with this noble game would do well to consult Hasbro, 'Hungry Hungry Hippos Commercial', https://www.youtube.com/watch?v=8HPI_HT6yjo (accessed 27 March 2016).

possibility that one character may be desperate to talk while another is equally desperate not to, or that the same character can be desperate to talk at one moment and reluctant to do so the next. It flattens out any sense that the dialogue is embedded in an evolving situation—any sense, that is, of the dramatic. It assumes that what Buckingham wants in the passage is to speak more than Richard and that he fails to achieve this aim. A more reasonable assumption is that what Buckingham wants is to be Earl of Hereford, as soon as possible, and without having to beg for it.

Similarly, while the exchange may look like look a duologue on the page—the kind of analysis proposed by Emrys Jones, for example, would produce a simple ABAB alternation through twenty-two turns—to treat it as such is to miss the point. Richard and Buckingham begin and end in a duologue, but what happens in between is an interactional arm-wrestle over precisely the question of whether or not that is how things will stay. It is an arm-wrestle that Buckingham wins, forcing Richard to acknowledge him at line 111 and finally to answer his question at line 119. This is a Pyrrhic victory for the duke, but a victory all the same. Short describes Richard's behaviour well:

> Richard deflects him time and again, mainly by changing the topic and by addressing Stanley when in conversational terms he should be responding to Buckingham's just requests. In his first speech Richard explicitly tells Buckingham not to pursue the topic he has raised, and begins a new one, Richmond's flight. The next time Buckingham asks for his reward, Richard ignores him and addresses Stanley instead. The third time Buckingham tries, Richard apparently goes off into a reverie about Richmond, a tactic he continues over Buckingham's next two attempts to get the topic back to what Richard owes him.[10]

These two tactics—addressing Stanley and going off into a reverie—are both forms of blanking.[11] Richard stonewalls Buckingham for five consecutive turns. Short is right to see this as a display of power at the interactional level. He is wrong, however, to present the dialogue as conspicuously one-sided. Just as important as the fact that Richard

---

[10] Short, p. 209.
[11] I have marked these turns as being self-addressed for reasons that will be become clear in Chapter 4.

refuses to acknowledge Buckingham's request is how far Buckingham is prepared to push him in pursuit of it. Both men are behaving in a conversationally aggressive way. Buckingham's words are all politeness, as Short points out (he 'uses a stream of status-marked address terms' when speaking to Richard), but he pointedly refuses to allow the king off the hook. There is a clear contradiction between the way in which Buckingham speaks and the fact he insists on speaking. The two men take eleven turns each. On all eleven occasions that Richard talks, he has been the addressee of the previous turn. Buckingham takes the same number of terms but is addressed on only six occasions. He intervenes twice between an instruction issued to Stanley and Stanley's acknowledgement of that instruction. It would be possible, of course, for Stanley to acknowledge Richard non-verbally, but it still would not follow that Buckingham should speak next. Part of what makes this scene dramatic is the mismatch between Buckingham's aggressive and insistent conversational behaviour and the reality of his powerlessness. A genuinely powerless supplicant—or one who better understands his own position—does not insist in this way. Buckingham ploughs on in the face of Richard's obvious displeasure. Short senses this tension but fails to make it explicit:

> Buckingham sticks to his request because it is so important to him. In spite of the fact that he is not as powerful as Richard, it is he who initiates the large majority of the conversational exchanges, and each time with the same topic, his unfulfilled reward for services rendered.[12]

It is not simply the importance of Buckingham's request that causes him to persevere but a mistaken sense of his own importance to Richard. The passage dramatizes the process by which he comes to realize that his influence has waned (or was never what he thought it). Rather than tell Buckingham that he will not be getting the earldom—and that, incidentally, he had better start making himself useful if he wants to

---

[12] There is a slight inaccuracy here that is nonetheless worth pointing out. It is only in his third turn (l. 91) that Buckingham makes his first attempt to claim what Richard has promised him. The 'late demand' he mentions in line 87 was Richard's request to Buckingham that he make away with the two princes—a request Buckingham deferred answering until he had thought it over. Richard's behaviour is motivated, in part, by his anger at this lack of alacrity—you deferred my request, now I'm deferring yours.

keep a head on his shoulders—Richard shows it to him, slowly, through his interactional conduct. And Shakespeare shows it to us through the shape of the dialogue.

* * *

My second example is a more sophisticated exploration of the relationship between dialogue and power, Lynne Magnusson's fine chapter on '"Voice potential": Language and Symbolic Capital in *Othello*'.[13] Magnusson uses an economic model of linguistic exchange derived from the work of Pierre Bourdieu to analyse power relations in Shakespearean dialogue. Her larger aim is to develop a 'sociological stylistics of Shakespeare's language'—an approach to dialogue that recognizes the various ways in which linguistic behaviour is both socially situated and socially determined.[14] Much of what critics usually attribute to 'personal style' or to the 'individual temperament' of a writer or character, she argues, is in fact the product of 'relative social position'.[15] Magnusson makes judicious use of politeness theory, Bakhtinian 'dialogism', conversation analysis, and (in this chapter) Bourdieu's essay on 'The Economics of Linguistic Exchanges'.[16] It is worth summarizing the latter.

Bourdieu's aim is to provide a sociological critique of several of the assumptions which underpin formal linguistics, most notably that language is 'an object of understanding rather than an instrument of action'.[17] According to him,

> Language is not only an instrument of communication or even of knowledge, but also an instrument of power. A person speaks not only to be understood but also to be believed, obeyed, respected, distinguished.[18]

---

[13] This was first published as '"Voice Potential": Language and Symbolic Capital in *Othello*' before becoming the seventh chapter of *Shakespeare and Social Dialogue* (pp. 163–82).

[14] Magnusson, *Shakespeare and Social Dialogue*, p. 11.

[15] Magnusson, *Shakespeare and Social Dialogue*, p. 148–9.

[16] Pierre Bourdieu, 'The Economics of Linguistic Exchanges', trans. by Richard Nice, *Social Science Information*, 16 (1977), 645–68. This was originally published in French as 'L'économie des échanges linguistiques', *Langue française*, 34 (1977), 17–34.

[17] Bourdieu, 'The Economics of Linguistic Exchanges', p. 645.

[18] Bourdieu, 'The Economics of Linguistic Exchanges', p. 648.

How we respond to what someone says—the price it fetches on the linguistic market—depends on the 'symbolic capital' possessed by the speaker. All speech 'owes a major part of its value to the value of the person who utters it'.[19] Conversely, the way in which someone speaks is an expression of what they understand (consciously or subconsciously) to be their own social value. As Magnusson puts it, an utterance 'inscribes an expectation of profit, an estimate of the likelihood that the speaker will be believed, recognized, obeyed'.[20] Crucially, however, one does not speak to 'any Tom, Dick or Harry'. Speech 'presupposes a legitimate transmitter addressing a legitimate receiver'.[21] One problem with traditional linguistics, Bourdieu points out, is that 'the linguist regards the conditions for the establishment of communication as already secured, whereas, in real situations, that is the essential question'.[22] It is unclear whether Bourdieu was familiar with the work of Sacks, Schegloff, and Jefferson, but Magnusson undoubtedly is—she quotes from it in the preceding chapter, in a discussion of conversational 'repair'.[23] And she invokes it again here, albeit less explicitly, in a neat summary of what this approach might mean for the study of dialogue:

> If we consider how it could be that speech patterns inscribe a speaker's expectation of profit, we need to look not only at the internal constitution of the speeches but also at turn-taking and access to the floor.[24]

What she does not do, however, is engage with the mechanics of the turn-taking model.

Magnusson's central example is 1.3 of *Othello*, in which the scandal of Othello's secret marriage to Desdemona is brought before the Venetian Senate. The duke and the senators already have their hands full trying to deal with the threat of a Turkish invasion of Cyprus, but they pause this urgent business to resolve the dispute. Brabantio accuses Othello of having bewitched his daughter, Othello denies this, and Desdemona is sent for as a witness. When she arrives, Magnusson points out, she

---

[19] Bourdieu, 'The Economics of Linguistic Exchanges', p. 652.
[20] Magnusson, *Shakespeare and Social Dialogue*, p. 167.
[21] Bourdieu, 'The Economics of Linguistic Exchanges', p. 649.
[22] Bourdieu, 'The Economics of Linguistic Exchanges', p. 648.
[23] Magnusson, *Shakespeare and Social Dialogue*, pp. 143–4.
[24] Magnusson, *Shakespeare and Social Dialogue*, p. 167.

shows herself to be 'a bold and self-confident speaker in a setting whose formality and importance would silence most speakers, especially—one might expect—a woman'.[25] Desdemona seems to possess, and to be aware that she possesses, a significant amount of symbolic capital.

> Answering the Duke's summons, she speaks first to confirm Othello's account of their courtship and later to make a request of her own, to accompany Othello to the war zone. In both cases her speech wins credit, in the first instance solidifying the Duke's acceptance of the marriage and silencing Brabantio's complaint and in the second instance gaining her permission to go with Othello.[26]

In support of this claim, Magnusson quotes the 'chorus of dissent' which greets the duke's suggestion that Desdemona return to her father's house while Othello is in Cyprus.

OTHELLO [...]
    Most humbly therefore bending to your state,
    I crave fit disposition for my wife,
    Due reference of place and exhibition,
    With such accommodation and besort
235   As levels with her breeding.
DUKE   Why, at her father's!
BRABANZIO   I will not have it so.
OTHELLO   Nor I.
DESDEMONA   Nor would I there reside,
    To put my father in impatient thoughts
    By being in his eye. Most gracious Duke,
    To my unfolding lend your prosperous ear,
240   And let me find a charter in your voice
    T'assist my simpleness.
DUKE   What would you, Desdemona?
DESDEMONA   That I love the Moor to live with him,
    My downright violence and storm of fortunes
    May trumpet to the world.

                             (1.3.231–44)

---

[25] Magnusson, *Shakespeare and Social Dialogue*, p. 166.
[26] Magnusson, *Shakespeare and Social Dialogue*, p. 165.

Magnusson remarks how Desdemona's voice 'momentarily amplifies Othello's before she strikes off on her own, claiming the floor and elaborating an alternative plan'.[27] This is true, but there is an opportunity to say more, I think, about exactly how she gains access to the floor.

The short passage quoted contains a seven-turn sequence in the following form:

$$
\begin{array}{cc|ccc|cc}
1 & 2 & 3 & 4 & 5 & 6 & 7 \\
A{\rightarrow}B, & B{\rightarrow}A, & C{\rightarrow}B, & A{\rightarrow}B, & D{\rightarrow}B, & B{\rightarrow}D, & D{\rightarrow}B
\end{array}
$$

It begins, that is, with the duke in a duologue with Othello and ends with him in a duologue with Desdemona. In between are three consecutive interventions. Brabantio answers a question addressed to Othello, Othello then answers it himself, and Desdemona chimes in with a third answer. It would be possible for an actor to play the duke's question more openly, turning to address Brabantio or even Desdemona as he delivers it, but that would not invalidate the basic point. What matters is that all three of them reply before he speaks again and that they do so in a particular order—first her father, then her husband, then Desdemona. On the one hand, she speaks without having been spoken to. On the other hand, she does so only after the speak-when-you're-spoken-to rule has temporarily been suspended—intervening off the back of two prior interventions. The 'chorus of dissent' Magnusson describes is accompanied, that is, by a corresponding outbreak of interactional dissent—a momentary deviation from the normative expectations about sequencing. The conversation flares up for a second, the reins slacken, and Desdemona seizes her chance. Consider what difference it would have made had she been the first to reply—answering the duke's question immediately without having waited to see how her father and husband would respond. Having acquired a turn in this slightly opportunistic manner—by jumping, as it were, on the dissenters' bandwagon—Desdemona uses it, as Magnusson points out, to claim a more extended run. There is a confidence in the way she does so—she knows that the duke will not refuse her a direct request to speak—but it is the sharpness of her conversational reflexes that has enabled her to manufacture the opportunity. It is only possible to request the floor, verbally, when you already have it. Desdemona wins the duke's attention not only because she has the symbolic capital to claim it but also because she understands the mechanics of turn-taking. Here, as elsewhere, she shows herself to be extraordinarily dextrous in negotiating for the conversational floor. Like so many of Shakespeare's heroines, Desdemona is a character of acute interactional intelligence.

Magnusson is right to stress that 'what one says, how one says it, and whether one speaks at all in any given situation' are all strongly influenced by the 'practical expectation [...] of receiving a high or low price for one's discourse', but this is not the only factor at play.[28] It is not simply a question of *whether* one speaks but *when*—and why one speaks exactly when one does. Bourdieu recognizes this when he suggests that linguistic competence rests as much on the ability to identify 'the opportune moment' as to produce grammatically recognizable utterances—but he does not specify what makes the moment opportune.[29] It is here that the mechanics of turn-taking—as opposed to the fact that people take turns—have something to contribute.

The example also raises a larger question that may as well be addressed here: whether the turn-taking model, like traditional linguistics, obscures the social dimension of speech by replacing it with abstract formal description. Sacks, Schegloff, and Jefferson were all sociologists by training and would have been appalled to think so. They had intended the model to 'have the important twin features of being context-free and capable of extraordinary context-sensitivity', and they elaborate on these two terms in a footnote:

> When we speak of 'context-free' and 'context-sensitive,' we cannot state the scope of reference of 'context' that is relevant. For now, let it suffice to employ a long-term understanding of 'context' in the social sciences—one which attends the various places, times, and identities of parties to interaction. What we mean to note is that major aspects of the organization of turn-taking are insensitive to such parameters of context, and are, in that sense, 'context-free'; but it remains the case that examination of any particular materials will

[28] Magnusson, *Shakespeare and Social Dialogue*, p. 167.
[29] Bourdieu, 'The Economics of Linguistic Exchanges', p. 655.

> display the context-free resources of the turn-taking system to be
> employed, disposed in ways fitted to particulars of context. It is the
> context-free structure which defines how and where context sensi-
> tivity can be displayed […][30]

What they attempt to provide, in other words, is a neutral framework
within which comparisons between different cultures, situations, and
social actors can be made, not an apparatus with which to erase
sociological distinctions. The systematics describes how turn-taking
would function between perfect psychological and intellectual equals
conversing disinterestedly in a social vacuum—not how it *does* functions in any real situation. Their claim is that certain features of the way
in which conversation is organized are universal and that it is precisely
this universality that allows us to grasp the significance of the different
ways in which they are employed. Turn-taking is like eating—different
cultures and individuals may do it differently, and the same individual
may do it differently in different situations, but there is no culture or
individual that does not do it. The point of the systematics is to separate
the essential from the contingent.

   The distinction seems to have caused some confusion, however,
amongst the very few literary critics who have engaged with their
work. Keir Elam, for example, rightly distinguishes between 'the supposed "spontaneity" of the dialogue on the part of the dramatic
speakers' and the fact that, for the playwright and the actors, 'the
succession, content, and sheer length of contributions are at all times
determined by the laws of textuality and narrativity'.[31] In reality,
nothing could be less spontaneous than the turn-taking in a play.
Elam goes on to claim:

> What the textual and narrative status of the dramatic turn means is
> the effective elimination of the most characteristic feature of the
> management of natural talk: namely, the strategic negotiating of the
> conversational floor.[32]

This is true, but only of the play itself—not of the fictional world the
play depicts. It is entirely possible for a playwright to script the

---

[30] Sacks, Schegloff, and Jefferson, p. 699.
[31] Elam, *Shakespeare's Universe of Discourse*, p. 188.   [32] Elam, p. 188.

'strategic negotiating of the conversational floor'. More than that, it is central to all good drama. Elam then makes a further claim:

> Turn-allocation and repair techniques derive from what we might term the *ceteris paribus* democratic premise on which natural talk is founded: all other things being equal (we are not, for example, conversing with a monarch, a president or an armed terrorist), every participant has an equal right to the floor, so that speaking turns, rather than being predetermined, have to be booked, assigned or fought for. [...] Rhetorical equality of this kind is quite alien to the drama, in which, obviously, the distribution of discourse is not democratic but dramaturgic. Dramatic speakers clearly do *not* have the same rights to the floor.[33]

This is wrong both ways round. It is never the case that 'all other things' *are* equal—as Magnusson and Bourdieu are at great pains to show—and Sacks, Schegloff, and Jefferson pointedly avoid making the claim that they can be. The monarch, the president, and the armed terrorist are extreme examples of a universal principle. When we choose to speak, whether and when we interrupt, how we take turns at talk: these decisions are always and necessarily affected by whom we are talking to, in what situation. There is no distinction, in this respect, between real conversation and fictional dialogue—at least, not within the fictional world that we are supposed to imagine produces that dialogue. Elam is right to insist that realism is not the playwright's only concern, but he is wrong to insist that the 'dramaturgic' principle is inherently in opposition to, and takes precedence over, the attempt to reproduce the patterns of natural conversation. What we get in plays is a stylized form of turn-taking, in which these patterns are heightened and made obvious—just as the rhythms of language are heightened into verse and syntactic structures are heightened into rhetorical figures. One of the playwright's main resources when it comes to individuating characters as distinct personalities and to sketching the social relations between them is showing how they take turns at talk. Part of what constructs a king as a king, a servant as a servant, or a fool as a fool is their place within the interactional pattern of a scene. This is what Magnusson describes as 'the inscription in the conversational

---

[33] Elam, p. 188.

organisation of the characters' relative social positions'.[34] What a turn-taking model does is give us a way of deciphering this inscription. It makes no claim about what the inscription will say.

* * *

My final example is taken from Stephen Orgel's classic essay 'What is a Character?'. Orgel bemoans the 'editorial energy that has been expended on the question of consistency of character'.[35] Characters, he observes, 'are not people, they are elements of a linguistic structure, lines in a drama, and more basically, words on a page'. To understand this is 'to release character from the requirements of psychology, consistency and credibility'.[36] One of Orgel's key examples comes from *The Tempest*—a play he had edited some ten years earlier.[37]

> From Dryden to Kittredge, Miranda's attack on Caliban, 'Abhorred slave, / Which any print of goodness wilt not take,' etc., was regularly reassigned to Prospero, being considered inappropriate to the character of Miranda—it is often still given to Prospero in performance. This is a very clear case of the character being considered both prior to and independent of her lines, but it also clearly springs not from the play but from notions of how fifteen-year-old girls ought to behave. It bears no relation whatever, needless to say, to any notion of how they really do behave, and to that extent it is a change that makes Miranda less rather than more credible.[38]

My interest here is in whether or not Orgel is right to claim that the decision to reassign the speech springs 'not from the play' but from the prejudice of its editors, and in whether these two things are quite so easy to disentangle as he supposes. The basic pattern of the controversy is not unusual—many emendations first made in the eighteenth century were handed down unchallenged until the twentieth. But the result of such challenges is usually a greater awareness of the instability of the text, not the establishment of a new orthodoxy. No major editor

---

[34] Magnusson, *Shakespeare and Social Dialogue*, p. 148.
[35] Orgel, 'What is a Character?', *Text*, 8 (1995), 101–9 (p. 106).
[36] Orgel, 'What is a Character?', pp. 102–3.
[37] *The Tempest*, ed. by Stephen Orgel, The Oxford Shakespeare (Oxford: Oxford University Press, 1986).
[38] Orgel, 'What Is a Character?', p. 107.

since Kittredge has given the 'Abhorred slave' speech to Prospero.[39]
What makes this particular emendation interesting is that we are as
certain now that the speech should not be reassigned as we once were
that it should. A greater awareness of dialogical form, I will suggest, can
help us to understand why.

The disputed speech occurs in the play's long second scene. Prospero
has just summoned Caliban, who comes on cursing and complaining.
The gist of his complaint is that the island on which Prospero and
Miranda live was once his. Now he is made a slave, confined to a hard
rock, and tormented at night by pinches. Or so he claims. Prospero
responds to this bitter lamentation with anger. The reason for Caliban's
torment, he points out, is that he attempted to rape Miranda—until
which time he had been treated as one of the family. Caliban makes no
attempt to deny this. If only he had been successful, he gleefully
remarks, he could have peopled the island with Calibans. It is at this
point that the disputed speech occurs. Caliban's gloating elicits the
following response:

> Abhorrèd slave,
> Which any print of goodness wilt not take,
> Being capable of all ill! I pitied thee,
> Took pains to make thee speak, taught thee each hour
> 355 One thing or other. When thou didst not, savage,
> Know thine own meaning, but wouldst gabble like
> A thing most brutish, I endowed thy purposes
> With words that made them known. But thy vile race,
> Though thou didst learn, had that in't, which good natures
> 360 Could not abide to be with; therefore wast thou
> Deservedly confined into this rock, who hadst
> Deserved more than a prison.
>
> (1.2.351–62)

[39] *The Tempest*, ed. by G. L. Kittredge, The Kittredge Shakespeares (Boston: Ginn &
Co, 1939). Orgel is right to point out, however, that it is still sometimes reassigned in
performance—as, for example, by Peter Brook in 1957 (with John Gielgud as Prospero),
Ron Daniels in 1982 (with Derek Jacobi), and Silviu Purcarete (with Gerrard McArthur)
in 1996. For a comprehensive survey of the performance history of the speech (and the
play), see *The Tempest*, ed. by Christine Dymkowski, Shakespeare in Production
(Cambridge: Cambridge University Press, 2000), p. 164n.

The only substantive text of the play, the First Folio, gives the lines to Miranda, as do the three subsequent folios, as does Shakespeare's first known editor, Nicholas Rowe, and his second, Alexander Pope.[40] Orgel's identification of Dryden as the first person to reassign them is only half accurate. Dryden had indeed rewritten *The Tempest*—in collaboration with William Davenant—retaining these lines almost verbatim but reassigning them to Prospero.[41] But the Dryden–Davenant alteration is precisely that, an alteration. Its purpose is to make the play more effective on the Restoration stage, not to provide an authoritative, corrected text. (As well as reassigning the speech to Prospero, the pair introduce multiple new scenes and characters.) The first editor to reassign the speech was Lewis Theobald, in 1733, and he explained in a footnote what he thought he was up to:

> In all the printed Editions this Speech is given to *Miranda*: but I am persuaded, the Author never design'd it for her. In the first Place, 'tis probable, *Prospero* taught *Caliban* to speak, rather than left that Office to his Daughter: in the next Place, as *Prospero* was here rating *Caliban*, it would be a great Impropriety for her to take the Discipline out of his Hands; and, indeed, in some sort, an Indecency in her to reply to what *Caliban* last was speaking of.[42]

Theobald gives three reasons for reassigning the speech, two of which have engendered considerable critical debate, one of which has not. The first is that the speaker of the disputed lines claims to have taught Caliban to speak. That Miranda had at least some hand in the monster's education is clear from what he later says to Stephano about his 'mistress' having shown him the man in the moon (2.2.119–20). That she could have been his teacher at a time when he did not know his own meaning and would 'gabble like | A thing most brutish', however, is less clear. This uncertainty has spawned a somewhat tedious debate about the chronology of events before the start of the play. One side contends

[40] *The Works of Mr. William Shakespear*, ed. by Nicholas Rowe, 6 vols (London: Jacob Tonson, 1709); *The Works of Shakespear*, ed. by Alexander Pope, 6 vols (London: Jacob Tonson, 1725).

[41] John Dryden and William Davenant, *The Tempest, or the Enchanted Island* (London: Henry Herringman, 1670).

[42] *The Works of Shakespeare: in Seven Volumes*, ed. by Lewis Theobald (London: A. Bettesworth et al., 1733), I, p. 18n.

that Miranda, not yet three when she arrived on the island, 'could hardly have been competent so early' to teach Caliban to speak.[43] The other argues that 'later on—by age 10 or so—she could have introduced him to European words and ideas that Prospero had recently taught her'.[44] A third position, adopted by Frank Kermode, is that any such quibbling is misguided, since it fails to take account of Shakespeare's 'habitual disregard for this kind of immediate probability'.[45]

Theobald's second reason for reassigning the speech—the 'Impropriety' of Miranda taking the discipline out of her father's hands—has been largely ignored. Or rather, it is habitually conflated with his third—that it would be 'an Indecency' for Miranda to respond to a remark about rape. Current critical consensus sees Miranda as more 'sexually aware than early editors seemed to prefer'.[46] Theobald and his followers are 'discomfited by harsh words in Miranda's supposedly tender mouth', their objections having more to do with their own preconceptions about femininity than they do with Shakespeare's play.[47] The reassignment of the 'abhorred slave' speech has come to be seen exactly as Orgel presents it—a classic example of an ideologically motivated textual intervention—the silencing of an unacceptably outspoken young woman by a male editorial tradition.

As a characterization of the attitudes prevalent amongst eighteenth- and nineteenth-century editors of Shakespeare, this may well be accurate. As a reading of Theobald's footnote, however, it is not. Miranda's outburst is improper not only because of *what* she says but *when* it is that she says it. Lurking in Theobald's footnote is a recognition of the speak-when-you're-spoken-to rule. It is Prospero who is rating Caliban, and it is Prospero to whom Caliban is complaining. Miranda intervenes in this exchange by replying on her father's behalf to what Caliban has just said—not to her but to him. As well as taking 'the

---

[43] *The Tempest*, ed. by H. H. Furness, A New Variorum Edition of Shakespeare (Philadelphia: J. B. Lippincott, 1892), p. 73n.

[44] *The Tempest*, ed. by Virginia Mason Vaughan and Alden T. Vaughan, The Arden Shakespeare: Third Series (London: Thomson Learning, 1999), p. 135.

[45] *The Tempest*, ed. by Frank Kermode, The Arden Shakespeare: Second Series (London: Methuen, 1954), p. 32n.

[46] *The Tempest*, Vaughan and Vaughan (eds), p. 135.

[47] Raphael Lyne, *Shakespeare's Late Work*, Oxford Shakespeare Topics (Oxford: Oxford University Press, 2007), p. 107.

discipline out of his hands', she takes the words out of his mouth. As well as speaking out, she is speaking out of turn. The question of what it means for her to do this—or for an editor to stop her from doing it—remains open. But the fact that she does it is a matter of dialogical structure, not of ideological prejudice.

A useful comparison can be drawn here between Miranda's intervention and Desdemona's. Both women speak at moments of acute interactional friction, but Desdemona does so only after this friction has already disrupted the shape of the dialogue. Miranda disrupts it herself. Her intervention comes in the ninety-third turn since she and Prospero entered the stage over 350 lines ago. Forty-six of the preceding ninety-two turns have been spoken by Prospero, and the other forty-six have been spoken to him. There has been a strict alternation, that is, between A and B—where A is Prospero and B is any one of the other three inhabitants of the island. The 'abhorred slave' speech breaks this pattern. Instead of ABAB we have ABCB—instead of *Prospero-other-Prospero-other* we have *Prospero-other-Miranda-other*. It's the dialogical equivalent of a false rhyme after a hundred lines of neat heroic couplets.

Add some flesh to the interactional bones and things become clearer still. The scene opens with an exchange between Prospero and Miranda, in which he assures her that no one was harmed in the making of the tempest she has just witnessed and explains, at some length, how the two of them first came to be marooned on the island. Prospero then puts his daughter to sleep and summons Ariel, from whom he receives a report on the shipwreck and to whom he issues instructions. When he has finished with this he wakes Miranda and continues chatting to her, with Ariel popping in and out for further reporting and further instruction. Then Prospero calls for Caliban, who enters, as we know, cursing and complaining. The other three characters take turns to interact with Prospero, and they do so at his bidding—he summons and dismisses them, puts them to sleep and wakes them up. Not only do they speak when they are spoken to, but they enter and leave, wake and sleep, when he tells them to do so. Prospero is the single centre of both the action and the dialogue. Miranda, Ariel, and Caliban rotate around him like planets around a star. They do so, that is, until the moment of the intervention. When Miranda addresses Caliban, Prospero is for the first time sidelined—excluded (albeit momentarily) from the axis of speaker and addressee, a dialogical bystander rather than a participant. It is the breaking of this pattern, I want to suggest, as much as anything Miranda actually says to Caliban, that causes Theobald to reach for his red pen.

At the moment of its occurrence, then, the intervention comes as a surprise. But this is not the only time in the play, or the scene, that Miranda intervenes between her father and another character. She does so again when Prospero accuses Ferdinand of falsely claiming to be the king of Naples and of plotting to supplant him on the island:

PROSPERO [...]   Thou dost here usurp
 The name thou ow'st not, and hast put thyself
455 Upon this island as a spy, to win it
 From me, the lord on't.
FERDINAND   No, as I am a man.
MIRANDA There's nothing ill can dwell in such a temple.
 If the ill spirit have so fair a house,
 Good things will strive to dwell with't.
PROSPERO *[to Ferdinand]*   Follow me.
460 *[To Miranda]* Speak not you for him; he's a traitor.
  [To Ferdinand] Come,
 I'll manacle thy neck and feet together.
 Sea-water shalt thou drink; thy food shall be
 The fresh-brook mussels, withered roots, and husks
 Wherein the acorn cradled. Follow.
FERDINAND   No;
465 I will resist such entertainment till
 Mine enemy has more pow'r.
  He draws, and is charmed from moving
MIRANDA   O dear father,
 Make not too rash a trial of him, for
 He's gentle, and not fearful.
PROSPERO   What, I say,
 My foot my tutor? Put thy sword up, traitor,
470 Who mak'st a show but dar'st not strike, thy conscience
 Is so possessed with guilt. Come from thy ward,
 For I can here disarm thee with this stick
 And make thy weapon drop.

MIRANDA   Beseech you, father!
PROSPERO   Hence! Hang not on my garments.
MIRANDA   Sir, have pity.
475   I'll be his surety.
PROSPERO   Silence! One word more
        Shall make me chide thee, if not hate thee. What,
        An advocate for an impostor? Hush!

                                        (1.2.453–77)

Orgel is one of several critics to have drawn a parallel between the two exchanges. The 'decidedly active Miranda [. . .] who energetically defends Ferdinand', he suggests, would be equally capable of an energetic attack on Caliban.[48] Editors who deny her the 'Abhorred slave' speech are refusing to recognize 'an important aspect of her nature'.[49] Orgel has a sharp ear for dialogue, but, like Theobald, he lacks a precise vocabulary with which to describe what he hears. What he identifies vaguely as an 'aspect' of Miranda's nature is really a habit of her speech. Miranda is 'active' in both exchanges in the sense that she speaks without waiting to be spoken to—the 'energy' Orgel senses here is produced by the dialogical figure that I call intervention.

An awareness of the dialogical structure of the passage also enables us to make some distinctions. Miranda intervenes three times on Ferdinand's behalf, at lines 457, 466 and 473—twice when the default next speaker is her father and once when it is her future husband. On the first two occasions she adds something to a reply that Ferdinand has already given, glossing the young man's behaviour in an attempt to influence how Prospero will interpret it. On the third occasion, rather than comment retrospectively on something Ferdinand has just said, Miranda speaks first—stepping into the firing line to plead with her father directly. All three examples differ from her attack on Caliban because what she says is addressed to Prospero. Throughout Miranda's defence of Ferdinand, the magician remains at the dialogical centre of the scene, the object of both the young man's challenges and the young woman's appeals—the speaker or addressee of every turn at talk. For this reason, despite the similarity of the two exchanges, the 'Abhorred slave' speech remains unique. It is the only time in the play that

---

[48] *The Tempest*, Orgel (ed.), p. 17.   [49] *The Tempest*, Orgel (ed.), p. 120n.

Miranda sidelines her father in this way, the only time she addresses anyone other than him or Ferdinand, and the only time that one of Prospero's three fellow islanders directly addresses another.[50]

None of which means that we should correct Shakespeare's dialogue by reassigning the speech to Prospero, any more than we should correct a sudden use of half-rhyme by inserting a word more satisfying to the editorial ear. What it does mean is that the shock felt by eighteenth-century editors is not purely a matter of prejudice. Theobald's intervention in the text is prompted by Miranda's intervention in her father's correction of Caliban. Whether we agree with his decision or not (personally, I do not), there are reasons for reassigning the speech that spring not from 'notions of how fifteen-year-old girls ought to behave' but from the play itself—from precisely those 'elements of a linguistic structure' that, according to Orgel, constitute a dramatic character. More importantly, what the example shows is that there are ways of understanding consistency of character that do not rest on unexamined impressions of psychological credibility. They rest instead on the distribution of turns at talk, on patterns of interaction and habits of speech—on figures of dialogue that can be identified in the text with as much confidence as alliteration, chiasmus, or feminine rhyme.

---

[50] There are two marginal cases. First, Caliban curses Miranda, along with Prospero, at 1.2.322–5. This is marginal because Miranda is included as part of a plural addressee. Second, Ariel addresses Caliban in 3.2 (lines 39 and 57) but not in his own voice. Instead, he impersonates Trinculo to make the monster believe he has been insulted.

| 3 |

Apostrophizing the King

Richard II opens with Richard II trying to resolve a dispute between his cousin, Henry Bolingbroke, Duke of Hereford, and his hench-man, Thomas Mowbray, Duke of Norfolk. Having summoned the two dukes and received their salutations, he calls them to account.

25   RIC. We thank you both: yet one but flatters us,
       As well appeareth by the cause you come;
       Namely, to appeal each other of high treason.__
       Cousin of *Hereford*, what dost thou object
       Against the duke of *Norfolk, Thomas Mowbray*?
30   BOL. First, (heaven be the record to my speech!)
       In the devotion of a subject's loue,
       Tend'ring the precious safety of my prince,
       And free from other misbegotten hate,
       Come I appellant to this princely presence.__
35   Now, *Thomas Mowbray*, do I turne to thee,
       And mark my greeting well; for what I speak,
       My body shall make good upon this earth,
       Or my divine soul answer it in heaven.
       Thou art a traitor, and a miscreant;
40   Too good to be so, and too bad to live;
       Since, the more fair and crystal is the sky,
       The uglier seem the clouds that in it fly.
                            (V, G1r–v, 1.1.25–42)

I quote from the text of Edward Capell.[1] His edition is notable for many reasons, not least the 'certain new marks' of punctuation it seeks to introduce into Shakespeare's text. Capell had a horror of footnotes, which he considered 'both a blemish to the page they stand in, and inadequate to the end proposed', and the new marks were intended to mitigate the need for them.[2] They included an elevated full stop to indicate irony, a cross with one bar to indicate 'a thing shown', a cross with two bars to indicate 'a thing delivered', and double inverted commas to indicate an aside. None of them appears to have caught on.[3] What makes Capell's Shakespeare of particular interest to a student of turn-taking, however, is his use of dashes:

> A similar arrangement of a mark, call'd by the printers a dash or break, affords a new distinction: This in present usage is single, and put always in the middle: in this work it is otherwise; ranging sometimes with the top, and then it serves the purposes to which it has hitherto been assign'd; and sometimes with the bottom, and has a new signification: All dramatic works abound in single speeches that pass from one person to another, often to very many; which cannot be understood, unless this point likewise be known and attended to: the mark spoken of is destin'd to this service; wherever it occurs, it denotes constantly a change of the address; if it be at all ambiguous to whom the words are spoken, a name is added; but it is in most cases sufficient to mark where the change begins, and where it ends, if not with the speech; for to persons of the least intelligence the context will speak the rest.[4]

[1] *Mr William Shakespeare his Comedies, Histories, and Tragedies*, ed. by Edward Capell, 10 vols (London: Dryden Leach for J. and R. Tonson, 1768). All Shakespeare quotations in the current chapter are from this edition unless otherwise stated. Citations give the volume and signature for Capell followed by the act, scene, and line numbers of the equivalent passage in the New Oxford Shakespeare.

[2] Edward Capell, *Prolusions; or, Select Pieces of Antient Poetry* (London: J. and R. Tonson, 1760), pp. ii (sig. A5v), v–vi (sigs A7r-v). Capell was so confident that the meaning of his new marks would 'occur immediately to the reader' that he did not explain them in the introduction to his edition. See Capell (1768), I, p. 28n (sig. C2v). The reader is referred instead to the *Prolusions*, published eight years earlier.

[3] One minor exception is the use of inverted commas for asides. This was adopted in a slightly modified form by Dover Wilson and Quiller-Couch for their 1921 Cambridge edition, *The Works of Shakespeare* (series title), ed. by John Dover Wilson, et al., 39 vols (Cambridge: Cambridge University Press, 1921–66).

[4] Capell, *Prolusions*, pp. v–vi (sigs A7r-v).

Instead of one type of dash Capell has two, differentiated by their relative heights. A dash level with the top of the letters works in the same way as any other dash. A dash level with the bottom of the letters (what we now call an 'underscore') is reserved for a specific purpose. It signals what Capell calls a 'change of the address' and I call a dialogical apostrophe—a turning of the voice from one addressee to another. Capell was the first—and remains the only—editor of Shakespeare to attempt to mark changes of address in a systematic and unambiguous way: systematic because he attempts to mark them all, unambiguous because he has a typographical sign dedicated to the purpose. The earliest editions are notoriously inconsistent in their use of punctuation.[5] Modern editions tend to use a conventional mid-height dash for changes of address, but only where the editor deems necessary. Capell's low dashes are thus a unique record of one reader's attempt to locate every change of address in Shakespeare and a unique resource for anyone interested in the dialogical apostrophe.

There are two in the passage I have just quoted. The first comes at the end of line 27, when Richard switches from addressing the two dukes together to addressing Bolingbroke alone, a switch signalled by the address-terms 'you both' and 'Cousin of *Hereford*'. Prior to the apostrophe he has thanked the two men for their good wishes and reiterated the reason for their summons. After it, he instructs Bolingbroke to explain his grievances. So the change of address functions, interactionally, to close off one part of the proceedings and to open up another. It also functions, in conjunction with the question, to select Bolingbroke to speak—to give him the opportunity to put his side of the story first. More than that, it projects a larger structure—already hinted at in line 17, when Richard describes the two dukes as 'the accuser, and the accused'. What appears to be unfolding is some kind of trial. Implicit in Richard's insistence that Bolingbroke go first is a promise that Mowbray will be allowed to go second—that the two men will get a fair and equal hearing.

The second example comes in line 34, when Bolingbroke switches from addressing what we will assume (for the moment) is Richard to addressing what is unmistakably Mowbray. This switch is signalled

---

[5] On the punctuation in early editions of Shakespeare, see Chapter 7.

both by the use of the duke's name as an address-term and by an ostentatious act of self-narration. Bolingbroke announces his apostrophe as he performs it—'Now, *Thomas Mowbray*, do I turne to thee'—an announcement, I suggest, of which we should be suspicious. He need only have said, 'Thomas Mowbray, mark my greeting well', and it would have been clear to whom he was speaking. That Bolingbroke feels the need to define his own behaviour in this way—to control the narrative about how the interaction is proceeding—suggests a self-consciousness about how else it might be defined. By emphasizing the fact that he is turning *towards* Mowbray, he distracts attention from the fact he is turning *away* from Richard. The king has just asked him a question. The answer to that question should therefore be addressed to the king. Richard will then be in a position to ask a similar question to Mowbray and to compare the two answers. This is the structure projected by the shape of the interaction so far and the structure we would expect from its quasi-legal framework. By turning to address Mowbray five lines into his answer, Bolingbroke imposes his own sense of what this occasion is and how it should proceed. Instead of the two men taking turns to plead their cases to the king, he instigates a direct confrontation between them.

In both instances, then, the apostrophe functions as a way of directing, or redirecting, interactional traffic. When Richard does this it is entirely appropriate, both to his role as king and to the business at hand. When Bolingbroke does it, something politically, socially, and interactionally loaded is happening. This chapter will be an exploration of what that something is. My central claim is that Bolingbroke's apostrophe in 1.1 is his first act of rebellion. His words profess loyalty to the crown, but they are undermined by his conversational conduct. By apostrophizing Richard he usurps the interactional role of the king in the same way that he will later usurp his throne. This moment is illustrative of the wider significance of apostrophe as a dialogical figure and its special significance in relation to the monarch. Apostrophe, I want to suggest, is the most regal of conversational moves. For all his eccentricities, Capell was right to insist on the importance of 'changes of the address'. Shakespeare's plays, like all dramatic works, 'cannot be understood, unless this point [...] be known and attended to'.

*　*　*

That apostrophe should be characteristic of kings is hardly surprising. It is a way of replying to someone without inviting a further reply—not because no further reply is possible but because you are now talking to someone else. There is nothing inherently rude or dismissive about doing this: it is, as we have seen, one of the most basic ways in which a conversation can have more than two speakers. For a group of friends sitting in the back of a pub it may simply be a way of passing around the speakership. At an awkward social gathering, a conscientious host might use it to ensure that no one is left out. In an argument it can be a way of having the last word. But in all of these cases, whether well or badly intentioned, appropriate or inappropriate, inclusive or exclusive, apostrophe is a means of influencing what happens next. To apostrophize is to take an active role, however small, in the organization of an interaction. It is to be one of those handing out turns at talk rather than one of those waiting passively for a turn to be handed to them. As such, it is characteristic of parents, teachers, chairmen, judges, and talk-show hosts—of all those involved in making sure that the right person speaks at the right time. Instead of simply returning the ball, the speaker traps it, swivels, and passes in another direction. In footballing terms, it is the action of a playmaker.

Robert Dingwall's description of what he calls an 'orchestrated encounter' provides a useful way of thinking about this:

> An orchestrated encounter is characterized by the cessation of the right to organise speech exchange to one of the parties for the duration of the encounter. Examples of such organisation include that that party may act as an authorised starter and closer and as an arbiter of the distribution of the right to hold the floor and to introduce new topics.[6]

What enables the orchestrator to organize the exchange of turns is an asymmetry in speaking rights. As well as having the exclusive right to open and close proceedings, an orchestrator is often the only participant who does anything other than speak when he is spoken to. The encounters in Dingwall's study are tutorials at a medical school, and the kind of orchestrator he has in mind is a teacher. But the interactional

---

[6] Robert Dingwall, 'Orchestrated Encounters: An Essay in the Comparative Analysis of Speech-Exchange Systems', *Sociology of Health and Illness*, 2 (1980), 152–73 (p. 169).

role he describes has a very long history. Take, for example, the Speaker
of the House of Commons, as described by Sir Thomas Smith in 1583:

> In the disputing is a mervelous good order used in the lower house.
> He that standeth uppe bareheadded is understood that he will
> speake to the bill. If moe stande uppe, who that first is judged to
> arise, is first harde, though the one doe prayse the law, the other
> diswade it, yet there is no altercation. For everie man speaketh as to
> the speaker, not as one to an other, for that is against the order of the
> house.[7]

The members stand to indicate their wish to speak, but they do not
actually do so until called upon by the Speaker. Everything they say is
addressed to him, because to address it to their opponent would be to
run the risk of an 'altercation'—of two members breaking out into an
angry duologue. The existence of the rule is a recognition of how hard it
is to refrain from speaking when you're spoken to—especially in the
context of a disagreement. Even in such formal surroundings, the
members cannot be trusted to control themselves. And this, I suggest,
is the principle that underpins all orchestrated encounters. The necessity of achieving some institutionally defined goal (passing a bill, reaching a verdict, learning Latin grammar) makes it prudent to constrain
the otherwise free play of turns. Without appointing someone to
orchestrate the exchange, and clearly defining that person's role, there
is a risk that the business at hand will not be attended to—that
discussion will be derailed, or unproductive, or will overrun.

There is a sense, then, in which a king is a kind of orchestrator in
the business of state. At least, that is the role taken by the kings
in Shakespeare's plays. We have seen how Lear orchestrates the love
auction and how Richard orchestrates, or attempts to orchestrate, the
dispute between the two dukes. Unlike a judge or a schoolmaster,
however, or the Speaker of the House of Commons, the king's right
to shape the interaction in which he is involved is not conferred 'for the
duration of the encounter'. Nor need it be directed towards any specific
goal. Rather, it is a part of what makes him a king, enshrined in the
common law principle of the 'royal prerogative'.

---

[7] Sir Thomas Smith, *De Republica Anglorum* (London: Henry Middleton for Gregory
Seton, 1583), sigs F4r–v.

Prerogatiua is as muche to saye as a priuilege or preeminence that any person hath before another whiche as it is tollerable in some, so it is most to be permitted and allowed in a prince or soueraine gouernor of a realme. [. . .] For whiche cause the lawes do attribute unto him all honour, dignitie, prerogatiue and preeminence, which prerogatiue doth not onely extend to his own person, but also to all other his possessions goods and cattals. As that his person shalbe subiect to no mans suite, his possessions cannot be taken from him by anye [v]iolence or wrongfull disseisin, his goods & cattals are under no tribute, tolle nor custome, nore otherwise distreinable: with an infinite number of prerogatifes more, whiche were to tedious here to recite.[8]

As well as the powers granted to him by statute, and those he has accumulated under the common law, the king has his social prerogatives—the countless tiny ways in which his pre-eminence is recognized and expressed, both by himself and by those around him. Amongst these 'infinite number of prerogatives more' are what we might call the monarch's prerogatives of speech.[9] Most obviously, he occupies a unique place within the address-term system. Terms such as 'your Majesty' and 'my liege' are reserved exclusively for use to the monarch.[10] He holds a unique place, too, in the pronominal system— only the sovereign can employ the plural of majesty. Less generally recognized is that there are rules about when, as well as how, a king or

---

[8] William Stanford, *An Exposicion of the Kinges Prerogatiue* (London: Richard Tottel, 1567), sigs A6r–v. This work went through six editions during Shakespeare's lifetime. The royal prerogative still exists, albeit in a much diminished form. See *The Governance of Britain: Review of the Executive Royal Prerogative Powers, Final Report* (London: Ministry of Justice, 2009).

[9] The phrase is Shakespearean. Fantasizing about how he will chastise Sir Toby once he has married Olivia, Malvolio imagines himself saying 'give me this prerogative of speech' before telling the knight to amend his drunkenness (2.5.59–61).

[10] These customs appear to have originated with the historical Richard. See Nigel Saul, 'Richard II and the Vocabulary of Kingship', *The English Historical Review*, 110 (1995), 854–77. For their use in Shakespeare, see Caroline Replogle, 'Shakespeare's Salutations: A Study in Stylistic Etiquette', *Studies in Philology*, 70 (1973), 72–86, reprinted in *A Reader in the Language of Shakespearean Drama*, ed. by Vivian Salmon and Edwina Burness (Amsterdam: John Benjamins, 1987), pp. 101–15; Roger Brown and Albert Gilman, 'Politeness Theory and Shakespeare's Four Major Tragedies'; and N. F. Blake, *A Grammar of Shakespeare's Language* (Basingstoke: Palgrave Macmillan, 2002), pp. 271–83.

queen should be addressed. Subjects are required to attend on the monarch in conversation, waiting to be called upon to speak in the same way that they wait to be called upon to do anything else—speaking, that is, only when they are spoken to.

For these reasons, then, we would expect apostrophe to be characteristic of the kings in Shakespeare's plays, and Capell's dashes enable us to confirm that this is so. In seven other scenes roughly comparable to the opening of *Richard II*—in which the king is conducting official business in the presence of his full court—Capell identifies forty-seven 'changes of the address', thirty-eight of them performed by kings and nine by their subjects.[11] In six of those nine cases, one subject apostrophizes another. This leaves only three examples, out of nearly fifty, in which a subject apostrophizes the king. In purely statistical terms, apostrophizing the king—turning away from the sovereign to address another character—is a rare occurrence on Shakespeare's stage. It is comparable in its rarity, and in its social meaning, to addressing the monarch as 'thou' rather than 'you'—not something that never happens, nor that is necessarily inappropriate, but rare enough and risky enough to be of interest. Unlike address-terms, however, the dialogical apostrophe has received little or no critical attention.[12]

One way of gauging the value of Bolingbroke's apostrophe, then, is to compare it with the other three examples identified by Capell. The first is Malcolm apostrophizing his father in 1.1 of *Macbeth*:

[11] These are: 1.1 of *King John*, in which the king receives the French ambassador and settles a dispute between two brothers; 1.2 of *Hamlet*, in which the king dispatches ambassadors to Norway, gives Laertes leave to return to Paris, and enquires after his nephew's melancholy; 1.3 of *1 Henry IV*, in which Henry chastises the Percies for withholding the prisoners Hotspur took at Holmedon; all three scenes from *Macbeth* in which Duncan appears; and 1.1 of *King Lear*. In Capell's (1768) edition they can be found at: V, sigs A4r–A7r; X, sigs H5r–H7r; V, sigs N6r–N8r; IV, sigs U2r–U3v, U6v–U7v, U8v–X1r; IX, sigs Q8v–R5v. I have excluded those parts of the scenes from *1 Henry IV* and *Lear* during which no king is on stage.

[12] See Albert Gilman and Roger Brown's classic essay, 'The Pronouns of Power and Solidarity', in *Style in Language*, ed. by Thomas A. Sebeok (London: John Wiley & Sons, 1960), pp. 253–76; as well as responses to it by Kathleen M. Wales, 'Thou and You in Early Modern English: Brown and Gilman Re-appraised', *Studia Linguistica*, 37 (1983), 107–25; and by Deborah Tannen, 'The Relativity of Linguistic Strategies: Rethinking Power and Solidarity in Gender and Dominance', in *Gender and Conversational Interaction*, ed. by Deborah Tannen (Oxford: Oxford University Press, 1993), pp. 165–88.

> *Alarums. Enter King* DUNCAN, MALCOLM,
>   Donalbain, Lenox *with Attendants*;
>   a Soldier *meeting them.*
> DUN. What bloody man is that? He can report,
> As seemeth by his plight, of the revolt
> The newest state.
> MAL. This is the serjeant,
> Who like a good and hardy soldier fought
> 5 'Gainst my captivity:__Hail, hail brave friend!
> Say to the king the knowledge of the broil
> As thou didst leave it.
>   (IV, U2r–v, 1.2.1–7)

Prompted by Malcolm, the soldier goes on to deliver his celebrated description of Macbeth unseaming Macdonwald from the nave to the chaps. What differentiates this example from the one in *Richard II* is that Malcolm here acts as an intermediary between the king and the soldier, and he does so at his father's request. Prior to the apostrophe, what Malcolm says is an answer to Duncan's question. After it, what he says is a response to Duncan's observation that the soldier 'can report [...] of the revolt | The newest state'. Malcolm understands this observation as an instruction to extract a report from the man. So he carries that instruction out—the king's immediate stated wish taking precedence over the taboo against subjecting him to an apostrophe. Notice that Malcolm specifically instructs the soldier to deliver his report to the king, thereby re-establishing the monarch as the centre of the interaction.

The second example is Kent apostrophizing Lear immediately after the king has pronounced his banishment:

> LEA. [...]
> Five days we do allot thee, for provision
> To shield thee from disasters of the world;
> And, on the sixth, to turn thy hated back
> Upon our kingdom: if, on the tenth day following,
> Thy banish'd trunk be found in our dominions,
> The moment is thy death: Away! By *Jupiter*,
> This shall not be revok'd.
> KEN. Fare thee well, king: sith thus thou wilt appear,

> Freedom live hence, and banishment is here.__
> The gods to their dear shelter take thee, maid,
> That justly think'st, and hast most rightly said!__
> And, you, large speechers, may your deeds approve
> That good effects may spring from words of love.__
> Thus *Kent*, o princes, bids you all adieu;
> He'll shape his old course in a country new.   [*Exit*.
>   (IX, R3r, 1.1.155–68)

This apostrophe is one of three in a speech with four distinct addressees. First Kent bids farewell to Lear, then to Cordelia, then to Gonerill and Regan, and finally to the court. At the end of the speech he leaves the stage. One explanation of what happens here is that, having been banished (at least in part for speaking out of turn), Kent no longer cares about decorum. Like an employee who has just been sacked, he is released from the need to worry about what his former boss may think of him. Another explanation is that leave-taking is a special class of conversational action, conventionally exempted from the rule against apostrophe. A departing character (and particularly a character who has been banished) is given licence to say his or her farewells. However we choose to explain it, there is a clear difference between what Kent does here and what Bolingbroke does to Richard. Kent's speech neither selects any other person to speak nor requires that person to reply to him (rather than the king)—no one *can* reply to him, because he leaves the stage as soon as he has finished speaking. His turn is an interactional dead end, with no consequences for the shape of the conversation that follows.

The final example is the Bastard apostrophizing King John:

> JOH. A good blunt fellow:__Why, being younger born,
> Doth he lay claim to thine inheritance?
>   BAS. I know not why, except to get the land.
> But once he slander'd me with bastardy:
> But whe'r I be as true begot, or no,
> That still I lay upon my mother's head;
> But, that I am as well begot, my liege,
> (Fair fall the bones that took the pains for me!)
> Compare our faces, and be judge yourself.
> If old sir *Robert* did beget us both,
> And were our father, and this † son like him;__

O old sir *Robert*, father, on my knee
I give heaven thanks, I was not like to thee.
   JOH. Why, what a mad-cap hath heaven lent us here!
   ELI. He hath a trick of *Cœur-de-lion's* face,
The accent of his tongue affecteth him:
Do you not read some tokens of my son
In the large composition of this man?
                      (V, A5r–v, 1.1.71–88)

Old Sir Robert is long dead, so the Bastard's apostrophe is rhetorical. (Capell makes no distinction between rhetorical and dialogical apostrophes when marking changes of address.) But apostrophizing the king rhetorically is still potentially rude. At any rate, it is rare—this is the only example in the seven scenes consulted—and it seems to get a reaction. Both John and Elizabeth are impressed by the Bastard. They believe his story and give him a prominent place at court. Their credence is based on his resemblance to Richard I, both physically (he has 'a trick of *Cœur-de-lion's* face' and the same large frame) and vocally (the 'accent' of Richard's tongue is audible in the way he talks). Part of what makes him sound royal, I suggest, is the habit of apostrophizing. This is one of four apostrophes he performs in John's presence but the only time he apostrophizes the king himself. None of them is an apostrophe of the most flagrant kind—turning away from the king to select someone else to speak—but they are all a little boisterous. The Bastard has the dialogical DNA of his father, King Richard, and he is struggling to contain it. The royal blood that pumps through his veins is visible in the turn-taking structure of the scene.

On closer inspection, then, none of the other examples identified by Capell carries the same weight as Bolingbroke's apostrophe. None of them instigates a duologue from which the king is excluded or takes the scene in a direction that the king has not sanctioned. And, on at least one occasion, the act of apostrophizing is interpreted as regal—as evidence of a royal lineage. We would appear, then, to be nearing a conclusion. By turning away from Richard to address Mowbray, Bolingbroke is acting like a king, attempting to supplant his cousin as orchestrator of the scene. Like Miranda intervening in her father's chastisement of Caliban, his conduct is both surprising and inappropriate

(Prospero, too, is a kind of orchestrator). This is true, I think, but it is not the whole truth. There are at least three factors that complicate the picture.

*　*　*

The first is that addressing a king is not quite so straightforward a matter as it sounds. Take, for example, George Puttenham's advice on where to look when in the presence of a prince:

> Nor in looking on them seeme to ouerlooke them, nor yet behold them too stedfastly, for that is a signe of impudence or litle reuerence, and therefore to the great Princes Orientall their seruitours speaking or being spoken vnto abbase their eyes in token of lowlines, which behauiour we do not obserue to our Princes with so good a discretion as they do: & such as retire from the Princes presence, do not by & by turne tayle to them as we do, but go backward or sideling for a reasonable space, til they be at the wal or chamber doore passing out of sight, and is thought a most decent behauiour to their soueraignes. I haue heard that king *Henry* th'eight her Maiesties father, though otherwise the most gentle and affable Prince of the world, could not abide to haue any man stare in his face or to fix his eye too steedily vpon him when he talked with them.[13]

Notice the tension in this advice. The subject must steer a middle course between overlooking the king and beholding him too steadfastly. On the one hand, Puttenham praises the 'Orientall' custom of not turning tail on the prince—physically apostrophizing him—until you have left the room. On the other hand, Henry VIII, he assures us, did not like to have his interlocutor's eye fixed too steadily upon him. Gaze direction is not, of course, the same thing as linguistic address, but the two are related— we tend to look at the person to whom we are speaking and to turn away from them, if only slightly, to speak to someone else. My suggestion is that a similar tension exists—between attending on the king and encroaching on him—in the language a subject uses to address the sovereign. On the one hand, this should be directed, like the subject's gaze, towards the king. On the other hand, it should not be fixed too intently or directly upon him. There is a linguistic equivalent of staring into the monarch's face, and it too needs to be avoided.

---

[13] George Puttenham, *The Arte of English Poesie* (London: Richard Field, 1589), sig. 2Kv.

This is why what tends to be addressed is not the monarch himself, but an attribute of his monarchy. Instead of saying 'you', the subject says 'your majesty' or 'your highness'. The language points in the direction of the king or queen but avoids eye contact. This is also why the monarch is plural, whether addressed by a subject or referring to himself. The plural of majesty is usually explained as a linguistic recognition that the monarch is more than an individual. To address the king in the singular would be to reduce him to the size of a man. And no doubt this is so. But the plurality of the monarch is also a form of linguistic avoidance, of trying not to stare—as though the singular were too direct, or too intimate, to obtain between a subject and their sovereign.

And these two taboos—against turning your language away from the king and pointing it too fixedly at him—are related. Both have a pronominal base. According to Henry Peacham,

> Apostrophe, is a forme of speech by which the Orator turneth suddenly from the former frame of his speech to another, that is, when he hath long spoken of some person or thing, he leaveth speaking of it, and speaketh unto it, which is no other then a sudden removing from the third person to the second.[14]

The most 'usual' form of the figure, at least according to Peacham, is a switch from the third person to the second—from speaking 'of' your subject to speaking 'unto' it. He is referring, of course, to the rhetorical apostrophe (*o tempora! o mores!*), but dialogical apostrophe works, grammatically, in the same way. In both cases the 'sudden removing' is a realignment of the pronominal compass, rotated by the speaker until the arrow that was previously pointing to *you* is instead pointing to *him*. Compare the 'cat's mother' taboo, according to which it is impolite to refer to someone in the third person when that person is present.[15] Somewhat more theatrically, we might think of apostrophe as a swapping of grammatical roles. To apostrophize someone is to recast them in the supporting part of *he* rather than the lead role of *you*.

---

[14] Henry Peacham, *The Garden of Eloquence*, rev. edn (London: Richard Field for H. Jackson, 1593), sig. K2v.

[15] OED, she, *pron.1, n.*, and *adj.* P1: '*who's she—the cat's mother?* and variants: said to a person (esp. a child) who uses the feminine third person singular pronoun impolitely or with inadequate reference'.

These tensions are at work in the part of Bolingbroke's speech that precedes his apostrophe, the part that I suggested earlier was 'presumably' addressed to the king:

> BOL. First, (heaven be the record to my speech!)
> In the devotion of a subject's loue,
> Tend'ring the precious safety of my prince,
> And free from other misbegotten hate,
> Come I appellant to this princely presence.__
>
> (V, G1r–v, 1.1.30–4)

Notice, first, that there is nothing in the language which settles the question of who is being addressed here. One candidate is 'heaven'. If we take the clause bracketed off by Capell to be an imperative—a contraction, that is, of 'heaven, be *you* the record to my speech'—then the reference to Richard as 'my prince' is in the third person. Alternatively, 'heaven' might be in the third person—'*let* heaven be the record to my speech'—and the reference to Richard in the second—a contraction, that is, of '*you*, my prince'. It is also possible to hear both of these phrases in the third person, in a speech that is addressed to the court. The expectation created by the speak-when-you're-spoken-to-rule is that, coming straight after a question from the king, what Bolingbroke says is a reply addressed to Richard, but it may be he exploits this expectation to wriggle off the hook. An actor might choose to settle the question one way or another, but the textual ambiguity serves a dramatic purpose. It shows Bolingbroke struggling with the competing demands of (on the one hand) a complex etiquette of royal address and (on the other) his own seething resentment towards the king—a resentment that bursts out moments later when he turns to face his adversary.

Now consider how the same tension works itself out in Mowbray's response. By physically and linguistically addressing the duke, Bolingbroke requests him to do the same in return. He is ostentatiously seeking to establish the mutual gaze of speaker and hearer, a gaze that doubles here as the stare of two combatants. A failure on Mowbray's part to meet that gaze, to face and answer the accusations, looks like cowardice. But to turn towards Bolingbroke is to join him in turning away from the king. To answer Bolingbroke is to admit his right to orchestrate the scene—is to collude with him, at the interactional level, against Richard. Mowbray is caught, in other words, between

the competing demands of his loyalty and his honour. Here is what
he does:

> NOR. Let not my cold words here accuse my zeale:
> 'Tis not the trial of a woman's war,
> The bitter clamour of two eager tongues,
> Can arbitrate this cause betwixt us twaine;
> The blood is hot, that must be cool'd for this.
> Yet can I not of such tame patience boast,
> As to be hush'd, and nought at all to say:
> First, the fair reverence of your highness curbs me,
> From giving reins and spurs to my free speech;
> Which else would post, until it had return'd
> These terms of treason doubl'd down his throat.
> I do defy him, and I spit at him;
> Call him⁻a sland'rous coward, and a villain:
>
> (V, G2r, 1.1.47–61)

Notice, first, that he excuses himself twice—once for speaking out and
once for not saying more. Mowbray is not of such 'tame patience' that
he can remain silent after what Bolingbroke has just said. This is an odd
thing for which to apologize, given that the hearing has been convened
precisely so that the two men can state their cases. There is no question
of Mowbray not being given the chance to speak. The apology is not for
speaking, but for speaking prematurely. Mowbray is aware that Richard
should speak next, both because Bolingbroke should have addressed
him and because he is the king. On the other hand, he does not want
anyone to think this is all he has to say, or for his silence to look like an
admission of guilt. So Mowbray answers Bolingbroke but excuses
himself for doing so and simultaneously makes it clear that he is
curbing his response only out of reverence for Richard.

Notice, secondly, the absence of an underscore. According to Capell,
this speech has a single consistent addressee. In the absence of any
reason to think otherwise, a reader is likely to assume that Mowbray is
replying to Bolingbroke—and the phrase 'us twaine' would seem to
confirm this. When, a few lines later, it becomes clear that Mowbray is
addressing Richard (possibly at 'your highness' but certainly at 'his
throat') we might be tempted to read this as an apostrophe. But Capell
is right. There is no distinction, in English, between the inclusive and

exclusive forms of the first-person plural—'us twaine' can mean either 'me and you' or 'me and him'.[16] So Bolingbroke's usurpation of Richard's conversational role is only half successful. He may have got a response, but he does not get a reply. Mowbray feels compelled to justify himself, but he'll be damned if he's going to justify himself to Bolingbroke. The point of the ambiguity over whom he is addressing is that it mimics this internal struggle. Like Mowbray, we must drag our attention away from Bolingbroke if we are to interpret the syntax correctly. The effort the reader must make to understand this—the slow realization that Mowbray is in fact addressing Richard—is a measure of the effort the duke must make to do it.

One critic to have noticed these syntactical contortions is Stephen Booth. He explains them as part of a larger strategy in the first three acts of *Richard II* to frustrate the audience. Frustration, he argues, 'not getting to the point, not letting actions and situations finish so that new ones can follow', is the essence of this play.[17] The opening scene is, in this respect, an emblem of the whole. It 'pushes each member of its audience toward being his own Pierce Exton—impatient to hear a decisive assertion in a muddle of indecisive verbal gestures'.[18] Crucially, what produces this muddle is the syntax *between* turns at talk—'characters regularly respond to questions and demands in syntaxes that—though clear enough in intent, and thus serviceable—do not mesh with the syntaxes they follow'.[19] Booth's prime example is Bolingbroke's attack on Mowbray:

> When Richard says 'What dost thou object / Against the Duke of Norfolk, Thomas Mowbray?', Bolingbroke sets off in orderly fashion on an answer removed from the question by an irrelevantly focused gesture [...] When at last he turns to—and cautiously approaches—the point, he answers Richard's question by demonstration—by charging Mowbray [...] The question is answered, but not in its own syntactical terms, not in a construction like 'I charge that Mowbray is, or did, so-and-so.' The scene is easy enough to follow, but we follow it without a syntactic thread from point to point and speech to speech.[20]

[16] See Michael Daniel, 'Understanding inclusives', in *Clusivity: Typology and Case Studies of the Inclusive-Exclusive Distinction*, ed. by Elena Filimonova (Amsterdam: J. Benjamins, 2005), 3–48 (p. 3).

[17] Stephen Booth, 'Syntax as Rhetoric in *Richard II*', *Mosaic*, 10 (1977), 87–103 (p. 89).

[18] Booth, p. 89.   [19] Booth, p. 90.   [20] Booth, p. 90.

This is sharply observed, but the syntax Booth describes is a symptom of the problem and not its cause. His analysis is a very fine example of traditional close reading, but it remains on the linguistic surface of the writing, without seeing the 'basic structural shaping' of the dialogue beneath.[21] What matters is not that Bolingbroke fails to answer Richard's question 'on its own syntactical terms' but that he turns away from Richard to address Mowbray. The dropped syntactical thread is caused by an act of apostrophe. Similarly, when in the subsequent turn Mowbray blanks Bolingbroke to address Richard, this is, according to Booth's logic, a further example of two speakers failing to mesh syntactically—and the whole sequence descends into 'a muddle of indecisive verbal gestures'. To read the scene in this way is to ignore the relationship between any two turns that are not directly adjacent to each other. Mowbray's response is a very precise attempt to correct the damage caused by Bolingbroke—to pick up the dropped thread of interaction and stitch it back together. By addressing Richard, he puts the interaction back where it should have remained—in the hands of the king. To see this we need only recognize that interaction has its own syntax—its own structural logic—which can sometimes be at odds with, or in counterpoint to, the syntax of the language in which it is effected. Erving Goffman, we recall, had set out to study 'the syntactical relations among the acts of different persons mutually present to one another'.[22] It is these relations that Booth ignores.

*   *   *

The second complication is the quasi-legal framework of the dispute. Here are the opening lines of the play, up until the entrance of the two dukes:

> RIC. Old *John of Gaunt*, time-honour'd *Lancaster*,
> Hast thou, according to thy oath and bond,
> Brought hither *Henry Hereford* thy bold son;
> Here to make good the boistrous late appeal,
> 5   Which then our leisure would not let us hear,
> Against the duke of Norfolk, Thomas Mowbray?
> GAU. I have, my liege.

---

[21] Jones, *Scenic Form*, p. 3.   [22] Goffman, *Interaction Ritual*, p. 2.

> RIC. Tell me moreover, hast thou sounded him,
> If he appeal the duke on ancient malice;
> 10 Or worthily, as a good subject should
> On some known ground of treachery in him?
>   GAU. As near as I could sift him on that argument,⁻
> On some apparent danger seen in him,
> Aim'd at your highness, no inveterate malice.
> 15   RIC. Then call them to our presence; face to face,
> And frowning brow to brow, ourselves will hear
> The accuser, and the accused, freely speak:—
>   *[Exeunt some Attendants.*
> High-stomach'd are they both, and full of ire,
> In rage deaf as the sea, hasty as fire.
>   (V, G1r, 1.1.1–19)

Much of the language is legal, and can be glossed from *De Republica Anglorum*:

> Now in all iudgements necessarily being two parties, the first we call
> the impleader, suiter, demaunder or demaundaunt and plaintiffe: In
> criminall causes if he professe to be an accuser, we call him appellant or
> appellour, and so accusation we call appeale. The other we call the
> defendant and in criminall causes prisoner, for he cannot aunswere in
> causes criminall before he do render himselfe or be rendred prisoner.[23]

The word 'appeal' is used twice to describe Bolingbroke's actions. First,
as a noun, to describe the event that appears to have caused this
assembly—the duke's 'boistrous late appeal' to the king. Secondly, as
a verb, to describe what Bolingbroke is here to do—to 'appeal' Thomas
Mowbray. Bolingbroke also describes himself as coming 'appellant
to this princely presence'. Richard's description of the two men as 'The
accuser, and the accused' is similarly recognizable from *De Republica*,
even if these are not the most technically correct terms. It seems clear,
then, that the two dukes are cast in the two roles Smith describes—
Bolingbroke as the appellant, Mowbray the defendant—and that what
we have here is a criminal trial. Except that in a fourth use of the word
(still within the first thirty-five lines of the play) Richard explains that

---

[23] Smith, sigs H1r–v.

the two dukes have come 'to appeal each other of high treason'. Instead of accuser and accused, we have accuser and accuser.

So the idea of a trial is invoked, but not straightforwardly. I will return, in due course, to this lack of straightforwardness. First I want to consider what it might mean, in turn-taking terms, for a scene in Shakespeare to be a representation of a trial. Fortunately, Smith describes the procedures of an early modern criminal court in some detail.

> The Iudge first after they be sworne, asketh first the partie robbed, if he knowe the prisoner, and biddeth him looke vpon him: he saith yea, the prisoner sometime saith nay. The partie pursuiuaunt giueth good ensignes *verbi gratia*, I knowe thee well ynough, thou robbedst me in such a place, thou beatest mee, thou tookest my horse from mee, and my purse, thou hadst then such a coate and such a man in thy companie: the theefe will say no, and so they stand a while in altercation, then he telleth al that he can say: after him likewise all those who were at the apprehension of the prisoner, or who can giue any indices or tokens which we call in our language euidence against the malefactor. When the Iudge hath heard them say inough, he asketh if they can say any more: if they say no, then he turneth his speeche to the enquest.[24]

The key word here is 'altercation'—the same word Smith uses to describe what does not happen in the House of Commons. Once the appellant has made his accusation, the two parties are expected to argue with one another directly. The judge and jurors sit watching this altercation until it has taken its course. This process is then repeated with each of the witnesses—they state their evidence, the defendant contradicts it, and an altercation ensues. There are no lawyers and there is no cross-examination. The kind of trial we are familiar with today, known as the 'adversary trial', in which the plaintiff and defendant never directly address one another, did not develop until the eighteenth century.[25] Prior to that, it was a principle of English law that the

---

[24] Smith, sigs L4v–M1r. Notice, in passing, how the judge ends the pleading by performing an apostrophe.

[25] See John H. Langbein, *The Origins of Adversary Criminal Trial* (Oxford: Oxford University Press, 2002), esp. pp. 1–67; and John Hostettler, *Fighting for Justice: The History and Origins of Adversary Trial* (Winchester: Waterside Press, 2006).

defendant should have no legal counsel—the innocence of an innocent man was the only help he could need.[26]

On the face of it, then, the process described by Smith is exactly what happens in *Richard II*. Bolingbroke's accusation triggers an altercation at which the king and court effectively spectate. Richard's promise that the two men will be able to speak 'freely', 'face to face, | And frowning brow to brow' suggests that he is expecting this. So one reading of what happens here is that Shakespeare structures the scene as an early modern 'altercation trial', in which it is normal for the two parties to address one another directly. Bolingbroke might have waited for Mowbray to contradict him on a question of fact before launching into his tirade—his apostrophe is perhaps premature—but there is nothing inherently wrong with him addressing Mowbray in this kind of trial.

Attractive as this interpretation is, there are factors it ignores. One has already been touched upon—the roles of the characters in this scene do not map neatly onto the roles of the participants at a trial. Bolingbroke is the self-proclaimed appellant, but Mowbray appears to be a counter-accuser rather than a defendant. Richard is presumably the judge, but there is no obvious jury. The king refers vaguely to 'ourselves' hearing the appeals, but it is not clear whom he includes in this. There is no mention of a verdict at any point. The aim of the proceedings appears to be to resolve the dispute between the dukes, rather than to try Mowbray's guilt. The presence of the king is a complicating factor because the interactional role of a judge overlaps with that of the sovereign—they are both kinds of orchestrator. There is a tension, in other words, between the two types of *court* scene, between the depiction of a trial and the depiction of the royal household.

* * *

The third and final complication is that these events are not fictional. Underpinning the scene is a historical narrative, drawn primarily from Holinshed's *Chronicles*, in which much that Shakespeare leaves obscure is known to the parties involved.[27] I am not suggesting that this knowledge should be read back into the play as though he had not

[26] See Langbein, pp. 10–13.
[27] Raphael Holinshed, *Chronicles*, 2nd edn, 3 vols (London: Henry Denham, 1587), III, sigs 3B5r–3B6r.

chosen to omit it—but comparing the two texts can shed light on why he might have chosen to do so. This is true at the level of plot but also at the level of scenic structure. The *Chronicles* are surprisingly detailed when it comes to matters of ceremony and procedure, including who speaks when, on whose behalf, and to whom.

The opening of *Richard II* compresses two separate royal assemblies—a parliament at Shrewsbury and a specially convened hearing at Windsor—into a single composite scene. In Holinshed the initial claim, made at Shrewsbury, is that, in a recent conversation with Bolingbroke 'as they rode togither [. . .] betwixt London and Brainford', Mowbray uttered 'certeine words [. . .] sounding highlie to the kings dishonor'. What these words were is unclear, but for 'further proofe thereof' Bolingbroke presents the king with a written supplication:

> This supplication was red before both the dukes [1], in presence of the king: which doone, the duke of Norfolke tooke vpon him to answer it [2], declaring that whatsoeuer the duke of Hereford had said against him other than well he lied falselie like an vntrue knight as he was. And when the king asked [3] of the duke of Hereford what he said to it: he taking his hood off his head, said [4]; My souereigne lord, euen as the supplication which I tooke you importeth, right so I saie for truth, that Thomas Mowbraie duke of Norfolke is a traitour, false and disloiall to your roiall maiestie, your crowne, and to all the states of your realme.
>   Then the duke of Norfolke being asked [5] what he said to this, he answered [6]: Right deere lord, with your fauour that I make answer vnto your coosine here, I saie (your reuerence saued) that Henrie of Lancaster duke of Hereford, like a false and disloiall traitor as he is, dooth lie, in that he hath or shall say of me otherwise than well. No more said the king [7], we haue heard inough: and herewith commanded the duke of Surrie for that turne marshall of England, to arrest in his name the two dukes.[28]

Including the reading of the document, Holinshed specifies seven turns at talk in the course of this exchange. It is not clear by whom the document is read, only that it is not the king nor either of the dukes. Mowbray then gives a response, possibly before it has been called for (the phrasal verb 'take upon [oneself]' had already acquired the sense

---

[28] Holinshed, III, sig. 3B5r.

of 'presume, make bold').[29] From this point onwards, however, the king orchestrates a tightly structured formal procedure, inviting each of the adversaries to respond in turn to the claims of the other, prompting them to speak when he wants to hear them, and bringing things to a close once he has 'heard inough'. Richard ends the proceedings with an apostrophe, turning from the dukes to the Lord Marshal to issue him with instructions for the hearing at Windsor. Neither of the dukes addresses a word to the other, nor to anyone other than the king. If there is a moment at which the order of the exchange is threatened, it is Mowbray's potentially unsolicited first turn. It is he, rather than Bolingbroke, who appears the more volatile.

The hearing at Windsor is even more elaborate. The proceedings begin with a declaration made on Richard's behalf by Sir John Bushy, announcing the reason for the assembly. The king then sends Aumerle and Surrey, respectively the Constable and Lord Marshal, to inquire of the two adversaries whether they are willing to be reconciled. It is only once they have both formally refused that they are admitted to the king's presence.

> When they were come before the king and lords, the king spake himselfe to them [1], willing them to agree, and make peace togither: for it is (said he) the best waie ye can tak. The duke of Norfolke with due reuerence herevnto answered [2] it could not be so brought to passe, his honor saued. Then the king asked of the duke of Hereford [3], what it was that he demanded of the duke of Norfolke, and what is the matter that ye can not make peace togither, and become friends?
>
> Then stood foorth a knight; who asking [4] and obteining [5] licence to speake for the duke of Hereford, said [6]; Right deare and souereigne lord, here is Henrie of Lancaster duke of Hereford and earle of Derbie, who saith, and I for him likewise say, that Thomas Mobwraie duke of Norfolke is a false and disloiall traitor to you and your roiall maiestie, and to your whole realme: [...] The king herewith waxed angrie, and asked the duke of Hereford [7], if these were his woords, who answered [8]: Right deere lord, they are my woords; and hereof I require right, and the battell against him.

There was a knight also that asked [9] licence to speake for the duke of Norfolke, and obteining [10], it began to answer [11] thus: [...]

The king then demanded of the duke of Norfolke [12], if these were his woords, and whether he had anie more to saie. The duke of Norfolke then answered [13] for himselfe: [...] This is that which I haue to answer, and I am readie to defend my selfe against mine aduersarie; I beseech you therefore of right, and to haue the battell against him in vpright iudgement.[30]

At this point the king dismisses them in order to 'commune' with his council. That done, the two adversaries are commanded to 'stand forth' and make a final, formal declaration as to whether or not 'they would agree and make peace togither'. When both parties again refuse, Richard loses patience and 'perceiuing this demeanor betwixt them' swears by Saint John the Baptist that he will 'neuer seeke to make peace betwixt them againe'. It is then Sir John Bushy, the same man who opened proceedings, who announces the decision to appoint a 'daie of battell' for the two men at Coventry.

Notice, first, how little direct access the dukes have to the king. Their initial pleas are requested and returned through intermediaries (Surrey and Aumerle). Their main arguments are made by a pair of knights, each of whom asks 'licence' from the court to speak on behalf of his lord. The exact status of these 'knights' is not clear, but they function as advocates, making what appear to be carefully crafted speeches on behalf of the two parties. The phrase 'who saith, and I for him likewise say' is repeated several times by both knights, suggesting it is a conventional legal formula. It is only after the speech of his advocate that either duke is asked to speak for himself—to confirm in person, directly to the king, that he stands by what has been said. Direct interaction between the dukes and the king is restricted to a kind of retrospective checking. Notice, secondly, that there is no interaction whatever between the dukes themselves. They are kept physically apart before the hearing, submitting their pleas independently to the king's officers, and they are kept apart interactionally once the hearing has started. The risk of the two men breaking out into a direct confrontation is lessened by the fact that they barely speak for themselves, let alone to each other.

---

[30] Holinshed, III, sig. 3B5v.

Notice, thirdly, that everything said at the hearing is spoken either to, by, or on behalf of the king, who is elaborately and ostentatiously addressed by all the other speakers. How accurate Holinshed's account is, and how typical the procedures he describes, are difficult questions to answer. What Shakespeare has done with that account, however, is clear. Most obviously, he has stripped away many of the speaking parts—Bushy, Surrey, Aumerle, and the two advocates are all either absent from or silent in the play. He has reshaped the scene, to look more like the kind of trial described by Sir Thomas Smith, but retained its careful balance between two competing appellants—the phrase 'appealed ech other' is one of the few to make it from Holinshed into *Richard II*. Crucially, both Bolingbroke's apostrophe and Mowbray's reaction to it are entirely Shakespeare's invention.

The result is a suggestively hybrid shape, which both hints at an altercation trial and recalls the *Chronicles*. The scene creates the impression of a formal, legal process, governed by clearly understood rules, but without it being clear exactly what that process is. So when Bolingbroke apostrophizes the king, there is room for disagreement about the level of his impropriety—amongst the audience, obviously, but also on the stage. By replying to Richard rather than Bolingbroke, Mowbray projects an understanding of the situation very different from that which Bolingbroke himself has just projected. He corrects the duke's behaviour by refusing to follow his lead. Neither man, Mowbray suggests, should be addressing anyone other than the king. They are arguing not only about which of them is a traitor but also about the conventions governing the interaction—the nature of the event in which they are participating. It is as though Bolingbroke is playing by Smith's rules, and Mowbray by Holinshed's.

It is a commonplace of the play's critical literature that *Richard II* presents 'a conflict between two contrasting worlds—the static, pictur-esque, ceremonial world of Richard's medieval court and the active, modern, practical world of Bolingbroke and his successors'.[31] The opening scene, in particular, with its 'elaborate pageantry [. . .] royal ceremony and formal verse', is often seen as 'a period piece'—a

[31] Phyllis Rackin, 'The Role of the Audience in Shakespeare's *Richard II*', *Shakespeare Quarterly*, 36 (1985), 262–81 (p. 262).

window, for its sixteenth-century audience, onto a quaintly formal past.[32] E. M. W. Tillyard draws a contrast between the dramatically purposeful use of ceremony in *Richard III* (he has particular praise for 5.5, in which Richard is visited by the ghosts of his victims) and the static, self-sufficient ritual of *Richard II*.

> With all the emphasis and the point taken out of the action, we are invited, again and again, to dwell on the sheer ceremony of the various situations. [...] We are in fact in a world where means matter more than ends, where it is more important to keep strictly the rules of an elaborate game than either to win or to lose it.[33]

It is worth asking, then, what the reading I have just given of 1.1 can contribute to this argument. On the face of it, my claims for the importance of Bolingbroke's apostrophe would seem to fit the schema neatly. Bolingbroke—the active herald of the modern—refuses to play a passive part in Richard's medieval ritual. Instead of speaking when and how he is supposed to, he breaks decisively with the past. But we might equally argue that his behaviour suggests a world that is never quite as static as Tillyard makes out. If the apostrophe is not a part of the script, it is Richard, not Mowbray, who should correct it. Either as king or as judge, or as both, it is his responsibility to direct and define what is happening here, and his failure to do so characterizes him as a weak or negligent orchestrator, of the kingdom as well as the dialogue. Rather than the timeless ritual of an unchanging medieval world, the scene dramatizes a court still clinging to an empty pageantry it cannot comfortably inhabit. Richard seems both to rely on the old forms and to be too lazy, or ineffective, to enact them properly.

One final comment, on another of the play's critical commonplaces. Whatever was or was not said 'as they rode togither [...] betwixt London and Brainford' is not the primary cause of the conflict between the two dukes. What Bolingbroke is really angry about is the murder of his uncle, Thomas of Woodstock—secretly ordered by

---

[32] Phyllis Rackin, *Stages of History: Shakespeare's English Chronicles* (Ithaca, NY: Cornell University Press, 1990), p. 120.

[33] E. M. W. Tillyard, *Shakespeare's History Plays* (London: Chatto & Windus, 1944), p. 252.

Richard and secretly carried out by Mowbray.[34] The Oxford editors have put this well:

> On the surface a spectacle of royal judgement, the scene is in essence a proxy attack on the King for the killing of Thomas of Woodstock that is couched as an appeal against Mowbray. That means that the various participants are saying more than they appear to be saying and that Richard is in the uncomfortable position of playing the impartial judge when he is implicitly the accused.[35]

The various participants are indeed saying more than they appear to be saying, but not just through the words they choose to use. Bolingbroke knows that Richard is guilty but cannot accuse the king directly. Shakespeare manages to imply this knowledge without stating it, and the manner in which he does so amounts to what we might think of as an irony of interactional structure. Like a man who has reached the point at which he just has to lash out at somebody, Bolingbroke turns away from Richard to lash out at Mowbray—and he does so precisely *because* the king is the real object of his rage. His apostrophe is a crack in the 'surface' described by Dawson and Yachnin, and Mowbray's response (so nearly addressed to the duke) is an unconvincing attempt to paper it over. One function of this crack is that it hints at what is to come—Bolingbroke really will become king, deposing Richard politically as he has deposed him conversationally. But, just as importantly, it hints at what has already happened. The impression is one of muffled conflict, seething unspoken resentments, a dam about to burst. We are never told that Richard is responsible for his uncle's murder, or that Mowbray was his tool, but Shakespeare does not need to tell us this—he has written it into the shape of the dialogue.

* * *

[34] 'Iustice Kikill hearing what he confessed vpon his examination, wrote the same as he was commanded to doo [...] and as it hath beene reported, he informed the king (whether trulie or not, I haue not to say) that the duke franklie confessed euerie thing, wherewith he was charged. Wherevpon the king sent vnto Thomas Mowbraie earle marshall and of Notingham, to make the duke secretlie awaie', Holinshed, III, sig. 3A3r. There is still some hedging, however—the source of this information is described as 'an old French pamphlet'.

[35] *Richard II*, ed. by Anthony B. Dawson and Paul Yachnin (Oxford: Oxford University Press, 2011), 1.1 (p. 135n).

Stepping back from the details of this particular scene, the example serves to illustrate a wider point. The analysis of turn-taking patterns in Shakespeare's plays is not a narrowly formalist concern. It is as historically grounded as the analysis of language itself. The investigation of turn-taking in Shakespeare must therefore go hand in hand with the investigation of turn-taking in Shakespeare's sources and his society. What I have tried to do here with Smith and Holinshed is to show how this might work. Turn-taking patterns can be excavated from handbooks on teaching, trial proceedings, conduct literature, *The Book of Common Prayer*, and any number of other historical documents, as well as from plays, chronicles, and legal textbooks. Only when this work has been carried out will we be able to gain an accurate sense of how Shakespearean dialogue is shaped.

| 4 |

Taking Asides

Towards the end of Samuel Beckett's *Endgame*, the two protagonists have a brief metatheatrical tiff:

> HAMM: Then let it end! [CLOV *goes towards ladder.*] With a bang!
> [CLOV *gets up on ladder, gets down again, looks for telescope, sees it, picks it up, gets up ladder, raises telescope.*] Of darkness! And me? Did anyone ever have pity on me?
> CLOV: [*Lowering the telescope, turning towards* HAMM.] What? [*Pause.*] Is it me you're referring to?
> HAMM: An aside ape! Did you never hear an aside before?[1]

The joke seems straightforward enough. Clov cannot possibly have 'heard' an aside before, because an aside is a remark that the other characters do not hear. If Hamm had been speaking aside, Clov would not have heard him. And the fact that Clov *did* hear him confirms what Hamm should already have known—that this is not the kind of drama in which speaking aside is possible. The misunderstanding is caused not, as Hamm thinks, by Clov's ignorance but by his own delusions of grandeur. He is the Don Quixote of dramatic convention—trying to play by one set of rules in a world that is governed by another. Hamm

[1] Samuel Beckett, *Endgame*, trans. by Samuel Beckett (London: Faber & Faber, 1958), p. 46.

fancies himself a Hamlet but fears he is only a ham, and his name, like the play, hovers between these two possibilities. Any doubts about who might be at fault here are settled by the text. We know that Hamm is deceiving himself because, had he really been speaking 'aside', a stage direction would have told us so.

Like his name, Hamm's failed aside invites us to compare him with Hamlet—a character who speaks aside the very first time he opens his mouth:

> *King.* Take thy fair hour, *Laertes*, time be thine;
> And thy best Graces spend it at thy will.
> But now, my cousin *Hamlet*, and my son—
>   *Ham.* A little more than kin, and less than kind.   [*Aside.*
>   *King.* How is it, that the clouds still hang on you?
>   *Ham.* Not so, my lord, I am too much i'th' Sun.[2]
>   (2[1.2].62–7)

At least, this is how he speaks in Lewis Theobald's 1740 edition of play. Prior to that, Hamlet's aside, like Hamm's, had not been accompanied by a stage direction. This does not mean, however, that the line only became an aside in 1740. Theobald may have been the first to mark it as such, but he is unlikely to have been the first to read it that way. That characters in Shakespeare do sometimes speak 'aside' is uncontroversial. When this is the case, and what exactly it means for them to do so, however, are not. Alan C. Dessen explains:

> The norm in the early printed texts is silence, no signal whatsoever [...] hundreds of speeches that seem obvious *asides* to editors and actors are not marked as such in the quartos and the Folio. [...] My point is not that asides (in our sense) did not occur in performances of Shakespeare's plays or those of his contemporaries. The phenomenon (or something closely akin to it) did exist, but Shakespeare apparently did not use the term as part of his working vocabulary.[3]

---

[2] *The Works of Shakespeare*, ed. by Lewis Theobald, 2nd edn (London: H. Lintott, et al., 1740), VIII, p. 111 (sig. E8r).
[3] Alan C. Dessen, *Recovering Shakespeare's Theatrical Vocabulary* (Cambridge: Cambridge University Press, 1995), pp. 50–2. As Dessen points out, 'The only examples in the Shakespeare canon of what today is deemed the normative use of aside' occur in '(1) a suspect part of *Pericles* and (2) a "bad" quarto' (p. 52).

So Shakespeare's early readers were, on the one hand, frequently at risk of failing to realize when an aside was dramatically necessary, and, on the other hand, free to decide for themselves. They were placed, that is, in precisely the position in which Hamm places Clov—expected to recognize the special interactional status of the aside from the shape of the dialogue in which it is housed, without the help of a paratextual marker.

By the middle of the eighteenth century the marking of asides had become *de rigueur* for editions of Shakespeare, and for drama more generally. Editors were faced with a binary choice—*aside* or *not-aside*. Leaving the question open was no longer an option. In the case of Hamlet's first words, they opted overwhelmingly for *aside*. Bernice Kliman collates thirty-six texts of *Hamlet* published between 1750 and 1920, only three of which do not include the stage direction.[4] More recent editors have begun to demur (as more recent editors are wont to do) and even, on occasions, to admit uncertainty. Bate and Rasmussen's RSC Works regularly uses *Aside?* to signal doubtful cases, although, curiously, Hamlet's first words are not one of them.[5] But even the stage direction *Aside?* is only uncertain in a specific sense. It expresses doubt as to whether or not the line in question is an aside—not about what an aside *is*. That we all know what an aside is, is still taken for granted. This is why Beckett can make a joke about it. Hamm asking Clov 'Did you never hear an aside before?' is just as contradictory, and just as characteristically Beckettian, as Winnie asking herself 'What is that unforgettable line?'.[6]

This chapter will challenge the assumption on which that joke rests by rethinking the aside as a potential turn at talk. It will argue that the Shakespearean aside is neither so stable nor so well understood as we tend to assume. My starting point is the recognition that when a play-text ascribes words to a character—by setting them to the right of his or her name—it does not necessarily follow that those words are to be

---

[4] 'Line 245—Material Textual Note (MTN)', *The Enfolded Hamlet*, ed. by Bernice W. Kliman, 1996–, http://triggs.djvu.org/global-language.com/ENFOLDED/ (accessed 3 March 2015).

[5] *Complete Works*, ed. by Jonathan Bate and Eric Rasmussen, The RSC Shakespeare (Basingstoke: Macmillan, 2007), p. 58.

[6] Samuel Beckett, 'Happy Days', in *The Complete Dramatic Works* (London: Faber & Faber, 1986), pp. 135–68 (p. 160).

understood as a fully fledged contribution to the conversation. There is a distinction, that is, between the typographical turn (what we would traditionally call a 'speech') and the conversational turn. An 'aside' is what happens when these two things are, or may be, at variance. By thinking of the aside as a *potential* turn at talk, we can begin to catalogue the ways in which it might fail to be one. What all asides have in common is that they are speeches which are not, or not quite, turns at talk.

* * *

The first way in which a typographical turn can fail to be a turn at talk is that which underpins Beckett's joke—by being inaudible to the other characters onstage. This is how the aside is understood in Aubignac's *The Whole Art of the Stage*—the earliest attempt to theorize the con-vention to appear in English—and this is how it has most frequently been understood since.[7] Aubignac recognizes that asides 'do sometimes make very good sport' but deplores them for breaking the 'probability of the Stage'. The problem, according to him, is that it 'seems a little hard to conceive [...] that an Actor shall speak loud enough to be heard by the Audience, and yet not be over-heard by another Actor who stands by him'.[8] Understood in this way, the aside is essentially a violation of the laws of acoustics—simultaneously audible forty feet away in the galleries and inaudible three feet away on the stage. Already a distinction is necessary. Some asides are inaudible to *all* of the other characters onstage—are heard, that is, only by the audience—while others are inaudible only to some of them. The former have been called 'monological' or 'solo' asides, the latter 'dialogical', 'conversational', or 'shared' asides.[9] A further complication is caused by the fact that asides are sometimes overheard, often by a character that the speaker does not realize is present. To account for such cases, some critics have chosen to

---

[7] François Hédelin, abbé d'Aubignac, *The Whole Art of the Stage*, translator unknown (London: Printed for the author, 1684). First published in French as *La pratique du théâtre* (Paris: Antoine de Sommaville, 1657).

[8] Aubignac, sig. H3r.

[9] These pairs of terms belong, respectively, to Manfred Pfister, *The Theory and Analysis of Drama*, trans. by John Halliday (Cambridge: Cambridge University Press, 1988), pp. 138–40; and Bernard Beckerman, *Shakespeare at the Globe, 1599–1609* (New York: Macmillan, 1962), p. 186.

define the aside by intention rather than effect. An aside is a remark 'not *intended* to be heard by all those present' rather than a remark which they do not in fact hear.[10] James Hirsh, who has written more extensively on the question than any other critic, gives this a further twist. For Hirsh, an aside is a speech 'guarded by the speaker from the hearing of at least one other character onstage'.[11] The shift of emphasis from hearer to speaker allows him to account for intercepted asides as 'imperfectly guarded', like carelessly spilt verbal milk. In all of these cases, however, what defines the aside—what prevents it from being a turn—is its inaudibility (achieved or intended) to at least one other character.

But consider old Queen Margaret's entrance in 1.3 of *Richard III*, in the midst of an argument between Richard, still only the Duke of Gloucester, and his brother's wife, Elizabeth, the current queen. The quotation is a long one, so the reader will have to bear with me.

> QUEEN My lord of Gloucester, I have too long borne
> Your blunt upbraidings and your bitter scoffs.
> By heaven, I will acquaint his majesty
> 105 Of those gross taunts that oft I have endured.
> I had rather be a country servant-maid
> Than a great queen with this condit'ion:
> To be so baited, scorned, and stormèd at.
> Small joy have I in being England's queen.
> *Enter old Queen Margaret*
> 110 MARGARET *[aside]* And lessened be that small, God I beseech him.
> Thy honour, state, and seat, is due to me.
> RICHARD DUKE OF GLOUCESTER *[to the Queen]*
> What, threat you me with telling of the King?
> I will avouch't in presence of the King.
> I dare adventure to be sent to th' Tower.
> 115 'Tis time to speak; my pains are quite forgot.
> MARGARET *[aside]* Out, devil! I do remember them too well.
> Thou killed'st my husband Henry in the Tower,
> And Edward, my poor son, at Tewkesbury.

---

[10] A. C. Sprague, as quoted in Beckerman, p. 186.
[11] James Hirsh, *Shakespeare and the History of Soliloquies* (London: Associated University Presses, 2003), p. 22.

RICHARD DUKE OF GLOUCESTER *[to the Queen]*
Ere you were queen, ay, or your husband king,
120   I was a packhorse in his great affairs,
A weeder-out of his proud adversaries,
A liberal rewarder of his friends.
To royalize his blood, I spent mine own.
MARGARET *[aside]*   Ay, and much better blood than his or thine.
RICHARD DUKE OF GLOUCESTER *[to the Queen]*
125   In all which time, you and your husband Grey
Were factious for the house of Lancaster.—
And, Rivers, so were you.—Was not your husband
In Margaret's battle at Saint Albans slain?
Let me put in your minds, if you forget,
130   What you have been ere this, and what you are;
Withal, what I have been, and what I am.
MARGARET *[aside]*   A murd'rous villain, and so still thou art.
RICHARD DUKE OF GLOUCESTER
Poor Clarence did forsake his father Warwick,
Ay, and forswore himself—which Jesu pardon—
135 MARGARET *[aside]*   Which God revenge.
RICHARD DUKE OF GLOUCESTER
—To fight on Edward's party, for the crown.
And for his meed, poor lord, he is mewed up.
I would to God my heart were flint, like Edward's,
Or Edward's soft and pitiful, like mine.
140   I am too childish-foolish for this world.
MARGARET *[aside]*
Hie thee to hell for shame, and leave this world,
Thou cacodemon: there thy kingdom is.
RIVERS   My lord of Gloucester, in those busy days
Which here you urge to prove us enemies,
145   We followed then our lord, our sovereign king.
So should we you if you should be our king.
RICHARD DUKE OF GLOUCESTER
If I should be? I had rather be a pedlar.
Far be it from my heart the thought thereof.
QUEEN   As little joy, my lord, as you suppose

150   You should enjoy were you this country's king,
        As little joy you may suppose in me
        That I enjoy being the queen thereof.
        MARGARET *[aside]*   Ah, little joy enjoys the queen thereof,
        For I am she, and altogether joyless.
155   I can no longer hold me patïent.—
            [Coming forward]
        Hear me, you wrangling pirates, that fall out
        In sharing that which you have pilled from me.
        Which of you trembles not that looks on me?—
        If not that I am queen you bow like subjects,
160   Yet that, by you deposed, you quake like rebels.
        [To Richard] Ah, gentle villain, do not turn away.
        RICHARD   DUKE OF GLOUCESTER
        Foul wrinkled witch, what mak'st thou in my sight?
                                        (1.3.102–62)

Everything in square brackets, including the seven indications that Margaret is speaking aside, is editorial. The Folio text, on which the New
Oxford edition is based, makes no distinction between Margaret's speeches
and those of the other characters. Nor does it have it her 'Coming forward'
from a position outside the field of interactional play. The logic of these
additions is not hard to see. None of Margaret's first six speeches is
acknowledged by any of the other characters. The argument between
Richard and Elizabeth carries on as if she had not spoken. It is therefore
reasonable to assume that what she says is inaudible, either because it is
'aside' in the fully conventional sense, or because she is physically distant
from (lurking somewhere 'behind') the action. At line 155 Margaret
announces 'I can no longer hold me patïent', which can be taken to mean
'I can no longer refrain from speaking'. This is immediately followed by
'Hear me, you wrangling pirates', which would appear to be the moment at
which the old queen bursts out of her aside and into the conversation.

    Reasonable as this interpretation is, it is not the only reasonable
interpretation. Considered as conversational turns, there is nothing
very wrong with what Margaret has to say. Her contributions are bitter
and accusatory, but so are those of the other characters. She says
nothing we have reason to believe she would be afraid to say publically.
She responds on each occasion to the previous speaker, even though

their words are not addressed to her. And, with the exception of line 135—apparently delivered while Richard's sentence about Clarence forswearing himself is still in progress—she always speaks at an appropriate moment (at what Sacks, Schegloff, and Jefferson call a 'transition-relevance place'). Her speeches can be read, in other words, as a series of attempted interventions—Margaret repeatedly tries to enter the conversation, to take her place as a contestant in this game of competitive complaint, but is repeatedly blanked and ignored. And it is this that she can no longer endure when she announces, 'I can no longer hold me patïent'. The phrase 'Hear me' is indeed the moment at which she first establishes a foothold in the conversation, but this need not be because everything she previously said has been inaudible. The verb 'hear' had a fair range of non-acoustic meanings in early modern English, as it does now. When, for example, Iago complains to Roderigo, ''Sblood! but you will not hear me!' (1.1.4), Roderigo's refusal to 'hear' him has nothing to do with the volume at which Iago is speaking—it is a refusal to take on board what Iago is saying. Margaret's use of the same phrase can be read in the same way—as an exasperated plea for recognition.

Understood in this way, none of what the old queen says is 'aside' in the sense that it violates the laws of acoustics. But there is still a sense in which it is spoken aside. What Margaret is looking for, and keeps being refused, is the status of a 'ratified participant' in the conversation.[12] She asks for this by making what would be an appropriate contribution at what would be an appropriate moment. The other characters refuse it by failing to acknowledge that she has spoken. They refuse it, that is, by denying to each of her utterances the status of a turn. You can throw your counters onto the table, but until somebody picks one up you have not been admitted to the game. For a remark to be 'aside' in this sense is nothing to do with audibility. It is about the status of what is said in relation to an ongoing thread of official (in this very specific sense) conversation. And this status is defined by the shape of that thread from the moment at which the aside occurs. What the example shows is that an attempted turn can be relegated to the status of an aside by being treated as though it were inaudible. Conversely, an attempted aside can be promoted to the status of a turn by being given a reply in the main conversational thread. Teachers often do this, on purpose, to embarrass a child that is whispering in class. Clov does it, by accident, to Hamm.

---

[12] The phrase is from Goffman, *Forms of Talk*, p. 132.

Now consider how a reader of the Folio text would experience the lines, without the stage directions added by later editors. At the moment of Margaret's first speech, there is nothing to indicate that what she says is an aside. It is only when Richard subsequently replies to Elizabeth, ignoring what Margaret has just said, that the possibility suggests itself. And the same is true for each of her subsequent turns. On each occasion, we do not know she is going to be ignored until she has been ignored, although the more times this happens the more we might come to expect it. Shakespeare plays on this ambiguity by making the phrase with which Richard begins line 119, 'Ere you were queen', equally applicable to both Elizabeth and Margaret. And perhaps Richard plays on it too—teasing the old woman with the possibility that she is getting a response before dashing her hopes again. Without the stage direction 'aside' to forestall any doubts, the reader is in the same position as Margaret herself—each time hoping, each time disappointed. These brief moments at which the status of an utterance is undecided are a part of what makes the writing dramatic at the microlevel of conversational exchange. They help to characterize Margaret as a bitter old woman—a ghost from Shakespeare's earlier plays—shut out from and irrelevant to the dialogue in the same way that she is shut out from and irrelevant to the unfolding drama, but loudly clamouring, at both levels, to get back in. By marking her speeches as asides, the editorial tradition flattens out the drama of her readmittance. We are told before she knocks that the door will not be opened.

This does not mean, however, that the aside is 'a crutch we can well do without' or that it imposes 'artificial clarity' on 'the labyrinth of Shakespearean character and motivation, which interests us in part because it is confusing and obscure'.[13] Compare Catesby, Richard's henchman, chuckling to himself about Hastings' impending execution, as presented in the First Folio:

> *Cates.* The Princes both make high account of you,
> For they account his Head vpon the Bridge.
> *Hast.* I know they doe, and I haue well deseru'd it.
> $\qquad$ (TLN 1869–71, 3.2.66–8)

---

[13] Leah S. Marcus, 'Editing Shakespeare in a Postmodern Age', in *A Concise Companion to Shakespeare and the Text*, ed. by Andrew Murphy (Oxford: Blackwell, 2007), pp. 128–44 (136–7).

The first of Catesby's two lines is addressed to Hastings, the second is an aside—of the kind that breaks the laws of acoustics. The joke of Hastings replying 'I know they doe' is predicated on the audience understanding that, in fact, he has no idea. His reaction makes no sense, psychologically, if he has heard Catesby, and the plot requires him to be ignorant of what is in store for him until it is too late to do anything about it. A sensitive reader will soon work this out, but—unlike in the previous example—the momentary confusion it causes serves no dramatic purpose. More damage is done, in this instance, by not taking the shortcut offered by the stage direction. Rather than dispense with the aside, we should be trying to use it more judiciously—with greater attention, that is, to the the turn-taking structure of the dialogue in which it occurs. What is needed is not 'unediting' but better editing.

An equally instructive example occurs in *The Two Gentlemen of Verona*. Julia is pretending to be angry with her maid, Lucetta, for having accepted a letter to her mistress from an admirer. I quote from the text of eccentric Victorian chess genius Howard Staunton.[14]

> JUL. This babble shall not henceforth trouble me.
> 100 Here is a coil with protestation !—   [*Tears the letter.*
> Go, get you gone; and let the papers lie:
> You would be fingering them, to anger me.
> LUC. She makes it strange; but she would be best pleas'd
> To be so anger'd with another letter.   [*Exit.*
> 105 JUL. Nay, would I were so anger'd with the same !
> O hateful hands, to tear such loving words !
> Injurious wasps ! to feed on such sweet honey,
> And kill the bees, that yield it, with your stings !
> I'll kiss each several paper for amends.

[14] *The Plays of Shakespeare*, ed. by Howard Staunton, 3 vols (London: Routledge, 1858), I, p. 7. Line numbering is borrowed from the New Oxford Shakespeare (Staunton's edition has none). According to the ODNB, Staunton 'was dubiously alleged to be the natural son of the Earl of Carlisle', 'had little or no formal education', 'received a legacy [possibly from Carlisle] which he rapidly spent' and 'claimed to have acted Lorenzo to the Shylock of Edmund Kean' (ODNB, Staunton, Howard (1810–1874), chess player and literary scholar). Staunton's writings on chess are still widely read. Bobby Fischer has described him as 'the most profound opening analyst of all time'. See *The Oxford Companion to Chess*, ed. by David Hooper and Kenneth Whyld, 2nd edn (Oxford: Oxford University Press, 1992), p. 391.

110 Look, here is writ—*kind Julia:*—unkind Julia !
    As in revenge of thy ingratitude,
    I throw thy name against the bruising stones,
    Trampling contemptuously on thy disdain.
(I, p. 7, 1.2.99–113)

Staunton feels sure that lines 103–4 must be an aside but refrains from marking them as such. Instead, he voices his dissatisfaction in a footnote.

> It is surprising that no one has hitherto pointed out the inconsistency of Julia's replying to an observation evidently intended to be spoken by her attendant aside, or remarked the utter absence of all meaning in such reply [sic]. I have little doubt that the line above is part of Lucetta's side speech. The expression of the wish 'would I were so anger'd with the same!' from her is natural and consistent. In the mouth of her mistress it seems senseless and absurd.[15]

On the one hand, Lucetta's remark is 'evidently' intended to be an aside (Staunton does not elaborate on what makes this evident). On the other hand, Julia hears it. Asides, as we know, can sometimes be overheard, but it is unusual for an aside to be overheard by someone whom the speaker knows to be present. Staunton is so irked by this apparent contradiction that he suggests reassigning Julia's first line to Lucetta. The maid could then be understood to be reflecting (inaudibly) on how she certainly wouldn't mind receiving such a letter herself. The result would be a plausible, if somewhat violently achieved, reading.

Staunton's quandary evaporates as soon as we realize that a turn need not be inaudible—nor intended to be so—in order to be an aside. What this example shows is that it need not even be ignored by the other characters. But if Staunton is right to intuit an aside here, on what basis is he doing so? E. A. J. Honigmann can explain:

> When an editor adds '*Aside*' he often implies that the speaker would not have dared to utter the same words openly; in short, he passes judgment on the relationship of two or more dramatic characters.[16]

---

[15] Staunton, I, p. 7n.
[16] E. A. J. Honigmann, 'Re-Enter the Stage Direction: Shakespeare and Some Contemporaries', *Shakespeare Survey*, 29 (1976), 117–25 (p. 120).

The beauty of this remark is the choice of the word 'openly'. Saying something 'openly' is not the same thing as saying it 'audibly'. Staunton's problem is that he fails to see this distinction. To speak openly is to take responsibility for what you say—to put it on the record, as it were, with your name attached to it. To speak audibly, on the other hand, is merely to speak so that someone can hear you. We might flesh out Honigmann's remark by adding that the editor does more than simply 'pass judgement' on the relationship between two (or more) characters. He also helps to fashion it. Whether or not we see this line as an aside depends on our understanding of the relationship between Julia and Lucetta. But our understanding of their relationship depends, in part, on whether or not we see the line as an aside. The editor treads a circle, adjusting the text according to his sense of the characters and his sense of the characters according to the text. The argument can be made that what Lucetta says here is inappropriate. She is reflecting unfavourably on her mistress by making it clear that, in her opinion, Julia's protestations are insincere—inappropriate, yes, but hardly unheard of. What we might call the 'snarky servant'—the servant, that is, who provides a running commentary on his master's hypocrisy and stupidity—is something of a stock character in Shakespeare, particularly in the early comedies.[17] For obvious reasons, this commentating is carried on primarily through asides. It is also possible that Julia and Lucetta have the kind of relationship in which the mistress accepts a bit of good-natured teasing from her maid or pretends not to hear her remarks precisely because they are not good-natured at all.

But it is not simply the impropriety of Lucetta's remark that suggests it may be spoken aside. If we consider that remark as a potential turn at talk, two further considerations come into view. First, if this is a turn, Lucetta is blanking her mistress. Instead of 'You make it strange' we have 'She makes it strange'. Julia is held up, as if for inspection, before some unspecified third party. And this turning away of the voice suggests (although it does not guarantee) a turning away of the head. Both grammatically and acoustically, Lucetta's words are pointing at something other than her mistress. This does not necessarily make them an aside, but it does signal a change of some sort. The fact that

---

[17] Compare the Dromios in *A Comedy of Errors*, Mote in *Love's Labour's Lost*, and the unnamed second lord who attends on Cloten in *Cymbeline*.

Lucetta blanks Julia reinforces the impression that she is being rude and, therefore, that she does not want to be heard.

Secondly, there is the position of Lucetta's speech in, or rather just outside, the conversational sequence she exchanges with her mistress. It is likely that she is already leaving the stage at the moment she says it. I say 'likely' because both her exit and (a few lines later) her re-entrance are editorial. Lucetta has already left and re-entered the scene once, however, and Julia's behaviour here—expatiating in a way that exposes her own hypocrisy, getting on her knees to examine the fragments of a letter in which she claims to have no interest—suggests she is alone. If we accept that Lucetta is leaving as she utters her lines then they are aside in the sense that they occur after the conversation has officially ended, in a kind of interactional limbo. And it may be that this is deliberate. Lucetta is trying to have the last word as she walks off and to ensure that it *is* the last word by walking off quickly. Even if Julia hears her, she will not have time to reply. I have already suggested that an attempt at an aside can, by being answered, be made into a turn—it can, but that is not what happens here. Julia only admits that she has heard Lucetta in the same way that she admits she cares about the letter, alone and in soliloquy. My point, once again, is that what is really at stake is the status of Lucetta's utterance in relation to the conversation she is officially having with Julia. It is an aside because it fails to register in that conversation, not because it is inaudible. And it fails to register (this time) not because nobody responds to it but because the conversation is already over.

* * *

Thus far, then, we have three different ways in which what is typographically a speech can fail to be a turn at talk—by being inaudible, by being ignored, and by standing just outside an interaction. What they all have in common is that they are off the record in some way. Asides are remarks that we pretend not to hear, or that we half-hear, as well as those that we do not hear at all. They are remarks that hover at the fringes of a conversation, whether seeking admittance, standing aloof, or terrified of being dragged in. Crucially, the status of a speech is not something that the speaker simply chooses for him- or herself. Nor is it something that is fixed at the moment the words are uttered. Which speeches turn out to be asides also depends on how, whether, and when the other characters choose to take notice of them. There are two important issues, however, around which I have so far been tiptoeing. Each of them concerns the monological aside, and each has been the subject of a long-running critical squabble. Each can be better understood by thinking of the aside as a potential turn at talk.

The first concerns to whom asides are addressed. After many years of research, James Hirsh is unequivocal. According to him, asides and soliloquies 'represented self-addressed speeches as a matter of course'.[18] This runs counter, however, to a long tradition of Shakespearean scholarship that sees the aside and the soliloquy as addressed to the audience. In medieval drama, it is pointed out, interaction between character and audience was commonplace—characters would often introduce themselves to the spectators when they first appeared on stage.[19] The question is how far, and in what form, this tradition survived into the sixteenth and seventeenth centuries. Doris Fenton finds 'a decided lessening in the amount of extra-dramatic material' in plays after 1616. Anne Barton concludes that 'audience address not only decreases, but tends to be relegated in its surviving forms to a position slightly outside the play' after 1550. Hirsh is adamant that it had come to seem 'outmoded and amateurish' by 1590. William Congreve, writing in 1694, was of the opinion that 'in any part of a Play, if there is expressed any knowledge of an Audience, it is insufferable'.[20] There is agreement, in other words, that direct address to the audience was going out of fashion in Shakespeare's lifetime, but disagreement as to how quickly it was doing so.

---

[18] Hirsh, 'Guarded, Unguarded, and Unguardable Speech in Late Renaissance Drama', in *Who Hears in Shakespeare?*, ed. by Laury Magnus and Walter W. Cannon (Madison, NJ: Fairleigh Dickinson University Press, 2012), pp. 17–40 (p. 17). See also his *The Structure of Shakespearean Scenes* (London: Yale University Press, 1981) and 'The "To be, or not to be" Speech: Evidence, Conventional Wisdom, and the Editing of *Hamlet*', *Medieval and Renaissance Drama in England*, 23 (2010), 34–62.

[19] As for example Garcio, in the second play of the Townley Cycle, who greets the audience with 'All hayll, all hayll, both blithe and glad' before entreating them to 'peasse youre dyn' so the play can be heard. *English Mystery Plays*, ed. by Peter Happé, Penguin Classics (London: Penguin, 1985), p. 79.

[20] See, respectively, Doris Fenton, *The Extra-Dramatic Moment in Elizabethan Plays* (Philadelphia: Westbrook, 1930), p. 3; Anne Righter [Barton], *Shakespeare and the Idea of the Play* (New York: Barnes and Noble, 1962), p. 56; Hirsh, 'Guarded, Unguarded, and Unguardable Speech in Late Renaissance Drama', p. 18; William Congreve, *The Double-Dealer* (London: Jacob Tonson, 1694), sig. A4r.

Like most disagreements between literary critics, this one is exacerbated rather than resolved by an examination of the evidence. Excluding choruses, prologues, and epilogues, Hirsh finds only 'three speeches, all in very early comedies', in which a Shakespearean character addresses the audience.[21] Fenton finds them in 'almost two thirds' of all plays published before 1616. The root of this discrepancy, I will suggest, is a misreading of the evidence on both sides. More specifically, it is caused by a confusion of two types of address—address as a targeted attempt at communication, and address as a grammaticalized feature of language. This matters because it is possible for the two types to be at variance, and in Shakespeare they often are.

According to Hirsh, the evidence that asides in Shakespeare are 'self-addressed as a matter of course' is 'plentiful, varied, and unambiguous'.[22] He lists ten varieties:

(i)   Stage directions
(ii) Declarations by the speaker
(iii) Descriptions by other characters
(iv) Self-address by name (or epithet)
(v)   Self-address by second-person pronoun
(vi) Self-directed commands
(vii) Self-directed questions
(viii) Apostrophes
(ix) Conspicuous absence of evidence of audience address
(x)   Mockery of audience address[23]

Six of them (iv–ix) concern what I have called 'address as a grammaticalized feature of language'. Three of them (i–iii) do not. These three are enough to prove, if proof were needed, that some asides in Shakespeare are self-addressed. But they do not prove that asides in Shakespeare are self-addressed 'as a matter of course', since Hirsh is able to produce only two examples of stage directions, one declaration by the speaker, and one declaration by another character.[24] The

---

[21] Hirsh, *Shakespeare and the History of Soliloquies*, p. 199.
[22] Hirsh, 'Guarded, Unguarded, and Unguardable Speech', p. 18.
[23] Hirsh, 'Guarded, Unguarded, and Unguardable Speech', pp. 19–20.
[24] The unambiguous stage direction is '*Speakes to himselfe*' in the Folio text of *Richard III*, TLN 791 (1.3.317). More doubtful is the direction '*A Song the whilst* Bassanio comments on the Caskets to himselfe' occuring in both early texts of *The Merchant of*

bulk of his evidence therefore concerns grammatical address. I am using 'grammatical' in a broad sense here, to mean any formal feature of language relevant to identifying the addressee of an utterance. This is distinct from what I will be calling 'pragmatic address', which is a targeted attempt at communication with a person or group of people. It's something like the distinction between pointing a gun and pulling the trigger. Like a gun, an utterance can be aimed—at someone else, at oneself, at no one. It can be waved around ostentatiously and fired into the air, or concealed beneath a jacket whilst trained on an unsuspecting victim. The socially contextualized meaning of such gestures is not currently my concern. For the moment what matters is how far we can tell, just by looking at it, the direction in which the gun is pointing.

Hirsh identifies several of the ways in which address can be grammaticalized (address-terms, pronouns, imperatives, questions) but fails to consider how these function or how they differ from one another. Thus he quotes Kent and Petruccio as examples, respectively, of 'self-address by second-person pronoun' and a 'self-directed command':

> KENT [...]   Now, banished Kent,
> 5   If thou canst serve where thou dost stand condemned,
>   Thy master whom thou lovest shall find thee full of labour.
>   (*Lear*, 1[1.1].4.4–6)
> PETRUCCIO [...]
>   But here she comes, and now, Petruccio, speak.
>   (*Shrew*, 5[2.1].176)

But it is neither the second-person pronoun nor the command that identifies what is said here as self-addressed. It is the use of the character's own name as an address-term. The second-person pronoun (like all pronouns) is deictic rather than referential.[25] As a marker of

---

Venice, TLN 1407 (3.2.62)—doubtful because it could indicate that the actor should mime talking to himself during the song rather than that he should address himself in the speech which follows it. The doubtful example of a declaration by the speaker is Cloten's 'I dare speake it to myselfe', *Cymbeline*, TLN 2224–5 (4.1.5). This one is doubtful because he is alone on stage when he says it, which technically makes it a soliloquy rather than an aside.

[25] See the chapter on 'Deixis' in Stephen C. Levinson, *Pragmatics*, Cambridge Textbooks in Linguistics (Cambridge: Cambridge University Press) pp. 54–96—in particular section 2.2.1 on '*Person deixis*'.

address, it indicates a relative rather than an absolute direction (like saying 'go left' rather than 'go West'). In an aside which we know to be self-addressed, 'thou' and 'you' refer to the speaker. But they are of limited value as evidence when what we are trying to do is determine whether an aside *is* self-addressed in the first place, since they could equally well refer to the audience or to another character. The referent is determined by the addressee, not the other way around. Something similar is true of questions and imperatives. These project a specific type of recipient—one capable of answering the question or performing the command—but do not specify, purely by virtue of being a question or a command, who that recipient is. A pronoun can help to narrow the range of possibilities (by indicating that the target is singular rather than plural, for example), but the only unambiguous way in which an utterance can stipulate its own addressee, grammatically, is by containing a referential address-term.

This does not mean that only those turns which contain formulations such as 'Hamlet' or 'good my lord' can confidently be ascribed an addressee. Unless we have a reason not to, we assume that what is said is addressed to the speaker of the previous turn. This assumption is either confirmed or confounded by what follows. In conversation analytic terms, when dialogue is functioning smoothly, each new turn is 'orientated' to the turn before.[26] It retrojects an understanding of that turn, including an understanding of whom it was addressed to, that is open to challenge by the other participants in the conversation. If person A speaks and person B answers, we assume that person A was speaking to person B (whether singly or as part of a group) so long as the other participants in the conversation seem to accept B's interpretation of himself as addressee. The reader takes her cue from the responses of the characters.

The monological aside, however, is by definition a turn to which no subsequent turn is orientated. If the dialogue did not appear to ignore it, it would not be considered an aside. The kind of context that usually resolves ambiguities of address is therefore not available. Other kinds of context are available, and these do sometimes provide a resolution but not in the same systematically pervasive way. Grammaticalized address is therefore of more importance in determining the addressee of an

---

[26] See Schegloff, *Sequence Organization in Interaction*, pp. 1–13.

aside than any other type of turn. And this is the reason for the massive discrepancy between Hirsh and Fenton when it comes to interpreting what is largely the same material. Compare his list of the evidence against audience address with her list of the evidence for it:

> Stage-directions indicating this fact do occur, but they are rare. Far more frequent are such forms of address as 'sirs' or 'masters'. There is also the less conspicuous use of the second personal pronoun, and sometimes of the imperative.[27]

Stage directions we know are rare. Referential address-terms, such as 'sirs' and 'masters', may be frequent in some dramatists, but they are not frequent in Shakespeare, from whose works Fenton does not provide an example. She relies instead, like Hirsh, primarily on grammaticalized address, of the weaker, deictic, kind. When Hamlet says 'soft you now, the fair Ophelia', Hirsh hears 'you, *Hamlet*' and Fenton hears 'you, *the audience*', and each has a further example in support of their position. It's a textbook case of confirmation bias.

But there is a further, more serious flaw in Hirsh's argument. Here is Iago, watching Cassio greet Desdemona in the first quarto of *Othello*:[28]

> *Iag.* He takes her by the palme; I well sed, whisper: as little a webbe as this will ensnare as great a Flee as *Cassio*. I smile vpon her, doe: I will catch you in your owne courtesies: you say true, tis so indeed. If such trickes as these strip you out of your Leiutenantry, it had beene better you had not rist your three fingers so oft, which now againe, you are most apt to play the sir in: good, well kist, an excellent courtesie; tis so indeed: yet againe, your fingers at your lips? Would they were Clisterpipes for your sake.
>
> (E1r, 2.1.163–70)

In a copy of this book in the Huntington Library, one early reader has helpfully added 'Asid to himselfe' in the margin.[29] By doing so he is

---

[27] Fenton, p. 8.

[28] *The Tragoedy of Othello, the Moore of Venice* (London: Nicholas Okes for Thomas Walkley, 1622).

[29] No. 69337 in the library catalogue. Reproduced in facsimile in *Shakespeare's Plays in Quarto: A Facsimile Edition of Copies Primarily from the Henry E. Huntington Library*, ed. by Michael J. B. Allen and Kenneth Muir (Berkeley: University of California Press, 1981), p. 801.

committing precisely the error of which I am accusing Hirsh. Pragmatically, these words are addressed 'to himselfe' in the sense that no one else on stage is intended to hear them. Grammatically, they are a little more complicated. Iago begins in explanatory mode, commenting on Cassio's behaviour in the third person ('He takes her by the palme') to an unidentified addressee. The phrase 'well sed' would appear to be addressed to Cassio—Iago is pleased that the Florentine is being so intimate with Desdemona as to whisper to her. A second switch occurs after the word 'whisper', back to that explanatory third person ('as great a Flee as *Cassio*'), before eleven consecutive second-person pronouns that, our old friend context tells us, must be addressed to Cassio. It's as though Iago were watching the couple from a rooftop through a pair of binoculars or using a camera he had hidden in a light-fitting. In either case it would be possible, and distinctly Shakespearean, for him to address what he says to Cassio, even though Cassio cannot hear him. To put it more starkly, if Prof. Hirsh has his back to me and I stick two fingers up at him, he will have no idea that I have done so. I might choose to do it while his back is turned for precisely that reason. But I would still be sticking my fingers up *at* Prof. Hirsh.

The value of Hirsh's work—and it is genuinely valuable—lies in his insistence on the 'conspicuous absence of evidence of audience address' in the plays. Scholars had previously noted that 'there are surprisingly few direct appeals in Shakespeare' but without pausing to consider on what basis they found this surprising.[30] Hirsh's determination to accept as audience address only what cannot be interpreted in any other way successfully demonstrates that very little in Shakespeare falls into this category.[31]

But consider the following example, again from *Richard III*, in which Richard, his nephew Prince Edward, and our old friend Buckingham (not yet fallen from favour) await the arrival of the prince's younger brother:

---

[30] M. L. Arnold, *The Soliloquies of Shakespeare* (New York: Columbia University Press, 1911), p. 106.

[31] He concedes only one example, Launcelot Gobbo tricking his old, blind father in 2.2 of *The Merchant of Venice*. Even here, however, we do not have the 'sirs' or 'masters' of Fenton's claim.

PRINCE […]
　Methinks the truth should live from age to age,
　As 'twere retailed to all posterity,
　Even to the general all-ending day.
RICHARD DUKE OF GLOUCESTER *[aside]*
　So wise so young, they say, do never live long.
80　PRINCE What say you, uncle?
RICHARD DUKE OF GLOUCESTER
　I say, 'Without charàcters, fame lives long'.—
　[Aside] Thus, like the formal Vice, Iniquity,
　I moralize two meanings in one word.
                                        (3.1.76–83)

Line 79 is marked as an aside on the grounds that it contains a thinly veiled threat that Richard would not want his nephew to hear. When given the chance to repeat what he has just said, the duke declines to do so, substituting a similar-sounding but less sinister remark. Following this remark are a further two lines, in which Richard appears to compare himself with Vice—a stock character of medieval drama, famous (among other things) for direct address to the audience. These lines are likewise considered an aside. In any case, the boy takes no notice of them, resuming his own rather pompous train of thought about fame and Julius Caesar without showing any sign of having heard them.

　Notice, first, that line 79 is demonstrably not a representation of unspoken thought: the prince hears something, although how much he hears is an open question. Enough to request a rerun and enough, in Richard's opinion, for it to be worth ending that rerun with the same two words. But also, possibly, everything. Instead of demanding a repetition because he has not heard well, the prince's response ('What say you, uncle?') could be an expression of anger, or panic, or confusion, precisely because he has heard perfectly. It would be possible to play the scene in such a way that Richard spoke the words audibly, realized from the prince's reaction that he had gone too far, and then tried to back-pedal. By offering a similar-sounding replacement he offers a sort of compromise: if you pretend not to have heard that, I'll pretend not to have said it. The two characters could thus be shown collaborating to edit the official record of their conversation, re-categorizing as an aside what was initially treated as a conversational turn.

The real point of the example, however, is Richard's reference to Vice in line 82. In the absence of any form of grammatical address, the addressee of this aside is ambiguous. He could be addressing Buckingham, and he could be addressing himself. But by evoking the medieval character at such a moment, Shakespeare is also evoking the medieval convention. Even if the aside is *not* addressed to the audience, it at least teases them with the possibility that it might be. Richard is threatening to get medieval. What I want to suggest is that the kind of ambiguity made explicit here—and the self-consciousness it suggests about the evolution of dramatic convention—is at work implicitly throughout Shakespeare's plays. So many of his monological asides are ambiguously addressed because his dramaturgy looks both forwards and back. The use of direct address may have come to seem outmoded to some in 1590s but not to others, scorned by the literati but craved by the groundlings. Shakespeare manages to suggest audience address without explicitly employing it. His characters simultaneously talk to those that like to be addressed and not to those who don't. They make you feel included without ever quite looking you in the eye. They skilfully cater, that is, to the tastes of both a Doris Fenton and a James Hirsh.

* * *

The final way in which a typographical turn can fail to be a turn at talk is by not being talk at all—by representing thought rather than speech. This is the second of the two controversies to engulf the monological aside. The first writer to make the claim explicitly (in English, at least) was William Congreve:

> I grant, that for a Man to Talk to himself, appears absurd and unnatural [...] if he supposes any one to be by, when he talks to himself, it is monstrous and ridiculous to the last degree [...] We ought not to imagine that this Man either talks to us, or to himself; he is only thinking [...] the Poet finds it necessary [...] to inform us of this Persons Thoughts, and to that end is forced to make use of the expedient of Speech, no other better way being yet invented for the Communication of Thought.[32]

---

[32] Congreve, sigs A3v–A4r.

Three things are worth noting here. First, that a convention existed in Restoration drama by which both soliloquy (appearing to talk to oneself) and aside (doing so when someone else is 'by') can be interpreted as 'only thinking'. Second, that this convention was not universally understood—Congreve feels obliged to spell it out in response to what he describes as 'Objections' to *The Double-Dealer*. Third, that the convention involves an awkward compromise. It is an 'expedient' adopted by the playwright for want of a better alternative.

Since at least the beginning of the nineteenth century, there have been those who read Shakespeare in precisely this way—imagining, as Congreve encourages them to do, that soliloquies and asides are 'only thinking'. Charles Lamb, for example, describes how Hamlet's 'silent meditations' are 'reduced to words for the sake of the reader'.[33] Una Ellis-Fermor sees soliloquy as a solution to the 'technical problem' of revealing 'unspoken thought' to the audience, a solution which 'by sacrificing verisimilitude, immeasurably enriches our experience of reality'.[34] More recently, Marcus Nordlund has coined the term *inside* (on the analogy of *aside*) to cover soliloquies and monological asides, both of which he understands as representations of internal thought.[35]

The problem with the *inside* is similar to that with the aside *ad spectatores*. The convention was demonstrably in use within a century of Shakespeare's death but is difficult to date with confidence. Congreve may have been the first to write about it, but he does so with the air of a man exasperated at having to explain what everyone ought to understand. Assuming that his exasperation is justified, the convention predates 1694. But how far back does it stretch? The early modern play-text is characteristically reticent. It has no typographical equivalent for the thought bubble in a comic strip, and we do not find *Thinks* being used as a stage direction.[36] Formally, there is nothing to

[33] *Charles Lamb on Shakespeare*, ed. by Joan Coldwell (Gerrards Cross: Smythe, 1978), p. 29.

[34] Una Ellis-Fermor, 'A Technical Problem: The Revelation of Unspoken Thought in Drama', in *The Frontiers of Drama*, 2nd edn (London: Methuen, 1946), pp. 96–126 (p. 99).

[35] Marcus Nordlund, *The Shakespearean Inside: A Study of the Complete Soliloquies and Solo Asides* (Edinburgh: Edinburgh University Press, 2017).

[36] See, or rather don't see, *A Dictionary of Stage Directions in English Drama, 1580–1642*, ed. by Alan C. Dessen and Leslie Thomson (Cambridge: Cambridge University Press, 1999).

distinguish the aside from the inside. So it is perhaps not surprising that James Hirsh finds 'no evidence of any kind that any passage in any play by Shakespeare was an interior monologue' and concludes that 'even a soliloquy guarded in an aside from other characters represents a speech by the character rather than the character's unspoken thoughts'.[37] Most asides and soliloquies can be interpreted in either way, just as they can be interpreted either as self-addressed or addressed to the audience.

Most, but not all. As we have seen, it is not uncommon for soliloquies to be overheard in Shakespeare or for asides to be 'intercepted'.[38] Hirsh makes such occurrences the cornerstone of his argument. But again, his logic is open to question. It does not follow from the fact that some asides in Shakespeare are at least partially audible, that all asides in Shakespeare represent speech rather than thought. The limitations of this view can be shown from one of Hirsh's own pet examples—and the most sustained series of asides in Shakespeare—the meeting of Suffolk and Margaret in 5.6 of *1 Henry VI*. I am using 'Shakespeare' in a loosely metonymic sense here, because the authorship of this particular scene is contested.[39] It would not necessarily invalidate Hirsh's point (or mine) if the scene were not Shakespearean—even in a play with multiple playwrights, it is in everyone's interests to follow a single set of conventions—but there is a limit to how much weight such an example can bear. The exchange takes place after a battle in which Suffolk, on behalf of the English crown, has been victorious. Margaret of Anjou (the same Margaret we have already met in *Richard III*) is now effectively his prisoner:

MARGARET   Say, Earl of Suffolk—if thy name be so—
              What ransom must I pay before I pass?
30   For I perceive I am thy prisoner.
SUFFOLK *[aside]*   How canst thou tell she will deny thy suit
              Before thou make a trial of her love?
MARGARET   Why speak'st thou not? What ransom must I pay?
SUFFOLK *[aside]*   She's beautiful, and therefore to be wooed;

---

[37] Hirsh, *Shakespeare and the History of Soliloquies*, pp. 26, 146.
[38] The term belongs to Pfister, p. 138.
[39] See Brian Vickers, 'Incomplete Shakespeare: Or, Denying Coauthorship in *1 Henry VI*', *Shakespeare Quarterly*, 58 (2007), 311–52; and NOS, *Authorship Companion*, ed. by Gary Taylor and Gabriel Egan (Oxford: Oxford University Press, 2017), pp. 513–15.

315   She is a woman, therefore to be won.
    MARGARET   Wilt thou accept of ransom, yea or no?
    SUFFOLK *[aside]*   Fond man, remember that thou hast a wife;
        Then how can Margaret be thy paramour?
    MARGARET *[aside]*   I were best to leave him, for he will not hear.
40   SUFFOLK *[aside]*   There all is marred; there lies a cooling card.
    MARGARET *[aside]*   He talks at random; sure the man is mad.
    SUFFOLK *[aside]*   And yet a dispensation may be had.
    MARGARET   And yet I would that you would answer me.
    SUFFOLK *[aside]*   I'll win this Lady Margaret. For whom?
45   Why, for my king—tush, that's a wooden thing!
    MARGARET *[aside]*   He talks of wood; it is some carpenter.
    SUFFOLK *[aside]*   Yet so my fancy may be satisfied,
        And peace establishèd between these realms.
        But there remains a scruple in that too,
50   For though her father be the King of Naples,
        Duke of Anjou and Maine, yet is he poor,
        And our nobility will scorn the match.
    MARGARET   Hear ye, captain? Are you not at leisure?
    SUFFOLK *[aside]*   It shall be so, disdain they ne'er so much.
55   Henry is youthful and will quickly yield.
    [To Margaret]   Madam, I have a secret to reveal.

                                        (5.6.28–56)

The question Margaret asks in line 29 ('What ransom must I pay before I pass?') does not receive a response until line 56 ('Madam, I have a secret to reveal'). The seven-and-a-half speeches ascribed to Suffolk in between—in which he discusses whether or not to woo her and, if so, on whose behalf—are all traditionally understood to be spoken aside. Like Macbeth on hearing that he has been made Thane of Cawdor, Suffolk is 'rapt'.[40] He withdraws from the conversation into a private deliberation, unable to respond until he has decided how to proceed. Unlike Macbeth, Suffolk has only one interlocutor. Margaret has just asked him a question, on the answer to which her whole life hangs, and there is no one else present who can provide a response. The

---

[40] *Macbeth*, 1.3.138.

conversation cannot move on, or even tread water, until Suffolk takes his turn to speak.

Two things are of interest here. The first is the length of the delay. The playwright manages to stretch this moment out for nearly thirty lines. It is followed by a similar sequence played out in reverse, during which Margaret works out her own position in a second series of asides. The two characters take turns, as it were, at not taking turns. This kind of dramaturgical over-exuberance is characteristic of early Shakespeare (compare the extended sequence in which the same Margaret is ignored by Richard and Elizabeth). But the lack of subtlety could also be because the scene is written by someone else. If this is Shakespeare, then it is Shakespeare in the process of learning his trade, exploring both the potential and the limitations of a dramatic technique he will eventually come to master. It is as though the aside were a water pistol he has just received for Christmas, and he wants to see how far it can squirt.

The second point of interest is that, judging by Margaret's responses, there are at least two different kinds of aside in the exchange. At the beginning of the passage, she does not recognize the words attributed to Suffolk as speech. From the reader's point of view he begins to speak as soon as she has finished, but two lines later Margaret asks him, 'Why speak'st thou not?'. At some point thereafter, his words become at least partly audible to her. She observes that he 'talks at random' in line 41, hears enough of line 42 to mirror its syntax in line 43, and picks the word 'wood' out of his reference to 'a wooden thing' in line 45. The precise moment of the switch—if it has a precise moment—is not easy to locate, but it seems to lie somewhere between lines 34 and 40. Before that Suffolk is 'speaking not', after it he is 'talking at random'—at least from Margaret's point of view. What makes the example unusual is that we are given so many cues as to how to understand what Suffolk says. What makes it interesting is that those cues are contradictory.

James Hirsh's explanation of what happens here is that Suffolk, 'after speaking to himself of his love' for Margaret, 'becomes so overwhelmed by emotion that he eventually ceases to speak in well-guarded asides'.[41] Speaking aside, it would seem, is like keeping your voice down when

---

[41] Hirsh, *Shakespeare and the History of Soliloquies*, p. 151.

drunk. Relax or become distracted for a moment and you will soon realize you are no longer doing it. The difference between our two kinds of aside is therefore one of execution rather than type. All asides are self-addressed, all asides are spoken aloud, some are more successfully guarded than others. But other explanations are also possible. For those like Congreve and Aubignac, unhappy at the inherent implausibility of the monological aside, Margaret's failure to recognize that Suffolk is speaking is a particular strain on credulity. Not only are we asked to imagine that Suffolk's speech is inaudible to her—we are also asked to imagine that the movement of his lips is invisible. An aside is one thing in a large group, when attention can be focused elsewhere. But Margaret is waiting expectantly to learn what ransom she will be required to pay. It is Suffolk's turn to speak, and she is presumably looking straight at him. If, on the other hand, we interpret his first three asides as unspoken thought, all such objections disappear. What we have instead is a switch from the inside to the half-aside, from 'only thinking' to audibly muttering.

Both of these explanations are plausible, but they both also ignore something important. A consideration of Suffolk's asides here as potential turns at talk can help to supplement either account. The first thing to notice is that none of what Suffolk says is addressed to Margaret, whose attainability and poverty he discusses in the third person. It is of course possible to address an aside to someone who is present (as Iago does to Cassio) or to discuss that person aloud in the third person (as Lucetta does of Julia), but these are what we might call special dialogical effects. The first hint that Suffolk is speaking aside is the fact that his words are not addressed to Margaret. The second thing to notice is that something tangible does change, or is in the process of changing, between the point at which Suffolk is 'speaking not' and the point at which he is 'talking at random'. Margaret's comments pick up on and help to point out a grammatical shift in his speech. Here is Suffolk without Margaret:

> How canst thou tell she will deny thy suit [*Speaking not*]
> Before thou make a trial of her love?
> She's beautiful, and therefore to be wooed;
> She is a woman, therefore to be won.
> Fond man, remember that thou hast a wife;

Then how can Margaret be thy paramour?
There all is marred; there lies a cooling card.   [*Talking at random*]
And yet a dispensation may be had.
I'll win this Lady Margaret. For whom?
Why, for my king—tush, that's a wooden thing!
Yet so my fancy may be satisfied,
And peace establishèd between these realms.
But there remains a scruple in that too,
For though her father be the King of Naples,
Duke of Anjou and Maine, yet is he poor,
And our nobility will scorn the match.
It shall be so, disdain they ne'er so much.
Henry is youthful and will quickly yield.
Madam, I have a secret to reveal.   [*Addressing Margaret*]
                                                    (5.6.31–56)

It is not until after his fourth aside ('There all is marred; there lies a cooling card') that Margaret shows any awareness that Suffolk is speaking. Prior to that, his words are unambiguously addressed to himself.[42] From then on, the addressee recedes into ambiguity. Instead of addressing himself in the second person, Suffolk begins to speak in the first. The moment of decision ('I'll win this Lady Margaret') is also the moment at which he grammatically takes ownership of what he is saying, an ownership confirmed in three subsequent possessives ('my King [...] my fancy [...] our Nobility'). In short, there are no first-person pronouns before the fourth aside—the first one Margaret half overhears—and no second-person pronouns after it.

My point is not that the self-addressed aside consistently represents unspoken thought in Shakespeare and the first person aside consistently represents half-audible speech. My point is that the distinction

---

[42] It might be objected that the question posed in lines 31–2 ('How canst thou tell she will deny thy suit') is answered in lines 34–5 ('She's beautiful, and therefore to be wooed') suggesting a second voice and a second addressee. But this is not the case. The point of the question is that Suffolk has reason to hope, and the maxim which follows it is further evidence in support of that point, urged by the same imagined speaker on the same imagined addressee. Line 37 does contain a change of tack, from having hope to seeing that hope as foolish, but this is addressed to a 'Fond man' who (context tells us) can only be Suffolk.

between them, a grammatical distinction, is something this playwright is aware of and able to exploit dramatically. He puts it to the use he does here because self-address is inherently more inward than addressing even an ambiguous and unspecified other. The self-addressed turn, whether used as an aside or not, starts and finishes in the same place. It is a way of short-circuiting the turn-taking system, like tossing the ball into the air and catching it yourself. The first-person aside, on the other hand, implies an addressee even when it does not specify one. It mimes looking outward even when there is nothing at which to look. This example hammers home the difference between the two by means of Margaret's rather crude interjections, but the difference is there whether she points it out or not. Later Shakespeare makes use of the same distinction without feeling the need to wave a flag and make an announcement.

Before leaving the subject it is worth sketching some further complications that arise from attempts to interpret the monological aside in a single and uniform way, whether as self-addressed speech or as unspoken thought. These can be only sketched because they involve the fairly large question of how language relates to thought. Hirsh is right to insist that both asides and soliloquies can potentially be overheard. But he is wrong to insist that 'plentiful evidence demonstrates' Shakespeare 'always rigorously maintained the distinction between thought and speech'.[43] He is wrong because the distinction between thought and speech is not one that *can* always be rigorously maintained, and because it would not have been in Shakespeare's interests to maintain it even if he could. One does not need to be Ludwig Wittgenstein in order to see this. When Margaret overhears Suffolk, this is not because he is speaking rather than thinking—it is because he is doing both. Andrew Gurr:

> [A] convention that seems less than natural today is the tradition of direct address to the audience. [...] Like explanatory prologues, the explanatory soliloquy or aside to the audience was a relic of the less sophisticated days that developed into a useful and more naturalistic convention of thinking aloud, but never entirely ceased to be a convention.[44]

[43] Hirsh, *Shakespeare and the History of Soliloquies*, p. 361.
[44] Andrew Gurr, *The Shakespearean Stage, 1574–1642*, 3rd edn (Cambridge: Cambridge University Press, 1992), p. 103.

This is not to say that characters in Shakespeare are incapable of silent thought. Nor is it to agree with Margreta de Grazia that Shakespeare 'collapses the distinction between inner and outer: as if thinking aloud were a form of talking'.[45] Thinking aloud *is* a form of talking. But it is also, crucially, a form of thinking. What Shakespeare does is to exaggerate how much, and in what circumstances, people make use of it. His characters suffer from a kind of collective coprolalia. They find it difficult not to speak the thoughts that pass through their minds, and the more inappropriate those thoughts are, the more difficult they find it to not to speak them. Brian Cummings has described the aside as 'somewhere between a social gaffe and an interior monologue uttered aloud'.[46] For 'somewhere' we should read 'wherever is most dramatically convenient at the time'. The convention of thinking aloud is no more damaging to the theatrical illusion than the convention of speaking in verse. It is an artistically heightened representation of a dramatically useful form of behaviour. People do in fact think aloud, sometimes involuntarily, and sometimes in the midst of conversation.[47] Thinking aloud and thinking in silence may not be the same thing, but they are at least partially equivalent—one can be made to substitute for the other. From the dramatist's point of view, thinking aloud has the triple advantage of being accessible to an audience, potentially audible to an eavesdropper, and possible for a character to fake when he thinks someone else may be listening.

* * *

This chapter has succeeded if it has managed to persuade the reader of two things. First, that the Shakespearean aside is an extremely capacious convention. It can be fully or semi-audible, inaudible, or impossible to gauge. It can be addressed to another character, to the audience, or to oneself. Characteristically, however, it is let off into the air and allowed to float, like a balloon, unaddressed. It can represent

---

[45] Margreta de Grazia, 'Soliloquies and wages in the age of emergent consciousness', *Textual Practice*, 9 (1995), 67–92 (p. 74).

[46] Brian Cummings, *Mortal Thoughts: Religion, Secularity and Identity in Shakespeare and Early Modern Culture* (Oxford: Oxford University Press, 2013), p. 205.

[47] Lev Vygotsky's celebrated work, *Thought and Language*, trans. by Alex Kozulin, rev. edn (Cambridge, Mass: MIT Press, 1986), argues that thinking aloud, like reading aloud, precedes the ability to do so silently.

thought, speech, or something between the two. The only real rule that Shakespeare seems to follow is the rule of dramatic convenience. Secondly, I hope to have persuaded the reader that identifying and interpreting asides is primarily a matter of conversational structure—of understanding how different utterances are related to one another, plotting their trajectories, and charting how these relationships develop over time. It is a matter, that is, of turn-taking.

PART TWO

Timing

| 5 |

Have I Finished?

The 1940s was a good time to be a social scientist. Anything seemed possible. Take Eliot D. Chapple, for example, and his 'interaction chronograph':

> After one crude attempt, a simple recorder was developed in which a tape was driven at a uniform speed and a series of keys, one assigned to each person, drew lines on the tape when the key was pushed down. [...] By pressing a key when a person started to act or to respond, whether by talking, smiling, or nodding his head, and releasing it when the action ended and doing the same thing for another person, we could record much of what had previously been regarded as the quality of relationships. Not only could one determine how much a person talked or acted and how much he was silent and allowed the other person to act in his turn, but one could also determine the nature of the adjustment of the two of them, whether one person habitually interrupted or rarely replied immediately, whether one tended to dominate, always talking the other person down if interrupted, and whether one took the initiative not merely at the beginning of the contact but at various opportunities when both became silent.[1]

[1] Eliot D. Chapple, 'The Interaction Chronograph: Its Evolution and Present Application', *Personnel*, 25 (1949), 295–307 (p. 297).

Chapple had high hopes for this machine. The interaction chronograph would it make it possible to 'evaluate personality and temperament' objectively by 'measuring the interaction pattern of an interview'.[2] Later iterations were more elaborate, automatically calculating a set of scores for each subject—'tempo' (how frequently they act), 'activity or energy' (how much longer they spend talking or responding than being silent or unresponsive), 'initiative' (how frequently they speak first after a period of silence), 'dominance' (how frequently they 'out-talk' or 'out-act' their interlocutor), and so on. Chapple was an 'applied' anthropologist—as well as conducting academic research, he ran a private company that offered practical advice to large corporations and government-run institutions.[3] He used the data generated by the chronograph to establish statistical norms that would allow him to identify good or bad candidates for jobs and to differentiate between patients requiring psychiatric care and what he amusingly refers to as 'normals'.[4]

In order to make the scores of the different subjects comparable, Chapple devised a standard interview.[5] Unlike the interviews devised by his competitors, however, Chapple's 'standard experimental stress interview' did not consist of a list of questions. It could be used with any questions to interview any subject for any purpose. The standardization lay not in the content of the interview but its shape. This was divided into five carefully timed periods. In the first, third, and fifth of these, the interviewer's behaviour is unremarkable. In the second and fourth, however, it is deliberately aberrant. In the 'Silence Period' the interviewer remains 'completely silent and unresponsive, neither smiling, nodding, speaking nor responding to the interviewee in any way' for fifteen seconds after the answer to each question.[6] If the interviewee fills the silence with an expansion of their answer, the fifteen seconds is

[2] Chapple, 'The Interaction Chronograph', p. 295.

[3] For more on Chapple, see Alice Beck Kehoe and Jim Weil, 'Eliot Chapple's Long and Lonely Road', in *Expanding American Anthropology, 1945-1980: A Generation Reflects*, ed. by Paul L. Doughty, Nancy K. Peske, and Alice Beck Kehoe (Tuscaloosa: University of Alabama Press, 2012), pp. 94–103.

[4] Chapple, 'The Interaction Chronograph', p. 301.

[5] Eliot D. Chapple, 'The Standard Experimental (Stress) Interview as Used in Interaction Chronograph Investigations', *Human Organization*, 12 (1953), 23–32.

[6] Chapple, 'The Standard Experimental (Stress) Interview', p. 24.

restarted. Only after it has been completed without further comment from the subject will the next question be asked. The point of the silence period is to test for 'initiative, and quickness in taking it, as well as ability to hold forth when there is a minimum of rapport'. An opposite approach is taken in the 'Interruption Period'. This time the interviewer lets the subject begin each answer then attempts to interrupt them. If they have not been 'talked down' within five seconds of competitive overlapping speech, the interviewer ceases the attempt and allows the interviewee to finish their answer unmolested. The aim, apparently, is to 'determine the subject's persistence, ability to dominate, or submissiveness in a situation in which he is continually interrupted'.[7]

At a distance of seventy years, the folly of Chapple's approach seems obvious. Reliable conclusions about someone's ability to do a job—or about their sanity—cannot be drawn purely on the basis of conversational timing. There are too many other variables at work in an interaction for Chapple's statistics to have the significance he claims. But that does not make them meaningless. However terrifying his overconfidence, Chapple was right to recognize the importance of turn-timing for understanding social interaction. What the interaction chronograph does is to isolate and quantify the conversational conduct of the two participants, regardless of what they are saying to one another. A decontextualized analysis of these data may not be able to tell us whether someone is sane or insane, but it is relevant to the question. A chronographic analysis of Hamlet's confrontation with Gertrude, for example, in 3.4 of *Hamlet* (the 'closet scene', as it sometimes called) would contribute much to our understanding of the prince's state of mind at this point in the play. The second half of this book will explore how far this kind of analysis is possible for fictional dialogue and will speculate about what might show up on the chronograph if Shakespeare's plays were run through it. It will be concerned, that is, with what the dramatic text does, and does not, tell us about the timing of transitions between turns—about interruption, pauses, and overlapping speech. Chapple's 'standard experimental stress interview' provides a useful starting point for thinking about turn-timing because

---

[7] Chapple, 'The Standard Experimental (Stress) Interview', p. 24.

it allows us to consider the two extremes of transitional behaviour. The interview is structured around two periods in which the interviewer deliberately mistimes the transitions between turns—first by being unaccountably late, then by being unaccountably early.

What characterizes the 'silence period' is the failure of the next question to arrive. The silence this produces is not neutral, however. In the context of an interview, it is likely to imply that the answer just given is in some sense inadequate. Chapple's aim, we recall, is to test for 'initiative, and quickness in taking it, as well as ability to hold forth when there is a minimum of rapport'. And he is right to suspect that a confident or interactionally alert interviewee will interpret the pause as an invitation to add to, or rephrase, their answer. No matter how many times they do so, however, the response will still be silence. It is only once the fifteen seconds has been completed that the next question will be asked—only once the subject has run dry that the interview can move on. As a technique for interviewing candidates for a job, this is little more than a cruel practical joke. As a conversational experiment, however, it demonstrates something interesting. Whether or not a person has finished speaking is not something that they simply decide for themselves. It is also determined, at least in part, by whether or not they receive a reply. This may seem obvious, but it runs counter to some of the most basic assumptions made about spoken interaction—even by theorists with a keen interest in dialogue. Take, for example, Mikhail Bakhtin:

> The speaker ends his utterance in order to relinquish the floor to the other or to make room for the other's active responsive understanding. The utterance is not a conventional unit, but a real unit, clearly delimited by the change of speaking subjects, which ends by relinquishing the floor to the other, as if with a silent *dixi*, perceived by the listeners (as a sign) that the speaker has finished.[8]

Bakhtin imagines that all conversation functions in a way analogous to the voice procedure used by military and aeronautical personnel—in which the end of each turn is unambiguously announced by the use of the word 'over' (short for 'over to you'). But the point of such a

---

[8] Mikhail Mikhaĭlovich Bakhtin, 'The Problem of Speech Genres', in *Speech Genres and Other Late Essays*, ed. by Michael Holquist and Caryl Emerson, trans. by Vern W. McGee (Austin: University of Texas Press, 1986), pp. 60–102 (71–2).

procedure is precisely to eliminate an ambiguity that is otherwise inherent to spoken interaction, as to whether or not someone has finished speaking. If there were no such ambiguity, the convention would not exist. There is a truth, of course, to Bakhtin's assumption—there is a sense in which the speaker does say 'over' to signal the end of a turn. But there is also a sense in which the hearer says 'when'. Pouring out speech for someone has this much in common with pouring them a glass of wine. If the hearer does not tell you to stop, you keep going—at least until you have given them what seems like a generous glassful. And even at that point, a failure to say thank you, a raised eyebrow, or a glance at the glass can indicate that more is required.[9] What Chapple's interviewer does is to keep demanding more wine until the glass has overflowed and the bottle has been emptied. No matter how many times the interviewee says 'over to you', the interviewer refuses to validate the transition—refuses, that is, to let the turn end.

Now consider the 'interruption period'. A slight overlap between turns does not, of itself, constitute an interruption. It can be an entirely appropriate way of saying 'when'. A longer overlap suggests impatience—implying that the listener is in some sort of a hurry or that the speaker is dragging things out unnecessarily. Moving quickly on to the next turn is a way of saying, at the interactional level, 'Yes, yes! I get the idea! Now back to me'. But to begin your own turn before the meaning of your partner's turn can possibly be clear is to dismiss what they are saying altogether. Rather than showing them that you under-stand their point, it shows them that you do not consider it worth understanding. The repeated interruptions of Chapple's interviewer are likely to come across, in each instance, as a rejection of the candidate's answer—as a rejection of the whole answer, that is, rather than an indication that it is now long enough. By persevering into an overlap, the interviewee can disagree. To keep talking is to say, at an inter-actional level, 'No, wait—I think you will want to hear this.' And this, of course, is the response Chapple is looking for—a demonstration of the subject's 'persistence' and 'ability to dominate' in a tussle over who will be heard and what is worth hearing.

[9] In conversation analysis this is known as 'back-channeling'. See Kent Drummond and Robert Hopper, 'Back channels revisited: Acknowledgment tokens and speakership incipiency', *Research on Language and Social Interaction*, 26 (1994), 157–77.

Chapple does not explain how he arrives at the intervals of five and fifteen seconds respectively, but they are both well outside what we would expect to find in ordinary conversation. Their function is to remove any ambiguity about whether or not the subject has finished speaking and whether or not they are being interrupted. Rather than negotiate the timing of transitions, Chapple's interviewer dictates terms. Real conversation is a little more nuanced. Between the extreme poles of prolonged silence and aggressive interruption is a range of expressive possibilities. The human ear is attuned to very fine gradations of pause and overlap, and the social meaning of an utterance can hinge on minute distinctions in conversational timing—it takes only a fraction of a second's delay to turn the phrase 'Yes dear' from an encouragement to go ahead and tell me about your day into an exasperated plea for silence.[10]

It would be useful to know, therefore, for each transition in Shakespeare, exactly how the change of speakers is 'timed' in at least two senses of that word. First, in the sense that is measured by Chapple's machine. If there is a gap between turns, we would like to know how long that gap is. If they overlap, we would like to know by how much. But it would also be useful to know how transitions are timed in a second, less tangible, sense. We would like to know, at the moment a transition occurs, whether it seems to the participants to be occurring early or late—how much it is a case of the speaker saying 'over' and how much it is a case of the hearer saying 'when'. As well as knowing when each speaker stops, we would like to know whether they have finished. Or rather—since the distinction is not binary—we would like to know *how much* they have finished at the moment the transition occurs. This chapter will address the question of how far it is possible to know either of these things. It will begin by reviewing what interactional linguistics and cognitive science have to say about turn-timing, before asking what this means for the study of Shakespearean dialogue. It will be followed by three further chapters which examine how our understanding of

---

[10] This is known as 'delayed minimal response'. See Don H. Zimmerman and Candace West, 'Sex Roles, Interruptions and Silences in Conversation', in *Language and Sex: Difference and Dominance*, ed. by Barrie Thorne and Nancy Henley (Rowley, Mass.: Newbury House, 1975), pp. 105–29.

turn-timing is affected, respectively, by Shakespeare's use of syntax, punctuation, and metre.

*   *   *

It is an observable fact that speakers are able to coordinate transitions between turns at talk to within a fraction of a second. Average response time in conversation is around 200 ms—less time than it takes to utter a single English syllable.[11] This is surprising because language production is, comparatively, slow—some 600 ms from conception to articulation, even for a single word.[12] Both speaker and hearer appear to know in advance exactly where the turn will end, even in an informal conversation with turns of varying lengths. And the hearer is able to produce, 200 ms later, what is recognizably a response—to answer a question, provide relevant information, or give some other proof of having understood the previous turn. The hearer appears to know not just when the speaker will finish but what they will have said when they do so. Traditional models of conversation, such as Saussure's *circuit de la parole*, are unable to account for these facts.[13] Conversation is not, as Saussure would have us believe, like an exchange of letters speeded up—in which person A composes an utterance and sends it to person B, who opens and reads it before composing a reply. The human brain is simply not quick enough to do this in the time available. For turn exchange at these speeds to be possible, the two cognitive processes it requires—language comprehension and language production—must overlap.[14] The brain does the equivalent of reading a letter and writing a response simultaneously. By the time A has finished speaking, B is ready to begin. But B still needs to be able to anticipate exactly when

[11] See Tanya Stivers, Nick Enfield, N. J. Brown, et al., 'Universals and Cultural Variation in Turn-Taking in Conversation', *Proceedings of the National Academy of Sciences*, 106 (2009), 10587–92.
[12] See Lilla Magyari, Marcel C. M. Bastiaansen, Jan P. de Ruiter, and Stephen C. Levinson, 'Early Anticipation Lies behind the Speed of Response in Conversation', *Journal of Cognitive Neuroscience*, 26 (2014), 2530–9.
[13] On the ubiquity and persistence of this model, see Roy Harris, 'The Speech-Communication Model in Twentieth Century Linguistics and its Sources', in *The Foundations of Linguistic Theory, Selected Writings of Roy Harris*, ed. by Nigel Love (London: Routledge, 1990), pp. 151–7.
[14] Stephen C. Levinson, 'Turn-Taking in Human Communication—Origins and Implications for Language Processing', *Trends in Cognitive Sciences*, 20 (2016), 6–14.

this moment will come. As well as the 'speaker sequencing problem', the parties to a conversation must continually solve a 'transition timing problem'. The question is how they do this.

The earliest answers to this question are of the kind envisaged by Bakhtin—in which the interlocutors use 'cues' or 'signals' to communicate their interactional intentions. This has been described, appropriately enough, as a 'signalling' model of turn-taking.[15] Like so much else in this sub-field, it was first seriously proposed by Erving Goffman in the early 1960s.[16] It is in the work of Starkey Duncan Jr, however, and his later collaborations with Donald Fiske that the signalling model finds its fullest expression. Duncan was a psychologist with an interest in non-verbal communication. The basis of his approach is the detailed recording of what else is happening at the moment transitions occur. He then tries to establish statistically significant correlations between a change of speakers and any other observable behaviours. What he would like to find is the interactional equivalent of the flashing yellow indicator lights on a car or the 'over' used in aeronautical voice procedure. What he does find is a little more complex. Duncan's two basic concepts are the 'turn-yielding signal' and the 'attempt-suppressing signal'.[17] The former notifies the hearer that the speaker has finished, the latter that he has not. The turn-yielding signal is 'the display of at least one of a set of six discrete behavioral cues' which can be displayed 'either singly or together'.[18] These cues include intonational patterns, physical gestures, recognized ending formulae, and the completion of syntactical units. The attempt-suppressing signal 'consists of one or both of the speaker's hands being engaged in gesticulation'.[19] Through

---

[15] Thomas P. Wilson, John M. Wiemann, and Don H. Zimmerman, 'Models of Turn Taking in Conversational Interaction', *Journal of Language and Social Psychology*, 3 (1984), 159–83 (p. 159).

[16] 'Once a state of talk has been ratified, cues must be available for requesting the floor and giving it up, for informing the speaker as to the stability of the focus of attention he is receiving. Intimate collaboration must be sustained to ensure that one turn at talking neither overlaps the previous one too much, nor wants for inoffensive conversational supply, for someone's turn must always and exclusively be in progress', Goffman, 'The Neglected Situation', p. 136.

[17] Starkey Duncan Jr, 'Some Signals and Rules for Taking Speaking Turns in Conversations', *Journal of Personality and Social Psychology*, 23 (1972), 283–92. See also Starkey Duncan Jr and Donald W. Fiske, *Face-to-Face Interaction: Research, Methods, and Theory* (Hillsdale, NJ: L. Erlbaum, 1977).

[18] Duncan Jr, p. 286.   [19] Duncan Jr, p. 287.

detailed analyses of video-taped interviews, Duncan is able to show that:

> (a) the occurrence of simultaneous turns will be associated primarily with the auditor's turn-taking attempts when zero yielding cues (i.e., the absence of a yielding signal) are being displayed by the speaker, and (b) display of the attempt-suppressing signal by the speaker will sharply reduce the auditor's turn-taking attempts in response to yielding cues.[20]

In short, he identifies several behaviours relevant to the occurrence of transition and shows that transitions are more likely to be mistimed when these behaviours are not 'displayed'.

The value of such research is obvious, but the signalling model also has its weaknesses. It has a tendency to treat the mouth as a sort of tap—turn it on and out flows speech, turn it off and the flow stops. There is little sense that talk has structure. Signals are made up of discrete cues that might be displayed at any moment—even syntactical completion is treated as something discrete, which either is or is not occurring when a transition takes place. Signalling is discussed as though it were incidental to talking, like raising a little red flag just as you finish eating your piece of toast. The alternative is what has been described as a 'sequential-production' model, and the chief proponents of this approach are our old friends Sacks, Schegloff, and Jefferson.[21]

Their model relies on a pair of awkwardly named but brilliantly conceived conceptual tools—the 'turn-constructional unit' and the 'transition-relevance place'. A 'turn-constructional unit' is any unit out of which a turn at talk can be constructed. Sentences, clauses, phrases, and words are all examples of turn-constructional units. But so too are jokes, anecdotes, speeches, and 'reading you the letter I have just received from my aunt'. The vagueness of the term is necessary in order to avoid the vexed question of exactly what kind of grammar is at work in spoken language and what kind of units it organizes.[22] All that matters for the model to function is that some such grammar is at work and some such set of units exists. A 'transition-relevance place' is any point at which a turn-constructional unit is potentially complete and

---

[20] Duncan Jr, p. 288.   [21] Wilson, Wiemann, and Zimmerman, p. 159.
[22] On the problems this can cause, see Taylor and Cameron, *Analysing Conversation*, pp. 12–13.

thus at which a speaker might have finished speaking. Two things matter about transition-relevance places. The first is that they are 'projectable'—it is possible to hear them coming. By parsing the syntax of the turn in progress, the hearer is able to project both where it might be going and when it is likely get there. Like an arrow in flight, a turn has a trajectory, and by recognizing that trajectory we can predict where it will land. The second thing that matters about transition-relevance places is that they are optional. The occurrence of a transition-relevance place does not necessitate a change of speakers, any more than the occurrence of an exit necessitates that I come off the motorway. As the exit approaches, the possibility of my coming off becomes relevant, but if I am going somewhere else I simply drive past it. Since various types of unit can operate within the same turn, and their various points of completion may or may not coincide, it follows that a single turn may contain a series of transition-relevance places— a series of potential endings—at which no transition occurs. Recognizing which exit the speaker intends to take requires sensitivity to more than just the emerging syntax of the turn in progress. A range of other factors is also involved, both linguistic and non-linguistic. Intonation, gaze, gesture, and a pragmatic sense of what your interlocutor is likely to be doing with his words at this moment in the conversation ('action ascription' as it is known in the literature) all play a part.[23]

Armed with these two concepts, Sacks, Schegloff, and Jefferson formulate the following set of rules, which I can now give (for the first time) in full:

(1) For any turn, at the initial transition-relevance place of an initial turn-constructional unit:

   a) If the turn-so-far is so constructed as to involve the use of a 'current speaker selects next' technique, then the party so selected has the right and is obliged to take next turn to speak; no others have such rights or obligations, and transfer occurs at that place.

   b) If the turn-so-far is so constructed as not to involve the use of a 'current speaker selects next' technique, then self-selection for next speakership may, but need not, be instituted; first starter acquires rights to a turn, and transfer occurs at that place.

---

[23] This last term is a more recent coinage. See Stephen C. Levinson, 'Action Formation and Ascription', in *The Handbook of Conversation Analysis*, pp. 103–30, for an overview.

   c) If the turn-so-far is so constructed as not to involve the use of a 'current speaker selects next' technique, then current speaker may, but need not, continue, unless another self-selects.

(2) If, at the initial transition-relevance place of an initial turn-constructional unit, neither 1a nor 1b has operated, and, following the provision of 1c, current speaker has continued, then the rule-set a–c re-applies at the next transition-relevance place, and recursively at each next transition-relevance place, until transfer is effected.[24]

There are several assumptions here that we might choose to question and one to which I have already objected. What matters is not that this explanation is perfect but that this is the right *kind* of explanation. The stroke of genius here is the concept of 'relevance'—a more precise way of describing what I earlier referred to as 'how much' a speaker has finished. Sacks, Schegloff, and Jefferson were the first to recognize that there are points in a turn at which transition might have occurred but did not—at which, if somebody else had spoken, it would not have been an interruption. This enables them to account both for the fact that turn-timing is so accurate and for the fact that turn-length is so elastic. Unlike a letter, or a WhatsApp message, the turn at talk is telescopic. Its length is the product of a fragile process of incremental expansion that might have stopped when it didn't and needn't have stopped when it did. And where it does stop is not determined solely by the speaker. What Montaigne says of the word is equally true of the turn—it is 'halfe his that speaketh, and halfe his that harkeneth vnto it'.[25]

*   *   *

So what does this mean for the study of dramatic dialogue? I want to answer that question in two stages. The first is to consider what happens when we try to write conversation down in the form of a transcript. The second is to consider what relation such a transcript bears to a script—to the text, that is, of a fictional conversation.

---

[24] Sacks, Schegloff, and Jefferson, p. 704.
[25] Michel de Montaigne, *The Essayes or Morall, Politike and Millitarie Discourses of Lo: Michaell de Montaigne*, trans. by John Florio (London: Valentine Sims for Edward Blount, 1603), sigs 3I2r–v. For a brilliant analysis of Montaigne on conversation, see Terence Cave, *Montaigne*, How to Read (London: Granta, 2007), pp. 101–4.

When Harvey Sacks first became interested in turn-taking in the late 1960s, the data on which he was working were sound recordings. Part of what made the kind of work he did possible was the ease with which he could carry these around with him and listen to them repeatedly.[26] The advantage of Sacks' approach (over that of Goffman, for example) was that it dealt exclusively with real data in a more or less empirical way. The disadvantage was that it dealt only with what was on the recording—sound, and thus, primarily, speech. Although sound recordings are overwhelmingly the material on which conversation analysts work, conversation analysis itself is overwhelmingly communicated in print.[27] Having gathered his material, one of the analyst's first tasks is to transcribe it. At the very least, he will need to transcribe those parts of the recording that he wishes to use as examples in his work. Again, something is lost. Just as an audio recording captures only part of what happens in an interaction, so a transcript captures only part of what is present on an audio recording. In the first case, what is lost are most of the non-linguistic aspects of the interaction— gesture, gaze, facial expression, posture, positioning, movement, and so on. In the second, it is what linguists call the 'prosodic features' of speech—pitch, pace, volume, pronunciation, stress, juncture, intonation.[28] The losses matter because, as we have seen, it is precisely these that enable the participants to differentiate between a transition-relevance place at which the speaker intends to stop and one at which she does not. Without them there is no way of telling whether A has interrupted B or forced B to keep talking by refusing to respond.

[26] See the 'General Introduction' to the Fall 1967 lectures, *Lectures on Conversation*, I, pp. 619–23.

[27] More recent conversation analytic work has attempted to combine these two approaches. For an overview, see Christian Heath, 'The analysis of activities in face to face interaction using video', *Qualitative Research: Theory, Method and Practice* (London: Sage, 1997), 183–200. This change of focus has been accompanied by a change in terminology. Conversation analysts no longer speak of 'conversation' but of 'talk-in-interaction' and, more recently still, of 'talk-and-related-conduct-in-interaction'. It is hard to believe this last term will gain much traction, but see, for example, Emanuel A. Schegloff, 'Conversational Interaction: The Embodiment of Human Sociality', in *The Handbook of Discourse Analysis*, ed. by Deborah Tannen, Heidi E. Hamilton, and Deborah Schiffrin (Chichester: Wiley-Blackwell, 2015), pp. 346–66.

[28] For a sharp analysis of these issues, see Eric Griffiths, 'Recorded Sounds: Linguistics and the Voice', in *The Printed Voice of Victorian Poetry* (Oxford: Oxford University Press, 1989), 13–36.

It is possible, of course, to annotate a transcript in such a way as to preserve some of these features. The system most commonly used by conversation analysts was devised by Gail Jefferson in the late 1970s. It has marks to indicate overlapping speech, stress, suppressed laughter, pauses, non-linguistic noises, and much else.[29] But there is always a compromise. To preserve everything is impossible. To preserve too much results in a text that is so difficult to decipher that it obscures more than it illuminates. Comparing her own transcription of one fragment of talk with an earlier transcription of the same fragment made by Sacks, Jefferson is willing to admit that one is 'concise, and readable', the other 'a nightmare'.[30] But the nightmare retains, or attempts to retain, more of what is present on the recording. Whatever system we choose to adopt, however, a transcript can only ever provide a partial record of a conversation, and the aspects of the conversation it captures most fully are those which lend themselves most easily to being written down—the order in which people speak and the words they use. In this respect, a transcript can be understood as the fossilized remains of a conversation. The skeleton of an animal gives us crucial information about it—information from which much can be deduced—but it is not the whole animal. When a dramatist writes dialogue, they are sketching the remains of a conversation that never took place, the skeleton of an animal that never existed. The task of putting flesh on the bones of that conversation is left to the reader or actors of the play. And the set of typographical conventions a playwright chooses to adopt—or has available to her—determines the extent to which she can specify the non-linguistic aspects of the interaction and the prosodic features of the language it contains.[31] It determines the extent, that is, to which she can specify how transitions between turns are timed and understood.

[29] Gail Jefferson, 'Glossary of Transcription Symbols with an Introduction', in *Conversation Analysis: Studies from the First Generation*, ed. by Gene H. Lerner (Amsterdam: John Benjamins, 2004), 13–31.

[30] Jefferson, p. 14. For a thorough treatment of the problem of transcription, from a conversation analytic point of view, see Carole Edelsky, 'Who's Got the Floor?', *Language in Society*, 10 (1981), 383–421.

[31] On the specific conventions available to Shakespeare, see T. H. Howard-Hill, 'The Evolution of the Form of Plays in English During the Renaissance', *Renaissance Quarterly*, 43 (1990), 112–45.

Before examining the particular set of conventions at work in Shakespeare's plays, it is worth considering the most basic convention of dramatic typography. The dramatic page is sequential rather than chronographic—it tells us what happened next but not when or how quickly it happened. To see this we need only compare it with a musical score, or with the roll of paper that runs through Chapple's interaction chronograph. Dramatic typography has evolved, quite rightly, to enshrine a fundamental principle of dialogue—that one character speaks at a time. There is a list of names down the left-hand side of the page to indicate the sequence of speakers, and each name is followed by the words the character speaks. A change of speakers is indicated by a hard return, and then, on the line below, the name of the next character to speak. Turns at talk appear to follow one another in an orderly and unbroken procession, at an even pace, without gaps, overlap, pauses, or stuttering. The musical score, on the other hand, has evolved to accommodate simultaneity rather than turn-taking. It tells us what each instrument is doing at each moment, even if it is silent. It would be possible, though inefficient, to present the text of a play in a similar form, with the speech-heading for each character occurring only once, and time running from left to right—much as it does on Chapple's roll of paper. It would be possible, in such a text, for the dramatist to indicate minute effects of timing, both within turns and between them, by positioning each speaker's words at the appropriate point on the x-axis of the page. I am not suggesting, of course, that such a system should be adopted. Since speech overwhelmingly does occur one-at-a-time, the typographical compromise involved in presenting as though it always occurs in this way is worth making. But it is important to remember that it *is* a compromise.

The remainder of this chapter will be devoted to exploring some of the ways in which Shakespearean dialogue manages to circumvent this basic limitation and to create the impression of an agile, elastic, and, above all, improvised exchange of turns—one that builds and crashes, accelerates and decelerates, with much of the same artistry as the music contained in a musical score. Having wearied the reader with fourteen pages of theoretical groundwork, I think I owe her an example. I'll start, like Chapple, with a period of silence. Interruptions will come later.

* * *

The climax of Plutarch's 'Life of Caius Martius Coriolanus'—as of Shakespeare's play—is an act of persuasion. A Roman mother persuades her Roman son not to sack the city of Rome. Thomas North's English translation helpfully adds a marginal note, describing what happens in the climactic moment as *'The oration of Volumnia, unto her sonne Coriolanus'*.[32] The choice of word is revealing. This is not an interview or a colloquy or a dialogue but an 'oration'. Volumnia speaks once—powerfully and at length—and the effect of her speech is to save the city from destruction. Or so the note would seem to imply. What we find in the text is not quite so simple:

> Martius gaue good eare vnto his mothers wordes, without interrupting her speache at all: and after she had sayed what she would, he held his peace a prety while, and aunswered not a worde. Hereupon she beganne againe to speake vnto him, and sayed. My sonne, why doest thou not aunswer me? doest thou thinke it good altogether to geue place vnto thy choller and desire of reuenge, and thinkest thou it not honestie for thee to graunt thy mothers request, in so weighty a cause?[33]

Having said what she has to say, Volumnia stops. Then, after a prolonged pause, she resumes speaking—but she does so, as the narrative voice makes clear, only *because* no reply has been forthcoming. Volumnia holds out the conversational baton and Coriolanus refuses to take it. She throws him the ball but he lets it drop, forcing her to bend down and pick it up herself. What precedes the pause might well be described as an oration. It's a skilfully constructed rhetorical set piece, in which Volumnia reasons with Coriolanus about the consequences of his actions. What follows it is something different. The mother begins to reprimand her son for his bad manners. Having run out of arguments, she resorts to chiding.

Here is the equivalent passage as it appears in Shakespeare's play:

> VOLUMNIA [...] Thou know'st, great son,
> The end of war's uncertain; but this certain:
> That if thou conquer Rome, the benefit

[32] Plutarch, *The Lives of the Noble Grecians and Romanes*, trans. by Thomas North (London: Thomas Vautroullier and John Wright, 1579), sig. Y2v.
[33] Plutarch, sig. Y3r.

Which thou shalt thereby reap is such a name
145   Whose repetition will be dogged with curses,
Whose chronicle thus writ: 'The man was noble,
But with his last attempt, he wiped it out,
Destroyed his country, and his name remains
To th' ensuing age abhorred.' Speak to me, son.
150   Thou hast affected the fine strains of honour
To imitate the graces of the gods,
To tear with thunder the wide cheeks o'th' air,
And yet to charge thy sulphur with a bolt
That should but rive an oak. Why dost not speak?
155   Think'st thou it honourable for a noble man
Still to remember wrongs? Daughter, speak you;
He cares not for your weeping. Speak thou, boy;
Perhaps thy childishness will move him more
Than can our reasons. There's no man in the world
160   More bound to's mother, yet here he lets me prate
Like one i'th' stocks. Thou hast never in thy life
Showed thy dear mother any courtesy,
When she—poor hen—fond of no second brood,
Has clucked thee to the wars, and safely home,
165   Loaden with honour. Say my request's unjust,
And spurn me back; but, if it be not so,
Thou art not honest, and the gods will plague thee
That thou restrain'st from me the duty which
To a mother's part belongs.
    [Coriolanus turns his back to Volumnia]
                  He turns away.
170   Down, ladies; let us shame him with our knees.
To his surname Coriolanus 'longs more pride
Than pity to our prayers. Down! An end.
This is the last.

                                    (5.3.141–73)

Down to line 154, the play and its source remain close. The speech is not, as has been claimed, taken 'word for word' from Plutarch, with only 'some additional graces of expression, and the charm of metre superadded'.[34] But Shakespeare does lift whole phrases from North's translation and expands or reshapes others with characteristic imaginative sensitivity. He enlivens the warning that Coriolanus will be 'chronicled the plague & destroyer' of his country, for example, by having Volumnia quote the words that a future chronicle might use. But there is one respect in which Shakespeare cannot follow Plutarch, even if he wants to. Lacking a narrator, he has no way of telling us that Volumnia has finished speaking, how long she pauses for, or why she decides to carry on.

Having reached the point at which Plutarch's Volumnia stops, Shakespeare starts to interpolate. The first of her five questions in Plutarch ('My sonne, why doest thou not aunswer me?') he splits in two, and stuffs it with an invented appeal to Coriolanus' sense of honour (lines 150–4). The question appears first as an imperative ('Speak to me, son') then in something closer to its original form ('Why dost not speak?'). In one sense, this doubling is a substitute for the intervention of Plutarch's narrator. Bracketed between the imperative and the interrogative is an implied pause, in which Coriolanus fails to speak. And this is followed, in Shakespeare, by two further speech imperatives, not to be found in Plutarch. Volumnia calls first on Virgilia (Coriolanus' wife) and then on young Martius (his son), unsuccessfully imploring them to plead on her behalf. We might hear the lines as an amplification, or refraction, of what we find in Plutarch. Volumnia reaches the end of her oration and fails to get the desired response from her son—fails to get any response at all. But rather than a single failure, Shakespeare scripts a whole series of them. Each new burst of speech is a further attempt to force the moment to its crisis. Each is followed by a pause, in which no reply is forthcoming. And on each occasion she finds herself compelled to speak again. Volumnia turns from character to character, like a beggar on the tram, but can get no change from any of them. Her speech stalls and splutters, grinds to a halt, and drags itself on. Crucially, these pauses are not rhetorical—not really pauses at all, but failed attempts to end.

---

[34] Anna Jameson, *Characteristics of Women* (1832), quoted in *Coriolanus*, ed. by David George, Shakespeare: The Critical Tradition (Bristol: Thoemmes Continuum, 2004), p. 115.

The situation would seem to be clear. Coriolanus treats his mother in much the same way that Chapple treats his interviewees, wringing every last drop of speech from her through his refusal to reply. Run the exchange through the chronograph and the roll of paper will show a series of pauses, after each of which Volumnia 'takes the initiative' by speaking first. These pauses are signalled in the text by questions and complaints. When Volumnia says, 'Why dost not speak?', what we have is (in effect) an implied stage direction. In order for her words to make sense, Coriolanus must have remained silent at what was intended to be the end of her turn. The character, if not the actor, has missed his cue. Things may not be quite this simple, however. Another possibility is suggested by a footnote in the edition of Charles and Mary Cowden Clarke:

> With what exquisitely artistic touches Shakespeare finishes his character-portraits! Here, in two half lines, he paints Virgilia's habitual silence, and Volumnia's as habitual torrent of words. She bids her daughter-in-law plead, yet waits not for her to speak.[35]

According to the Cowden Clarkes, Volumnia's appeal to Virgilia in lines 156-7 ('Daughter, speak you; | He cares not for your weeping') is no more than a rhetorical gesture—a kind of conversational feint, in which she shapes as if to pass but never lets go of the ball. And the same is true of the other points in her speech at which Volumnia seems to be looking for a response. Any or all of them may be rhetorical. Rather than drying up in a series of Plutarchan pauses, we might equally hear her rushing on in an unstoppable torrent of words. Appearing to be hung out to dry in this way—to be left, as she puts it, to 'prate' like one in the stocks—casts Volumnia as the victim of Coriolanus' interactional behaviour as well as his political strategy. Or rather, it mobilizes one as a metaphor for the other. In this reading of the scene, Virgilia and young Martius might keep their mouths shut for another reason—not because they are too overcome to speak, and not because Volumnia will not let them, but because they recognize that the spectacle of his mother in this humiliating predicament is the thing most likely to make Coriolanus relent.

---

[35] *The Plays of Shakespeare*, ed. by Charles and Mary Cowden Clarke, 3 vols, Cassell's Illustrated Shakespeare (London: Cassell, Petter, & Galpin, 1864–8), III, p. 131 (n. 50).

My point is not that the Cowden Clarkes are right but that either interpretation is plausible. Meta-communicational comments made by a fictional character can provide us with evidence about how a transition may be timed, but they do not constitute proof. It is perfectly possible to accuse someone of interrupting you when you know that they have not done so. Frequent invocation of the rules of conversation is characteristic of the bully as well as the victim—an aggressive move as well as a defensive one. Volumnia's castigation of her son for his silence is the most sustained and unambiguous series of complaints about the turn-taking conduct of any character in Shakespeare. But it does not, and it cannot, prove that he is guilty as charged. The dramatic text tells us only where speeches do end, not where they might have done—only that a character doesn't respond, not why they fail to do so.

The point is important, so I am going to labour it just a little longer. The fragile process of incremental expansion by which turns at talk are built becomes obscured when we write them down. The reader of *Coriolanus* can see at a glance that Volumnia is making a long speech and is tempted to hear what she says as single coherent unit—as the 'oration' described in North's note. On the stage, the same speech plays rather differently. An audience has no way of knowing, in advance, when Volumnia will finish. What sounds like the end can turn out to be a pause, and what sounds like a pause can turn out to be the end. So the speech as acted is both more and less ambiguous than the speech on the page. Less ambiguous because the actress takes specific decisions about where and how to pause—more ambiguous because the length of the turn is hidden from view. Shakespeare exploits these ambiguities to brilliant dramatic effect. Not only does Volumnia repeatedly reach a point at which she might have finished, she repeatedly claims to have finished, asks questions, issues speech imperatives, threatens to leave, and reprimands her son for his failure to reply. However rhetorical, in one sense, these gestures are, it is a rhetoric that relies for its effect on the possibility of reply.

There is also a third way of interpreting what happens here. Recognizing when a speaker intends to finish—which of several transition-relevance places is likely to harden into a transition—is, as we have seen, a complex business. It involves a range of cues, both verbal and non-verbal. Crucially, however, it is possible for some of these cues to be at variance with others. In the same way that tone, gesture, or facial expression can be used to cancel or undercut a statement (to imply 'I don't really mean what I am saying here'), they can also be used to nullify the relevance of transition (to imply 'I don't really expect you to reply to this'). The reading suggested by the Cowden Clarkes, in which the pace of Volumnia's delivery negates the possibility of Virgilia being able to respond, is one such example. The Volumnia they imagine does the equivalent of offering Virgilia a Hobnob and then shoving it into her own mouth before the younger woman's hand can get within striking distance of the plate. But speed of movement is only one way of negating the likelihood of transition. The kind of ambiguity I have already identified as a feature of the written text (or, more properly, as a consequence of its prosodic featurelessness) can also occur in real conversation. There are times at which we do not know whether we are supposed to speak—times at which we hesitate and end up missing what must have been our cue. Often this is simply the result of a misunderstanding or a moment of inattention. But such an ambiguity can also be engineered deliberately, as a way of baffling or upsetting someone or of putting them awkwardly on the spot.

Not only is this possible, it is an interactional technique habitually used by adults to reprimand children. Parents, teachers, and (of course) grandmothers specialize in what we might call the ambiguously rhetorical question: *What the hell do you think you're playing at? What time do you call this?* and so on.[36] Such questions seem to demand a reply—to invite the child to justify herself—whilst at the same time making it clear that any reply would be dangerous. The child is thus caught between two competing imperatives—*Speak when you're spoken to* and *Don't answer back*. And the flustered, panicky awkwardness of having something to say but not knowing whether to say it, is itself a form of punishment. I do not mean to suggest that this is exactly what is happening between Volumnia and Coriolanus, only that it lurks somewhere in the background of the scene—a ghost in the form of a dialogical pattern, an archetype of parent–child confrontation.

---

[36] Interestingly, this is no longer considered good pedagogical practice, precisely because it gives the student a chance to speak. See Irena Barker's article in the *TES*, 'Don't ask students to quit mucking about—tell them', 2 January 2015, https://www.tes.com/news/dont-ask-students-quit-mucking-about-tell-them (accessed 16 January 2019).

Here is the end of that same speech, as it appears in the First Folio:

	Volum. […]	Come, let vs go:
3535	This Fellow had a Volcean to his Mother:	
	His Wife is in *Corioles*, and his Childe	
	Like him by chance: yet giue vs our dispatch:	
	I am husht vntill our City be afire, & then Ile speak a litle	
	Holds her by the hand silent.	
3540	*Corio.* O Mother, Mother!	
	What haue you done? Behold, the Heauens do ope,	
	The Gods looke downe, and this vnnaturall Scene	
	They laugh at. Oh my Mother, Mother: Oh!	
	You haue wonne a happy Victory to Rome.	

(TLN 3534–43, 5.3.178–87)

This time the silence is unambiguous. It comes not from the mouth of a character but with the authority of a stage direction. This is one of only two stage directions in Shakespeare to indicate silence, and the only one to indicate the timing of a transition between two turns.[37] What happens to Coriolanus in the gap between the end of his mother's speech and the beginning of his own has been described as a 'breakdown', a 'collapse', and a 'capitulation', as the moment at which he 'comes to know himself and to understand the meaning of life for the first time', a 'failure of male autonomy' and 'the death of the male self'.[38] So it is hardly surprising if this pause, rather than any other, should be deemed worthy of special treatment. The longer Volumnia's turn goes on, the more vociferously she demands an answer, and the longer Coriolanus makes her wait for one, the more obvious it becomes that this is the play's climactic moment. Colin Burrow has suggested

[37] Dessen and Thomson find only ten in the whole of early modern drama. See their *A Dictionary of Stage Directions in English Drama, 1580–1642*, p. 200. The other one in Shakespeare is in *Henry VIII* (TLN 1363–5, 2.4.10).

[38] Respectively: Philip Brockbank, *Coriolanus*, The Arden Shakespeare: Second Series (London: Methuen, 1976), p. 59; Ralph Fiennes, quoted in Julian Curry, *Shakespeare on Stage: Thirteen Leading Actors on Thirteen Key Roles* (London: Nick Hern, 2010), p. 54; John Dover Wilson, *The Tragedy of Coriolanus*, The Cambridge Shakespeare (Cambridge: Cambridge University Press, 1960), p. xxxiv; Janet Adelman, *Suffocating Mothers: Fantasies of Maternal Origin in Shakespeare's Plays, Hamlet to The Tempest* (London: Routledge, 1991), p. 162.

that Shakespeare may have 'constructed *Coriolanus* effectively by reading Plutarch's "Life" backwards'—that his reshaping of the material is 'dominated by the need to motivate its final scene'.[39] We might go further and suggest that the scene itself is dominated by the need to motivate the silence between these two turns at talk. Burrow describes the scene as being run 'in slow motion'.[40] This is a sharp observation, but it might be worth adding that the effect is primarily one of dialogical structure. This final, torturous silence comes after a long series of failed transitions. The rhythmic pulse of turn-exchange—the interactional heartbeat of the play—has been labouring badly for over fifty lines. Now, finally, it seems to have stopped—a mere blank on Chapple's chronograph, like the flat-lining electrocardiogram in a hospital drama. We know that it must recover because we know that the play must end, but we hold our breath all the same. The drama of the moment lies not in *whether* Coriolanus will speak, nor even in what he will say, but in *when* he will finally open his mouth. The moment he does so the tension is released, like air hissing out of a tire.

Notice, by way of a coda, Volumnia's long last line (TLN 3538). The most likely explanation for it is compositorial expedience. A slight misjudgement in the process of casting-off appears to have left the compositor with an urgent need to save space. By shortening a couple of spellings, availing himself of an ampersand, and dropping the terminal punctuation, he successfully manages to 'cram one and one-half lines of verse into one line of type'.[41] But the accident is a happy one. It is fitting that a speech which has been failing to end for over thirty lines should succeed in doing so, finally, with a line that itself fails to end where it should, and that stops without coming to a full stop. It is fitting too that the line should contain both an act of self-silencing and a threat to speak again. It is fitting, finally, that these are Volumnia's last words. The city does not burn, and she never speaks again.

* * *

---

[39] Colin Burrow, *Shakespeare and Classical Antiquity*, Oxford Shakespeare Topics (Oxford: Oxford University Press, 2013), p. 234.

[40] Burrow, p. 235.

[41] Lee Bliss, 'Scribes, Compositors, and Annotators: The Nature of the Copy for the First Folio Text of *Coriolanus*', *Studies in Bibliography*, 50 (1997), 224–61 (p. 258).

Fascinating as Volumnia's exchange with Coriolanus may be, it is also untypical. It is rare that we can use one of Shakespeare's sources to shed light on why a character pauses, and equally rare that we can rely on a stage direction to tell that there is a silence between turns. For the vast majority of the transitions in Shakespeare's plays, we must rely on other, less explicit, kinds of evidence. The first and most obvious of these is dramatic context. Our understanding of what might be happening at a transition is shaped by our sense of what is happening in the scene of which it is a part and on an accumulated sense of how the two characters conduct themselves in the play as a whole. But this kind of amorphous context is not something that can be discussed in the abstract. It is, by definition, specific to a given scene and a given pair of characters. What can be discussed in the abstract are the three basic means by which Shakespeare's plays suggest how turns at talk are timed—syntax, punctuation, and metre—and it will be the work of the next three chapters to discuss them.

None of these, however, nor even the three of them combined, can provide us with the kind of clarity we would get from an interaction chronograph. The deep ambiguity of the dramatic text in this regard can be frustrating, and the modern editor works hard to reduce it. But it is also, potentially, liberating. One of the central differences between a piece of dramatic writing and the record of a real interaction—between literary criticism and conversation analysis—is that, for the linguist, the gap between a conversation and its transcript is always a loss. For the critic, there can be no loss, because there never was a conversation. A script looks forward rather than back. It is a recipe for a meal rather than the detritus left on the table after a meal has been eaten—a set of possibilities for the future rather than an imperfect record of the past. The critic's task is not to lament the gap between script and performance, or to attempt to close it, but to explore the space it opens up.

| 6 |

Aposiopesis and the Comforts of Rhetoric

Like his life, Hotspur's last turn at talk comes to a premature end.

> *The Prince killeth Percy*
> HOTSPUR   O Harry, thou hast robbed me of my youth.
>   I better brook the loss of brittle life
>   Than those proud titles thou hast won of me.
>   They wound my thoughts worse than thy sword my flesh.
> 80   But thoughts, the slaves of life, and life, time's fool,
>   And time, that takes survèy of all the world
>   Must have a stop. O, I could prophesy,
>   But that the earthy and cold hand of death
>   Lies on my tongue. No, Percy thou art dust
> 85   And food for—   *[He dies]*
> PRINCE   For worms, brave Percy.
>   (*1 Henry IV*, 5.4.76–86)

Both the terminal dash and the stage direction which follows it are editorial, but neither is controversial. It seems clear that Hotspur is cut off part way through a sentence because the preposition 'for' has no complement. And it seems clear that what cuts him off is his own death because, as he recognizes himself, he has just been given his death blow. Even once he knows he is dying, Hotspur remains unrealistic about what he will be able to achieve—about how much he can say in the time he has left. He might have stopped, appropriately enough, at the word 'stop', but he goes on, gesturing towards a prophecy that it is now too late to deliver. And he dies just one word short of what would have been a plausible ending for his turn—agonizingly close, that is, to a final syntactical resting place. The speech is patterned on a repeated scaling-down of its own scope, a foreshortening of the projected end, which ultimately Hotspur still fails to reach. It mimes, in miniature, the shape of his life—ill-weaved ambition attempting too much and shrinking at last into death.

Hotspur's dying words have become a textbook example of *aposio-pesis*, a rhetorical figure in which 'something is said and then the rest of what the speaker had begun to say is left unfinished'.[1] They are frequently used to illustrate the figure in lists of rhetorical terms, and the figure is frequently used to describe them in works of literary criticism.[2] So clear is this example that it has even been used to illustrate the function of rhetorical figures more generally, not just in Shakespeare but in the whole of Renaissance literature.[3] The importance of rhetoric for understanding Shakespeare's language is now beyond doubt. As a succession of scholars have shown, Shakespeare was the product of an educational system that put rhetoric at the heart of the school curriculum and the figures at the heart of rhetoric:

---

[1] *Rhetorica ad Herennium,* trans. by Harry Caplan, The Loeb Classical Library 403 (Cambridge, MA: Harvard University Press, 1954), IV. 30. 41 (p. 331).

[2] Richard Lanham, *A Handlist of Rhetorical Terms: A Guide for Students of English Literature,* 2nd edn (Berkeley: University of California Press, 1991), p. 20; Michael Neill, '"To know my stops": *Hamlet* and Narrative Abruption', in *Issues of Death: Mortality and Identity in English Renaissance Tragedy* (Oxford: Oxford University Press, 1997), pp. 216–42 (217); Abigail Rokison, 'Laurence Olivier', in *Gielgud, Olivier, Ashcroft, Dench,* ed. by Russell Jackson, Great Shakespeareans (London: Bloomsbury, 2013), xvi, 61–109 (p. 83); Hélène Cixous in conversation with Nicholas Royle, 'Rites of Tenderness, Killing the Dead, Living On: Thoughts for the Times on Shakespeare and Death', *Oxford Literary Review,* 38 (2016), 279–88 (p. 282).

[3] Brian Vickers uses them to make a larger point about the 'polysemous' nature of rhetorical figures. Sylvia Adamson, Gavin Alexander, and Katrin Ettenhuber use them to illustrate the 'meta-rhetorical' processes characteristic of Renaissance literature. See, respectively, Vickers, *In Defence of Rhetoric,* p. 336; and Sylvia Adamson, Gavin Alexander, and Katrin Ettenhuber (eds), *Renaissance Figures of Speech* (Cambridge: Cambridge University Press, 2007), p. 10.

[F]rom their schooldays onwards, renaissance writers studied, memorised and internalised sets of figures and, under the same influence, renaissance critics—and ordinary readers—analysed a text or an author's style in terms of the repertoire of figures it deploys.[4]

What the rhetorical approach seems to offer, then, is a way of understanding both how Shakespeare wrote and how he came to write in the way he did. Having memorized and internalized the figure at school, he had it ready to hand, some twenty years later, when he came to write this scene. Nor is that all. When an early modern playwright employs a rhetorical figure, we are told, he is 'simultaneously thinking with the figure and about the figure'.[5] Like a plumber selecting the right size of spanner, Shakespeare thinks 'aposiopesis' to himself as he tries to work out how Hotspur should die. An understanding of rhetoric thus provides us with more than an explanation for his highfalutin style—it gives us access to the mind of a genius at the moment of creation. Or so the argument runs.

I have my doubts about that last claim, but the point of this chapter is not (at least, not primarily) to air them. Rather, I want to use Hotspur's death to open up the larger question of what syntax does—and does not—tell us about the timing of transitions between turns. 'Aposiopesis', as A. E. Housman long ago remarked, 'is a comforting word', but sometimes that comfort comes at cost.[6] It is not a word, I will argue, that can adequately account for what happens when Hotspur fails to complete his final sentence. But the inadequacy of the term is also instructive. It can help us to develop a more precise vocabulary—or at least one better suited to the analysis of dialogue—with which to talk about the relationship between syntax and turn-taking. I'll start by reviewing what a sixteenth-century grammar school boy is likely to have understood by the word 'aposiopesis' before tackling the more difficult subject of syntax in dramatic dialogue. I'll finish by returning to Hotspur and Prince Hal.

* * *

[4] Sylvia Adamson, 'Literary Language', in *The Cambridge History of the English Language*, ed. by Roger Lass, 6 vols (Cambridge: Cambridge University Press, 2000), III, pp. 539–653 (p. 548).

[5] *Renaissance Figures of Speech*, p. 3.

[6] A. E. Housman, 'On Soph. Electr. 564, and Eur. I. T. 15 and 35', *The Classical Review*, 1 (1887), 240–1 (p. 241).

The two rhetorical handbooks in which Shakespeare is most likely to have encountered aposiopesis are the anonymous *Rhetorica ad Herennium* (once thought to be by Cicero) and Quintilian's *Institutio Oratoria*. These are the books most frequently recommended by humanist pedagogues for teaching the figures and the books most frequently stipulated for that purpose in the statutes of Tudor grammar schools.[7] We know that Shakespeare was familiar with the *Ad Herennium* because fragments of it sometimes find their way into his work.[8] We know that he had it in mind as he was writing *1 Henry IV* because Hal's soliloquy in 1.2 recalls a passage in Book 3 on 'artificial memory' (or memorization techniques).[9] There is less direct evidence that Shakespeare had read the *Institutio Oratoria*, but it would be odd if he had not. T. W. Baldwin has described Quintilian as 'the Supreme Authority' on rhetoric in early modern England, and scholars have assembled a long list of passages in Shakespeare that seem to show an awareness of him.[10] These two authorities can be supplemented by comparison with rhetorical handbooks written in English by Shakespeare's (rough) contemporaries. It has been suggested, for example, that he may have owned a copy of Thomas Wilson's *The Arte of Rhetorique*, but it is hard to be certain.[11] Even if he were not directly familiar with them, the English handbooks provide us with a second kind of evidence. They are parallels rather than sources for Shakespeare's understanding of rhetoric—a record of how other Tudor schoolboys reacted to, expanded upon, or transformed what they had learned from Quintilian and the *Ad Herennium*.

Whether classical or early modern, these handbooks contain two types of information about rhetorical figures—definitions of them (often with examples), and lists of the effects they can be used to produce. Information, that is, about the form of the figures and information about

---

[7] See Quentin Skinner, *Forensic Shakespeare* (Oxford: Oxford University Press, 2014), pp. 28–9.

[8] See T. W. Baldwin, *William Shakspere's Small Latin & Lesse Greeke*, 2 vols (Urbana: University of Illinois Press, 1944), II, pp. 69–107.

[9] See Colin Burrow, '"Rare Accidents" in *1 Henry IV* and the *Ad Herennium*', *Notes and Queries*, 62 (2015), 107–9; and (also Burrow) 'Shakespeare's Authorities', in *Shakespeare and Authority*, ed. by Katie Halsey and Angus Vine (London: Palgrave Macmillan, 2018), pp. 31–53 (38).

[10] Baldwin, II, pp. 197–238.   [11] Skinner, p. 3.

their functions. Formal definitions of aposiopesis can be situated along a spectrum, from those that define it most narrowly to those that give it the widest scope. At the broad end is the *Ad Herennium* and at the narrow end is Quintilian. According to the *Ad Herennium*, aposiopesis occurs whenever 'something is said and then the rest of what the speaker had begun to say is left unfinished'.[12] There is no stipulation as to what this 'something' should be. It is incompletion that defines the figure, regardless of what is left incomplete. Quintilian, on the other hand, is a lot more specific, distinguishing between aposiopesis and 'another Figure, not indeed an Aposiopesis (which would involve an unfinished sentence) but a cutting short, as it were, of a passage before its proper end'.[13] The key distinction is between breaking off a sentence and breaking off some larger unit of speech (the Latin *oratio* has a wider range of meanings than the English 'passage').[14] For Quintilian, it is only the former that counts as aposiopesis.

Early modern writers tend to steer a middle course, vaguer than Quintilian but more specific than the *Ad Herennium*. Thomas Wilson calls aposiopesis a 'stop, or half telling of a tale' which occurs when 'we breake of our tale before we have told it'.[15] Richard Sherry uses 'tale' and 'sentence' interchangeably.[16] Henry Peacham, George Puttenham, Abraham France, and Angel Day all describe aposiopesis in terms of breaking off 'a speech' or 'speech'.[17] This jumble of terms suggests both dissatisfaction with the Latin definitions and disagreement about how to improve on them. These writers seem reluctant to follow Quintilian by confining the figure to the sentence and equally reluctant to follow the *Ad Herennium* by leaving it unconfined. Some larger unit is needed, and both 'tale' and 'speech' are attempts to provide it. How Shakespeare

[12] The Latin is 'cum dictis quibus reliquum quod coeptum est dici relinquitur inchoatum', in which *dictis* and *dici* neatly avoid the question of *what* is being said. *Rhetorica ad Herennium*, IV. 30. 41 (p. 330).

[13] In Latin: 'Est alia non quidem reticentia, quae sit inperfecti sermonis, sed tamen praecisa velut ante legitimum finem oratio'. Quintilian, *The Orator's Education*, trans. by Donald A. Russell, The Loeb Classical Library 124–8, 5 vols (Cambridge, MA: Harvard University Press, 2002), IX. 2. 57 (p. 66–7).

[14] See OLD, *oratio*, n.

[15] Thomas Wilson, *The Arte of Rhetorique* (London: Richard Grafton, 1553), sig. 2A4r.

[16] Richard Sherry, *A Treatise of the Figures of Grammer and Rhetorike* (London: Robert Caly[?] for Richard Tottel, 1555), sig. B2v.

[17] Peacham, *The Garden of Eloquence*, sig. R3v; Puttenham, *The Arte of English Poesie*, sig. T4r; Abraham France, *The Arcadian Rhetorike* (London: Thomas Orwin, 1588), sig. F6v; Angel Day, *The English Secretorie* (London: Richard Jones, 1592), sig. N1v.

would have defined aposiopesis we do not know. All that matters for the moment is to be aware of the tension between the two most important authorities. The distinction between an unfinished sentence and an unfinished speech, or tale, will become important later.

So much for form. Before looking at what rhetoricians have to say about the function of aposiopesis, it is worth stressing where such information was understood to have come from. 'From Aristotle to the end of the eighteenth century,' Vickers tells us, 'the figures and tropes were regarded mimetically, as capturing specific and clearly defined emotional states'.[18] Puttenham puts this well:

> [A]ll your figures Poeticall or Rhetoricall, are but observations of strange speeches, and such as without any arte at all we should use, and commonly do, even by very nature without discipline [...] so as we may conclude, that nature herselfe suggesteth the figure in this or that forme, but arte aydeth the judgement of his use and application.[19]

Rhetorical handbooks are, amongst other things, a record of such observations. They preserve not just the figures themselves, but the circumstances under which they have been observed to occur—the emotional states that, experience teaches us, can spontaneously give rise to them. As Vives remarks of aposiopesis, 'if someone were to express his true feeling of anger or fear by a moment of silence, this would be natural, for excitement does impede the power of reason'.[20] It follows that a rhetorician, armed with a list of rhetorical figures and the emotional states that are known to produce them, can reverse-engineer his language to look like the product of real emotion. If he wishes to appear angry, he can mimic in his speech what he knows to be an authentic sign of anger by breaking off part way through a sentence. This is not to say that the figures map neatly onto the emotions with a one-to-one correspondence. Aposiopesis can be a sign of mental states other than anger, and anger can be mimicked with figures other than aposiopesis (this is why Vickers describes the figures as 'polysemous').[21]

---

[18] *In Defence of Rhetoric*, p. 304–5. Vickers provides an impressive array of evidence in support of this claim.

[19] Puttenham, sig. T4r.   [20] Quoted by Vickers, *In Defence of Rhetoric*, p. 337.

[21] *In Defence of Rhetoric*, p. 331.

What the handbooks provide for each figure is a list of possible causes it might have, and thus of possible effects it can be used to produce.

For aposiopesis the list is a long one. Quintilian gives four reasons a speaker might break off a sentence—'anger', 'anxiety', 'scruple', and 'to contrive a transition' from one part of a speech to another.[22] The *Ad Herennium* gives only one, but it is a reason not mentioned by Quintilian—'a suspicion, unexpressed, becomes more telling than a detailed explanation would have been'.[23] Notice that whilst Quintilian is more focused on the causes of aposiopesis, the *Ad Herennium* is more focused on its effect. Most early modern writers simply repeat what they find in these two authorities. The exception is George Puttenham in *The Arte of English Poesie*. Puttenham lists seven basic reasons a speaker might break off—'it needed no further to be spoken of', 'that we were ashamed', '[that we were] afraide', 'by way of threatning', 'to shew a moderation of anger', 'for feare of offence', and '[that] it would be indecent to tell all'.[24] This much is in keeping with the classical tradition and his own contemporaries. What he says next has no precedent (that I can find) in any other writer:

> If it be for none of all these causes, but vpon some sodaine occasion that moues a man to breake of his tale, then thus.
>
>> *He told me all at large: lo yonder is the man*
>> *Let himselfe tell the tale that best tell can.*
>
> This figure is fit for phantasticall heads and such as be sodaine or lack memorie. I know one of good learning that greatly blemisheth his discretion with this maner of speach: for if he be in the grauest matter of the world talking, he will vpon the sodaine for the flying of a bird ouerthwart the way, or some other such sleight cause, interrupt his tale and neuer returne to it againe.[25]

All other rhetorical theorists agree that aposiopesis is caused by something *internal*—either an emotional state experienced by the speaker or an attempt to mimic the effect that such an emotional state would cause. Puttenham attributes it to something *external*—the flight of a bird or the sudden arrival of the man you were talking about. These are

[22] Quintilian, IX. 2. 54–7 (pp. 65–7).
[23] *Rhetorica ad Herennium*, IV. 30. 41 (p. 331).   [24] Puttenham, sig. T4r.
[25] Puttenham, sig. T4r.

not simply more reasons that a speaker might break off what they are saying: they are reasons of a fundamentally different type.

To explain why this matters, we will need to address the larger question of what it means to apply rhetorical description to the language of a play. A neat summary is provided by Adamson, Alexander, and Ettenhuber:

> To ask questions about the role of the rhetorical figures in English Renaissance literature is to engage with a theoretical system that at first glance might not seem to fit at all. The system of classical rhetoric inherited by the Renaissance had theorised public speaking, rather than private writing, and was an expression of the political and legal cultures of ancient Greece and Rome, a world away from those of early-modern Europe.[26]

Seen in this way, drama would appear to be the most rhetorical of literary forms. It might be written in private, but it is performed in public. And it frequently dramatizes just those situations that rhetoric was developed to theorize—trials, debates, ceremonies, and various other forms of public speaking. When, following Caesar's murder, Brutus and Mark Antony take turns to address the multitude, the speeches Shakespeare scripts for them are classic—and thoroughly classical—rhetorical set pieces. Adamson, Alexander, and Ettenhuber continue:

> But what about a scene between two lovers—does that count as rhetoric? It may well do so, once we remind ourselves that rhetoric is able to describe any situation in which a speaker tries to persuade a particular auditor or audience to believe something.[27]

This is true in the sense that a lover may employ some of the same techniques to persuade the beloved that an orator uses to persuade an audience. But there is also a fundamental difference between the two situations. What an orator delivers is a speech—a single extended turn at talk. Everyone present recognizes that it is his turn to speak, that he is speaking for a specific purpose, and that he will speak, without interruption, for a more or less predictable length of time. What he says is likely to be scripted in advance—if not word for word, at least in the sense that he is following a predetermined argument to a predetermined

---

[26] *Renaissance Figures of Speech*, p. 1.   [27] *Renaissance Figures of Speech*, p. 4.

conclusion. Rhetorical theory teaches the orator how to make the best use of this single turn at talk—how to structure, write, and deliver a speech to maximum effect.

It is useful to the early modern dramatist because one of the things he wants to be able to dramatize is people giving speeches. But he also needs to be able to dramatize the innumerable other ways in which people talk—the improvised, informal, elastic exchange of turns that characterizes ordinary conversation—and rhetorical theory does not help him to do this. Emrys Jones is no doubt right to insist that Shakespeare was a 'Tudor genius' who had been 'taught expertly in an age outstanding for its educational achievements'.[28] It is no doubt true that the extraordinary flowering of English drama in the late sixteenth century had its roots in the educational ideas of Colet and Erasmus and in the schools founded by Edward VI. Copious young men abounded, but good positions for them did not. So they began to compete with one another at writing rhetorically brilliant plays, full of mighty bombastic lines and ranting tyrants. My purpose here is not to try to overturn this narrative. It is merely to point out that, for the playwright, rhetorical exuberance also has its downside. When early modern English drama is bad, it is usually because the characters are making speeches at one another when they should be conversing. The kind of play that a rhetorical education equips a man to write is *Gorboduc*, not *King Lear*. To write *King Lear* requires both a grounding in rhetoric and an understanding of turn-taking—an understanding that neither Quintilian nor the *Ad Herennium* can provide.[29]

Something similar is true of rhetoric as a tool of analysis. It is beautifully adapted for the job it was designed to do—describing the single, extended, persuasive turn at talk. It is not well adapted for the analysis of dialogue. The answer to the question posed by Adamson & co. is thus both 'yes' and 'no'. Some of what happens in a scene between two lovers does count as rhetoric, and rhetorical theory can describe it. But unless the two lovers are exchanging orations, rather than talking

---

[28] Emrys Jones, *The Origins of Shakespeare* (Oxford: Clarendon Press, 1977), p. 263.

[29] This is not to deny that other parts of the Tudor curriculum could have been useful to Shakespeare when it came to understanding turn-taking. An early acquaintance with Roman comedy, for example, or Erasmus' *Colloquies*, is likely to have been formative. See Burrow, *Shakespeare and Classical Antiquity*, pp. 133–61.

to one another, there is likely to be more going on than a purely rhetorical description can capture.

This is why Puttenham's innovations are important. Unlike Quintilian or the author of the *Ad Herennium*, and unlike most of his contemporaries, Puttenham is writing about 'poesie'—in the broad sense of imaginative or fictional writing—rather than oratory or the art of persuasion. His extension of the remit of aposiopesis is part of a larger attempt to adapt rhetorical theory to literary purposes—to improve what Adamson and friends call the 'fit' between the two. The extra items he adds to the list of possible causes for aposiopesis are of little use to an orator. In order for a sentence to be broken off because of 'some sodaine occasion', for example, some such occasion must suddenly occur. It would be possible for an orator to stage his own occasion—by planting an accomplice in the crowd with instructions to release a dove or let off a firework while he is speaking—but, realistically, this is not an effect he can use. To a dramatist, on the other hand, these same observations are extremely handy. The voices in a play are situated in relation to a fictional world, a world containing fictional happenings which could potentially distract or disrupt a speaker in the course of what they are saying. Even more suggestive is the couplet Puttenham invents to illustrate his point: 'He told me all at large: lo yonder is the man | Let himselfe tell the tale that best tell can'. The lines conjure a little dialogue in which A is relating something to B—apparently an anecdote concerning C—when C himself arrives. A then selects C to speak, and C takes up the anecdote interrupted by his arrival. Puttenham stops short of recognizing the most common reason for a broken or unfinished sentence in conversation—interruption by another speaker—but not far short. It is because C arrives, not because he speaks, that A breaks off. That one person might stop talking because another person has started, or that two voices might cut across or compete with one another, does not appear to have occurred to him.

Puttenham's couplet is as close as early modern rhetoric comes to a theorization of dialogue rather than speechmaking. His attempt to extend the range of the figure shows us where its boundaries lie. It also makes clear why it is misleading to describe Hotspur's last words as an aposiopesis. To do so is to imply that it is Hotspur himself who breaks off his final sentence—that what causes his silence is internal rather than external. This is possible (as we shall see), but it is not how the lines are usually understood. The simpler interpretation is that Hotspur dies in the act of speaking—interrupted by the 'sodaine occasion' of his death, just as he could have been interrupted by a roll of thunder, a slap in the face, or the speech of another character. The distinction matters because of the dramatic freight this moment carries and the size of the critical claims that have been made on its behalf. 'The broken-off sentence,' Brian Vickers has observed, is 'a peculiarly appropriate way of symbolizing death'.[30] This is true, but it still matters *why* the sentence is broken off. A sentence cut short by another character, or by something external to the speaker, symbolizes a different kind of death from a sentence that he or she voluntarily leaves unfinished. Similarly:

> [Hotspur's] death in mid-speech represents Shakespeare's reflection on the abruption of a promising life by untimely death. Events are being read like texts. A figure is being interpreted figuratively and applied to the world beyond language.[31]

The 'abruption of X by Y' is interruption, not aposiopesis. Aposiopesis is the 'abruption of X by X'. Read figuratively, what aposiopesis signifies is suicide, not death on the battlefield. Hotspur's end is untimely because Hal kills him, interrupting his life in the same way that death interrupts his sentence. Rather than read this event like a 'text', we should be reading it like a dialogue. Rather than reading Hotspur's last words as a speech, we should be reading them as turn at talk. The problem with the term aposiopesis—and the weakness of the rhetorical approach to drama—is that it makes it harder for us do this.

*   *   *

If I am right that critics have been overzealous in their invocation of the figure, and if we accept that this is a problem, the answer would appear to be simple. All we need do is distinguish more carefully between aposiopesis (in which a speaker stops of her own accord) and interruption (in which she is prevented from going on by someone, or something, else). Unfortunately, as Thelonious Monk long ago observed, simple ain't easy. It is one thing to draw such a distinction in the abstract but another to

---

[30] *In Defence of Rhetoric*, p. 336.   [31] *Renaissance Figures of Speech*, p. 10.

apply it in a dramatic text. Consider, for example, Macbeth, as he receives the news that the English army is approaching:

> *Enter Servant*
> MACBETH [...]
>   The devil damn thee black, thou cream-faced loon!
>   Where gott'st thou that goose-look?
> SERVANT   There is ten thousand—
> MACBETH   Geese, villain?
> 15 SERVANT   Soldiers, sir.
> MACBETH   Go prick thy face and over-red thy fear,
>   Thou lily-livered boy. What soldiers, patch?
>   Death of thy soul!—those linen cheeks of thine
>   Are counsellors to fear. What soldiers, whey-face?
> 20 SERVANT   The English force, so please you.
> MACBETH   Take thy face hence.
>
> (5.3.11–21)

The dash in line 13 is editorial, but its logic is clear. The servant stops speaking without having told Macbeth what it is that there are 'ten thousand' of. In a different context, one in which 'soldiers' is already the subject of discussion, 'there is ten thousand' could function as a complete turn at talk—in answer to the question, 'How many soldiers are there?', for example. But soldiers have not yet been mentioned. The servant's turn syntactically projects a noun that it does not reach. Pragmatically, too, it is incomplete—he has not yet accomplished the task he entered the stage to perform, which is to provide the king with information. It is a reasonable assumption, then, that Macbeth's sarcastic completion of the servant's sentence is an interruption. One man has not yet finished speaking when the other man starts. Psychologically this makes sense. Deserted by his allies and hemmed in by his adversaries, an increasingly manic and interactionally impatient Macbeth cannot even wait for the end of a sentence before jumping down his interlocutor's throat.

But it is equally possible that Macbeth only starts talking because the servant dries up—either because fear brings him stammering to a halt or because he is trying to avoid responsibility for the bad news. By failing to complete the sentence, the servant can invite Macbeth to complete it for him, so that the approach of the soldiers seems to be the consequence of the king's guess rather than his own message. Interactionally, this is a desperate measure, but dramatically it is plausible. What else could there be ten thousand of? And the kind of king who will abuse a man for having a pale face might just as easily punish one for bearing bad tidings. Either way, the servant's reluctance to say the crucial word would help to characterize Macbeth as a tyrant, an impression confirmed by his own sarcastic suggestion that it ought to be 'geese'.[32]

My point is that, syntactically speaking, aposiopesis is indistinguishable from interruption. In the absence of reliable punctuation, we have no way of knowing why a character stops speaking part way through a sentence.[33] Incomplete syntax may suggest interruption, but other explanations are always possible. Compare another king, receiving equally bad news with equal impatience. This is Richard II, just after his return from Ireland:

> KING RICHARD [...]
> Where is the Earl of Wiltshire? Where is Bagot?
> What is become of Bushy? Where is Green?
> 120   That they have let the dangerous enemy
> Measure our confines with such peaceful steps,
> If we prevail, their heads shall pay for it:
> I warrant they have made peace with Bolingbroke.
> SCROPE   Peace have they made with him indeed, my lord.
> 125   KING RICHARD   O villains, vipers, damned without redemption!
> Dogs easily won to fawn on any man!
> Snakes in my heart-blood warmed, that sting my heart!
> Three Judases, each one thrice worse than Judas!
> Would they make peace? Terrible hell,

---

[32] For reasons that are not intuitively obvious, geese seem to be associated with cowardice in Shakespeare. Compare, for example, Coriolanus, as he rallies the retreating Roman troops, 'You souls of geese | That bear the shapes of men, how have you run | From slaves, that apes would beat!' (1.5.5–7). I can only conclude that Shakespeare had never actually met a goose—either that, or the species has become considerably more aggressive in the last four centuries.

[33] The unreliability of Shakespearean punctuation is the subject of the following chapter.

130   Make war upon their spotted souls for this.
       SCROPE   Sweet love, I see, changing his property,
       Turns to the sourest and most deadly hate.
       Again uncurse their souls. Their peace is made
       With heads and not with hands. Those whom you curse
135   Have felt the worst of death's destroying wound,
       And lie full low, graved in the hollow ground.
                                          (3.2.118–36)

The issue here is what on earth Scrope thinks he is playing at in line 124. Richard has just accused Bagot, Bushy, and Green of betraying him ('I warrant' has the force of 'I bet') and Scrope appears to confirm that they have done so. What he says is syntactically complete, and it ends at what is clearly a transition-relevance place, but it is hard to believe he has finished speaking. Unless Scrope intends to mislead the king—which seems unlikely—then he must be about to explain that Richard's former favourites have only made peace with Bolingbroke in the sense that they are dead. Or rather, he *does* intend to mislead the king, but only for a second, as a dramatic opening to a longer explanation. No sooner are the words out of his mouth, however, than Richard interrupts. What was meant to be a fleeting rhetorical flourish hardens into the whole of Scrope's turn, and he finds himself in the awkward position of having lied to the king. The change of speakers occurs, in other words, at what is *syntactically* a transition-relevance place but with a larger turn-constructional unit—the delivery of the news about Bushy, Green, and Bagot—left incomplete. Scrope has completed his sentence but not his 'tale'. Like Macbeth, Richard's impatience characterizes him as an interactional tyrant, dictating to others not just when it is their turn to talk but how long that turn will be. Characteristically, however, his domineering behaviour only succeeds in making him look histrionic and unregal. This is true at the level of plot, and it is true too at the level of dialogue—in the tiny matter of how transitions are negotiated.

What the two examples show is that, while syntax is a relevant consideration when it comes to the timing of transitions between turns, it is ultimately inconclusive. It can help us to sharpen the ambiguity over a transition into a set of more or less distinct possibilities, but it cannot remove that ambiguity. It is not the case that interruptions occur only at syntactically awkward moments—skilled interrupters time them precisely so that they coincide with a plausible ending point. The fact that a turn is syntactically complete does not mean that the speaker has finished. The fact that a turn is syntactically incomplete does not mean the speaker has more to say. Many complete turns at talk are incomplete sentences, either because they can rely on the foregoing dialogue to provide what is missing (as in the case of a one-word answer to a question) or, as we have seen, as deliberate acts of aposiopesis. Which is not to say that it makes no difference when, syntactically, a transition occurs—only that the syntactical shape of the join between two turns does not determine, on its own, what kind of transition we have.

What is needed, therefore, is a more neutral term—one that recognizes that a turn is in some sense incomplete but without committing us to any particular explanation of why this is so. Such a term is provided by M. B. Parkes to describe the development, early in the sixteenth century, of a new kind of typographical symbol—one that indicates omission, incompletion, or ellipsis (more on this in the next chapter). Parkes calls this mark the sign of 'suspension' and that is the term I propose to adopt.[34] *Suspension* is what happens when, at the moment of transition between two turns, something is left incomplete. Like the *Ad Herennium*, I leave open the question of what is left incomplete. All that matters is that the turn has promised something it has not yet delivered. The most obvious kind of suspension is syntactical in the narrowest sense of that word. Hotspur's 'food for' promises a noun, as does the servant's 'ten thousand'. But other kinds of suspension are also possible—a passage, a tale, an oration, an anecdote—anything that can function as a turn-constructional unit can potentially be suspended. Crucially, however, the term implies nothing about what has caused the speaker to break off. Aposiopesis and interruption are both types of—or, rather, they are both explanations for—suspension. The difference is that suspension is an observable fact about the shape of the text—about what is happening syntactically at the moment a transition occurs—while the other two are ways of accounting for that fact. Which is not to say that there can never be disagreement about whether, or how, a turn is suspended—

only that this is a disagreement about the shape of the turn, not about whether one character has interrupted another.

Even an obvious case, such as Hotspur's death, admits of uncertainty. The dramatic context strongly suggests that what prevents him from finishing his sentence is his own death. Without the intervention of an editor, however, the exact moment of that death is ambiguous. It may or may not coincide with the moment at which Hotspur stops talking. Consider, for example, Laurence Olivier's performance of the role at the Old Vic in 1945.[35] Olivier played Hotspur with a stammer, but only on the letter *w*. His failure to say 'worms' was thus presented as more than simply a failure of breath—it became the product of a neurological and psychological flaw, a stifling rage that prevented him, throughout the play, from speaking and acting clearly. It also created a gap between the moment the sentence is suspended and the moment at which Hotspur dies—a gap long enough to for him to recognize his own impotence. But while a stammer can provide a rationale for such a gap, a gap can exist even without the stammer. Since we do not know when Hotspur dies, we do not know why he stops speaking. We do not know, that is, whether what we have here is interruption, aposiopesis, or something halfway between.

*   *   *

Recognizing this ambiguity is a step forward, but hardly a giant leap. There is a second and more fundamental way in which the rhetorical figure 'aposiopesis' fails to capture what happens on the battlefield at Shrewsbury. Just as important as the fact that Hotspur does not complete his final sentence is the fact that somebody else does it for him:

HOTSPUR [...]   O, I could prophesy,
    But that the earthy and cold hand of death
    Lies on my tongue. No, Percy thou art dust
85 And food for—   *[He dies]*
    PRINCE   For worms, brave Percy.
                            (5.4.82–6)

---

[35] Rokison, 'Laurence Olivier', p. 83.

The drama of the moment is as much about continuity as abruption. What we have is not, strictly speaking, an unfinished sentence at all but a sentence that is split between two speakers. This may seem obvious, but critics have been surprisingly slow to grasp its importance. Brian Vickers describes Hal as 'a bystander' at Hotspur's death, despite the fact that it is Hal who kills him and Hal to whom his final speech is addressed. Vickers moves on to his next example by remarking that 'a different kind of incompleteness is created when *aposiopesis* is used in dialogue'.[36] This is no more than a slip—a moment's reflection would have shown Vickers that this *is* dialogue—so it would be churlish to make too much of it. But the nature of the slip is revealing. It is caused by the fact that Vickers reads Hotspur's last words as a speech rather than a turn at talk, as rhetoric rather than drama. Hal is a 'bystander' because what is important here, from Vickers' point of view, is not the passing of the syntactical torch between two fictional characters but the fact that William Shakespeare is using a rhetorical figure.

Unsurprisingly, rhetoric has no way of describing this kind of dialogical effect. We must look instead to conversation analysis, where the first person to pay serious attention to the phenomenon was Harvey Sacks.[37] 'Collaborative utterances', as he calls them, have subsequently developed a substantial critical literature and a messy and inconsistent terminology.[38] There is no agreement as to what they should be called, nor how the various types should be differentiated. In order to avoid becoming embroiled in this dispute—a dispute that has its roots in the vexed question of segmentation in spoken language—I propose to adopt two further terms that at least have the virtue of intuitive clarity. These are 'completion' (borrowed from Gene Lerner) and 'addition' (my own coinage, on the analogy of 'completion'). Along with 'suspension', these make up my second trio of dialogical figures.

---

[36] *In Defence of Rhetoric*, p. 336.

[37] *Lectures on Conversation*, I, pp. 144–7, 167–8, 321, 528, 649–51.

[38] The two best recent studies are both by Gene H. Lerner: 'Collaborative turn sequences', in *Conversation Analysis: Studies from the First Generation* (Amsterdam: John Benjamins, 2004), 225–56; and 'Turn-Sharing: The Choral Co-Production of Talk in Interaction', in *The Language of Turn and Sequence*, ed. by Cecilia E. Ford, Barbara A. Fox, and Sandra A. Thompson, Oxford Studies in Sociolinguistics (Oxford: Oxford University Press, 2002), pp. 225–56.

Completion is what happens between Hotspur and Hal. It occurs when one turn at talk is suspended—whether through interruption or aposiopesis—and a subsequent turn supplies what was missing. Hal completes Hotspur's sentence by supplying the word 'worms'. Macbeth completes the servant's message by supplying the word 'geese'. The resolution need not occur immediately, and it need not be provided by a different speaker. Consider, for example, Iago reporting to Othello what (he claims) Cassio has said about Desdemona:

> OTHELLO   Hath he said anything?
> 30   IAGO   He hath, my lord. But, be you well assured,
>   No more than he'll unswear.
> OTHELLO   What hath he said?
> IAGO   Faith, that he did—I know not what he did.
> OTHELLO   What, what?
> IAGO   Lie—
> OTHELLO   With her?
> IAGO   With her, on her, what you will.
> OTHELLO   Lie with her? Lie on her? We say 'lie on her' when they belie
> 35   her. Lie with her? 'Swounds, that's fulsome!
>
>   (4.1.29–35)

Iago is a good rhetorician, and he begins, in line 32, with an aposiopesis of which even Quintilian would approve. But because this is dialogue rather than oratory, Othello can press him—can insist (as in fact he does) that the abandoned sentence be pursued to its bitter end. This enables Iago to appear reticent—to be breaking off, in Puttenham's words, 'for feare of offence' or because 'it would be indecent to tell all'— even as he is gleefully administering his poison.[39] And it forces Othello to take responsibility for what he is about to hear. The full horror of the sentence is revealed incrementally, like the monster in a horror film, and is all the more horrifying for precisely that reason. When, after a second suspension, Othello completes the thought himself, Iago's work would appear to be done. He has managed not only to persuade Othello that the report is true but also to make him speak it aloud. But Iago is

---

[39] Puttenham, sig. T4r.

no ordinary villain. He is the Michelangelo of stage Machiavels, and this is his masterpiece. He cannot resist adding one final stroke. To lie *with* someone is a fairly standard early modern euphemism for sex. To lie *on* them is a physical description of the sexual act. Unsatisfied with the former, Iago nudges Othello towards the latter. Rather than simply planting the information—Cassio says he slept with your wife—he infects Othello's mind with an image of Desdemona mounted by Cassio. And he does so in such a way as to appear to be trying to soothe the general's distress. *Let's keep things vague shall we—with her, on her, all over her—what do the details matter?* In reality what this achieves is not a dilution of meaning but an accumulation. While appearing to want it neither way, Iago has it both ways at once—as we can see from the fact that Othello immediately begins to weigh and compare the two possibilities.

Addition occurs when a character adds something to a previous turn, even though that turn is already complete. It is to treat a completed turn as though it were suspended—to render it retrospectively incomplete by extending or expanding it. Take, for example, the following description of Falstaff:

> *Enter Sheriff and the Carrier*
> PRINCE   Now, master sheriff, what is your will with me?
> SHERIFF   First, pardon me, my lord. A hue and cry
>   Hath followed certain men unto this house.
> PRINCE   What men?
> 420 SHERIFF   One of them is well known, my gracious lord,
>   A gross, fat man.
> CARRIER   As fat as butter.
> PRINCE   The man, I do assure you, is not here [...]
>   (*1 Henry IV*, 2.5.416–22)

The carrier's simile is syntactically and pragmatically superfluous. Both the sheriff's sentence and his description are already complete. By adding to it, the carrier implies that the previous turn was in some way inadequate or imprecise—that without the vivid extra detail he provides (*not just fat—as fat as butter!*), the prince may not be able to identify the culprit. Notice too that the addition coincides with an intervention. The carrier has not been addressed, so there is no reason for him to speak. By framing what he says as a continuation of the previous turn, however, he can mitigate the impoliteness of butting in. He is not *quite* speaking out of turn, because what he says is not *quite* a turn in its own right—it is a part of the sheriff's own sentence that he somehow forgot to add. Alternatively, the addition might be a sign of the prince's dishonesty, with Hal pretending not to understand the sheriff until the carrier pipes up. The actors might add a lengthy pause here in which Hal mimes the process of trying to remember (by scratching his head and looking quizzically round at his companions, for example) followed by a sudden faux-realization after the carrier's addition. *As fat as butter! Why didn't you say so! I know just the man.* Either way, the point of the simile remains its superfluity. There is only one fat man in this play, and we all know who that is. By feigning ignorance—if he does feign ignorance—Hal only succeeds in drawing attention to his own insincerity.

This, then, is my second trio of dialogical figures. If *intervention*, *blanking*, and *apostrophe* are figures of dialogical sequence, then *suspension*, *completion*, and *addition* are figures of dialogical syntax. The former help us to describe how strings of turns are built, the latter how they relate. I am using the word 'syntax' in a broad sense here. What is completed need not be a sentence, and what is added need not be a clause. The terms describe the relationships between turns at talk, not (or not necessarily) between the parts of a sentence. Anything that qualifies as a turn-constructional unit, anything that can be hearably complete or incomplete, can be used in the same way.

One final point before we return to Hotspur and Hal. Like all figures, collaborative utterances are polysemous. Often they suggest cooperation or intimacy—as between lovers who finish one another's sentences—but they can also suggest competition or hostility. Partly this depends on timing, both in the sense measured by Chapple's chronograph and in the less tangible sense of whether or not the speaker has finished. It is one thing to help someone out as they struggle to find the right words and another thing to cut them off unexpectedly with an impatient completion of their turn. Macbeth's 'geese' and Hal's 'worms' are syntactically similar but dramaturgically quite different. There is no room here for an exhaustive list of the uses to which these figures can be put, any more than there would be for an exhaustive list of uses to which rhyming couplets can be put, or syllepsis, or anaphora. What matters, as ever, is to be flexible—to be aware that these are shapes, not words—dialogical patterns that can take on different meanings in different contexts.

*   *   *

Which brings us back to the battlefield at Shrewsbury. Hal's completion of Hotspur's final sentence is the most dramatically charged collaborative utterance in Shakespeare—a tiny dialogical gesture that turns a brutal act of violence into a rite of tender sacrifice. It symbolizes not only the fact of Hotspur's death but the meaning of that death to each of the characters involved. It is a moment of both vindication and communion. And, just as importantly, it is a moment of narrative resolution. When Hal completes Hotspur's sentence, the plot of the play snaps shut with a satisfyingly audible click. To hear all this we will need to step back from the moment itself and retrace the paths by which the two Harrys, and the play as a whole, have come to it.

The first thing to understand about Hal's defeat of Hotspur is that it is entirely Shakespeare's invention. Harry Monmouth did not kill Harry Percy at the Battle of Shrewsbury in 1403. He did not do so in fact, and he does not do so in any of Shakespeare's sources.[40] Nor were the two men remotely the same age. Hotspur was older than Hal's father, let alone Hal. It is Shakespeare who makes them rivals and who makes that rivalry a central feature of his play. That the two Harrys are in some way interchangeable—that one can potentially substitute for the other—is not something it requires a literary critic to point out. It is repeatedly pointed out by the other characters in the play. This begins in the opening scene, when Henry IV wishes it could be proven that 'some night tripping fairy' (1.1.86) had swapped the two boys in their cradles, so that Hotspur rather than Hal would turn out to be his son. And it ends in the closing scene, when one Harry kills the other. Their rivalry is the engine which drives the plot of the play. The madcap Prince of Wales must somehow become the hero of Agincourt, Henry V. To do so he must first see off the threat of his alter ego—this other Harry, a 'Mars in swaddling-clothes' (3.2.112)—who seems to everyone,

---

[40] See Geoffrey Bullough (ed.), *Narrative and Dramatic Sources of Shakespeare*, 8 vols (London: Routledge and Kegan Paul, 1957–75), IV, pp. 155–79; and *King Henry IV, Part One*, ed. by David Scott Kastan, The Arden Shakespeare: Third Series (London: Thomson Learning, 2002), pp. 339–44.

including Hal's own father, to be a much more promising candidate for the throne. The contrast between the two men, and the question of which of them would make a better ruler, is thus of central importance to the drama. Nowhere is this contrast more strikingly or skilfully drawn than in their habits of interaction.

It has often been observed that Hal has a special talent for catching the manner of other people's speech. Wherever he goes, the Prince of Wales seems able to talk to the natives in their own language, be they soldiers, courtiers, rogues, tapsters, or the royal family. After a few pints he will even boast of this talent, as when he claims to have learnt so much slang in a quarter of an hour that he can 'drink with any tinker in his own language during my life' (2.5.15). Some critics see Hal's linguistic versatility as evidence of his common touch. It is because he understands people from all walks of life that he will make such a fine king.[41] Rather than a lamentable and degrading dissipation, Hal's fondness for rogues and taverns is really a kind of research. As Warwick puts it in 2 Henry IV, the prince 'studies his companions, | Like a strange tongue, wherein, to gain the language' (13[4.3], 68–9). Other critics see the same behaviour as evidence of a horrifying insincerity. Rather than an ideal ruler, Hal is a calculating and cold-blooded Machiavel, the 'prince and principle of falsification', who will cast off his former companions the moment it suits him to do so.[42] The more perfectly he seems to speak their language, the deeper his treachery.

Less frequently observed is that Hal's ability to charm those around him, to seem to understand them and deserve their loyalty, has as much to do with the sharpness of his interactional reflexes as it does with the flexibility of his vocabulary. Like Hamlet, he is a master of conversational timing. His drunken teasing of the 'puny drawer' Francis, for example, relies on this talent:

> PRINCE   Nay, but hark you, Francis. For the sugar thou gavest me, 'twas a pennyworth, was't not?

[41] The classic statement of this position is Tillyard, *Shakespeare's History Plays*, p. 269–82. For a neat summary of the arguments, see the section on 'The "Education" of Prince Hal' in *Henry IV, Part One*, ed. by David Bevington, The Oxford Shakespeare (Oxford: Oxford University Press, 1987), pp. 59–63.

[42] Stephen Greenblatt, *Shakespearean Negotiations* (Oxford: Oxford University Press, 1988), p. 42.

FRANCIS   O Lord, I would it had been two!
PRINCE   I will give thee for it a thousand pound. Ask me when
   thou wilt, and thou shalt have it—
POINS   [*within*] Francis!
FRANCIS   Anon, anon!
PRINCE   Anon, Francis? No Francis; but tomorrow, Francis; or,
   Francis, o' Thursday; or indeed, Francis, when thou wilt.

(2.8.48–56)

For the trick to work, Poins must call for Francis at precisely the moment
Hal finishes offering him a thousand pounds. Either that, or Hal must
continue to expand his offer until he hears Poins call. Then, when Francis
answers Poins, Hal must jump back in immediately, to end the young
man's turn before he has a chance to answer Hal too. By pretending to
take 'anon' as a response to his own offer rather than Poins' summons, he
puts Francis in the difficult position of having accidentally declined a
thousand pounds. What has put him in that position is a carefully
calibrated turn-taking ruse, orchestrated by the prince—a trick, that is,
of conversational timing.

   The fun with poor Francis may be a special case, but it illustrates
something important. Hal does more than simply adopt other characters' vocabulary and style. He masters the rhythms of their conversation. This enables him to go a step further, when he wants to make
himself agreeable, by sharing in the syntax of their turns and sentences.
The collaborative utterance is his dialogical signature tune. Here he is
with Falstaff, in their first scene together:

FALSTAFF   [. . .]
   'Sblood, I am as melancholy as a gib cat, or a lugged bear.
PRINCE   Or an old lion, or a lover's lute.
FALSTAFF   Yea, or the drone of a Lincolnshire bagpipe.
PRINCE   What sayst thou to a hare, or the melancholy of Moorditch?
FALSTAFF   Thou hast the most unsavoury similes, and art indeed the
   most comparative, rascalliest sweet young Prince.

(1.2.58–63)

The two men take turns to refine Falstaff's simile, producing a range of
possible alternatives—competing, comparing, and suggesting them to

one another as though the melancholy, and the sentence, belonged equally to both. We have an addition to an addition to an addition— a comic structure collaboratively produced. Falstaff's delight in this kind of game, and in Hal's skill at it, produces his tenderest expression of affection for the prince—an affection rooted in the pleasure of his company rather than the advantages of his status vicariously enjoyed. We never again see these two characters alone together for more than a few lines, and never so together in the shape of the lines they share. But Falstaff is wrong. It is not Hal who has the most unsavoury similes but himself. The joy he takes in these rascally comparisons is the joy of self-recognition. What Hal has done is to learn the trick of the old man's voice and then speak it back to him—speak it *with* him, rather, in an intimate act of syntactical collaboration.

Compare the prince's handling of his father, before the battle at Shrewsbury, in one of their rare moments of communion:

> *Enter the King, Prince of Wales, Lord John of Lancaster, Earl*
> *of Westmorland, Sir Walter Blunt, Falstaff*
> KING   How bloodily the sun begins to peer
>   Above yon bosky hill! The day looks pale
>   At his distemp'rature.
> PRINCE   The southern wind
>   Doth play the trumpet to his purposes,
> 5 And by his hollow whistling in the leaves
>   Foretells a tempest and a blust'ring day.

$$(5.1.1-6)$$

The effect is very different, but the move is the same. Once again we see Hal expanding on someone else's turn by a species of ventriloquism— slotting in after his father to amplify and extend this rather tedious act of portentous narration. But the collaboration here is less intimate. Hal does not encroach upon his father's syntactical territory—they share a speech, and a line, but not a sentence. He adds, but not in such a way as to imply that what was previously said was incomplete or inadequate. Either turn is whole on its own, even if the two turns are organized in such a way that, written out as one, you would not be able to spot the join.

The elephantine reader, with a memory long enough to recall the introduction to this book, may wish to object here. Aren't these the same two characters whom I have already described repeatedly mis-timing their conversation with each other? And didn't I make great play of the symbolic importance of these fumbled transitions? The short answer to both questions is 'yes'. The longer answer is that part of what gives the two reconciliation scenes their force is that Hal's timing is usually so good. The only person with whom he is ever out of sync is his father. Their shared speech before the battle at Shrewsbury is the exception to this rule. It comes shortly after the first reconciliation and offers us a confirmation, in the shape of the dialogue, that the reconciliation has been a success. It also takes place in public rather than private. Whatever problems the father may have with the son, or the son may have with the father, this is not the time to air them. With the fledgling Lancastrian dynasty facing possible extinction, the two men collaborate to present a smooth public front.

Hotspur, by way of contrast, has all the subtlety of a child on Christmas morning. He approaches a conversation in much the same way he approaches a battle—'responsibility, prudence, caution, strategy mean nothing to him', his only concern is honour, and honour, to Hotspur, means 'fighting, with a complete disregard of personal safety or the probability of victory'.[43] This is clear from his very first turn at talk. Summoned by the king to explain his failure to hand over the prisoners he took at Holmedon, Hotspur gives a long and seemingly rehearsed speech. His explanation hinges on having answered 'neglect-ingly, I know not what' (1.3.51) to the king's messenger when the prisoners were first requested—on his inability, that is, to filter what he says. He is equally incapable of filtering when he says it. Here is Hotspur's second turn, spoken in defence of his brother-in-law, Edmund Mortimer, whose ransom the king is reluctant to pay:

> KING [...]
> Shall we buy treason and indent with fears
> When they have lost and forfeited themselves?

---

[43] A. D. Nuttall, 'Henry IV: Prince Hal and Falstaff', in *Modern Critical Interpretations: William Shakespeare's Henry IV, Part 1*, ed. by Harold Bloom (New York: Chelsea House, 1987), pp. 115–34 (132).

No, on the barren mountains let him starve;
For I shall never hold that man my friend
90   Whose tongue shall ask me for one penny cost
To ransom home revolted Mortimer—
HOTSPUR 'Revolted Mortimer'?
He never did fall off, my sovereign liege,
But by the chance of war. To prove that true
95   Needs no more but one tongue [...]
                              (1.3.86–95)

The dash added by the Oxford editors seems a little strong. An unambiguous interruption of the king is rare in Shakespearean drama, and it
is not necessary to see one here. More likely, it seems to me, is that
Hotspur exploits an ambiguity over whether or not Henry has finished.
Like a drunk walking back from the pub, he is unable to contain
himself. So he makes use of the first thing that looks vaguely like an
opportunity—in the drunk's case a lamppost, in Hotspur's a transition-
relevance place. Notice, too, that this is an intervention. Henry's disavowal of Mortimer is addressed to Blunt, not Hotspur. At the moment
he opens his mouth, then, it is not clear that the king has finished, and it
would not be Hotspur's turn to speak even if he had. What he goes on
to say is a flat contradiction of Henry, in front of the whole court, on a
point of fact. No other character is ever this disrespectful to the king,
even when in open rebellion.

And Hotspur's interactional behaviour gets worse, rather than better,
after Henry leaves. He is no more capable of listening to something he
does want to hear than to something he does not. This is his uncle
Worcester (the brains of the Percy clan) trying to lay out their next move:

WORCESTER [...]
    Good cousin, give me audience for a while.
210 HOTSPUR I cry you mercy.
    WORCESTER   Those same noble Scots
        That are your prisoners—
    HOTSPUR   I'll keep them all.
        By God, he shall not have a Scot of them;
        No, if a Scot would save his soul he shall not.
        I'll keep them by this hand.
    WORCESTER   You start away,

215   And lend no ear unto my purposes.
        Those prisoners you shall keep.
HOTSPUR   Nay, I will, that's flat.
        He said he would not ransom Mortimer,
        Forbade my tongue to speak of Mortimer;
        But I will find him when he lies asleep,
220   And in his ear I'll hollo 'Mortimer!'
        Nay, I'll have a starling shall be taught to speak
        Nothing but 'Mortimer', and give it him
        To keep his anger still in motïon.
WORCESTER   Hear you, cousin, a word.
                                          (1.3.209–24)

Having made a first attempt at line 186, Worcester does not succeed in
explaining the plan until line 254. Hotspur, as his father points out, is
incapable of 'Tying [his] ear' to any tongue but his own (l. 235). And
even as he rides roughshod over his uncle's admonishments, this young
man is fantasizing about further untrammelled speech. He cannot stop
himself from talking about how he will not be stopped from talking.
The starling he describes—trained to chirrup the word 'Mortimer'
continually—is an image of Hotspur as well as his messenger. Like
him, it does not respect the rules of turn-taking or the social hierarchy
of which they are an embodiment. Like him, it harps constantly on its
own obsessive string. Unlike him, it has an excuse.

    This pattern continues throughout the play. Hotspur is continually
'crossing' (3.1.143) people—the king, Worcester, Glendower, his wife—
both in the sense that he mocks or contradicts them and in the sense
that he encroaches on their turn-taking territory. And, in the same way
that the exchange of conversational turns between Hal and his father
comes to stand for the exchange of the crown, so Hotspur's interruptions and interventions come to characterize him as a usurper. Hal's
ability to expand upon and complete other people's turns, on the other
hand—his genius for well-timed continuity—characterizes him as the
rightful heir. All this, it seems to me, is in play in those final moments
on the battlefield at Shrewsbury. Hotspur's death halfway through his
final sentence is an ironic form of interactional justice. Harry Percy—
the arch-interrupter—finds himself interrupted. The man who cannot
refrain from talking finds himself unable to talk, slain by the man
whose turn on the throne he has tried to take.

All this is in play, but this is not all. The significance of Hotspur's death is given its fullest explanation by Hal, in the reconciliation scene, when he promises to redeem his indiscretions 'on Percy's head'.

> And that shall be the day, whene'er it lights,
> That this same child of honour and renown,
140   This gallant Hotspur, this all-praisèd knight,
> And your unthought-of Harry chance to meet
> For every honour sitting on his helm,
> Would they were multitudes, and on my head
> My shames redoubled; for the time will come
145   That I shall make this northern youth exchange
> His glorious deeds for my indignities.
> Percy is but my factor, good my lord,
> To engross up glorious deeds on my behalf;
> And I will call him to so strict account
150   That he shall render every glory up,
> Yea, even the slightest worship of his time,
> Or I will tear the reckoning from his heart.
>
>   (3.2.138–52)

No clearer description could be given of Hotspur's function in the play. He busily accumulates honour and glorious deeds while Hal sits in the tavern, enjoying himself but shamed by the comparison. The more Hotspur achieves, the more praise he garners, the more credit he builds up—the greater the glory for Hal in defeating him. The process is imagined in strictly financial terms.[44] Hotspur is merely a 'factor', collecting rent for the landlord, Hal. Glorious deeds are the currency of honour, and Hal will call him to a strict account. This final transaction is imagined as an 'exchange' and a 'reckoning'—the moment at which Hal will empty Hotspur's metaphorical bank account.

Events transpire exactly as Hal has promised. What pains Hotspur in his final moments is not 'the loss of brittle life' but 'those proud titles thou hast won of me'. His death is conceived by both men as a kind of

---

[44] On the play's financial metaphors, see Angus Vine, ' "A Trim Reckoning": Account-ability and Authority in *1* and *2 Henry IV*', in *Shakespeare and Authority*, pp. 157–78.

transfer, an exchange of symbolic capital—the moment at which the two Harrys switch places, fulfilling, in a sense, the wish expressed by Henry in the opening scene. And this is why the writing is shaped in precisely the way it is. If aposiopesis is a kind of syntactical suicide and interruption is a kind of syntactical murder, completion is a kind of syntactical transfer. Hal takes possession of Hotspur's sentence and with it all 'those proud titles' he has spent his life collecting.

But this is not simply an act of triumph and humiliation. Like a pair of boxers who turn to embrace each other at the final bell, the animosity between the two men evaporates as soon as the outcome is no longer in doubt. There is no need for Hal to tear his reckoning from Hotspur's heart, because Hotspur's final words are an act of bestowal.

> HOTSPUR [. . .]   O, I could prophesy,
>   But that the earthy and cold hand of death
>   Lies on my tongue. No, Percy thou art dust
> 85   And food for—   *[He dies]*
>   PRINCE   For worms, brave Percy. Fare thee well, great heart.
>   (5.4.82–6)

Hotspur switches, in line 84, from addressing Hal to addressing himself. On the one hand, we might see this as a turn inwards. With death approaching, his sphere of reference contracts, like a dimming circle of light, to include only himself. But the apostrophe also facilitates the transfer of the sentence from one man to the other. Hotspur turns his language around, so that when Hal takes possession of it the pronouns are already pointing in the right direction—with the handle, as it were, towards the prince's hand. He invites Hal to complete the sentence for him, asks him to do so in exchange for the honour he has won. By accepting the offer, Hal provides Hotspur with a kind of closure, symbolic as well as syntactical. It is the turn-taking equivalent of closing a dead man's eyes. And, just in case we missed it, the gesture is repeated ten lines later:

> 95   But let my favours hide thy mangled face,
>   *[He covers Hotspur's face]*
>   And even in thy behalf I'll thank myself
>   For doing these fair rites of tenderness.
>   (5.4.95–7)

Again Hal speaks for Hotspur—thanking himself on Hotspur's behalf—
and again he performs a rite of tenderness, covering the dead man's face
with a cloth. Hélène Cisoux has described Hotspur's death as 'pure,
beautiful tragedy' and 'a moment of total love'.[45] She is right. And the
verbal gesture that gives expression to this love—the dialogical shape
that Shakespeare finds for it—is syntactical completion.

*　*　*

Syntax, then, is both crucial to our understanding of the relationship
between turns and a source of deep ambiguity about them. As the
impatient reader may have noted, in the process of trying to explore
that ambiguity I have repeatedly had recourse to such phrases as
'the dash is editorial' and 'the editors see an interruption here'. I have
repeatedly postponed, that is, any real discussion of the status of the
punctuation in these plays. If this or that dash is editorial, why not
simply go back to the earliest editions and look at Shakespeare's own
punctuation? Surely that would tell us when one character is interrupting another? Unfortunately, things are not quite that simple, as the next
chapter will show.

---

[45] Cisoux and Royle, pp. 283 and 281.

| 7 |

The Terminal Comma

At the bottom of sig. G4r in the first quarto of *A Midsummer Night's Dream* is what looks like comma.[1] I say 'looks like' because it lacks the clear distinction between head and tail that characterizes most other commas in the text but is of the same approximate size and shape. It looks, in fact, like this (Figure 1):

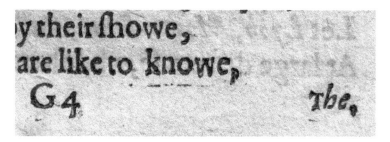

FIGURE 1   Detail from Q1 of *A Midsummer Night's Dream*, sig. G4r, copy TCC, by permission of the Master and Fellows of Trinity College, Cambridge.

---

[1] *A Midsommer Nights Dreame* (London: Richard Bradock for Thomas Fisher, 1600), sig. G4r (5.1.117). For details of the various copies see Henrietta C. Bartlett and Alfred W. Pollard, *A Census of Shakespeare's Plays in Quarto, 1594–1709*, rev. edn (New Haven: Yale University Press, 1939), pp. 70–1. For more up-to-date information on their locations, see the ESTC.

At least, this is how it looks in the copy of Q1 in the Wren Library at Trinity College, Cambridge. Of the seven other extant copies, four have something similar. The copy in the Houghton Library at Harvard, for example, has a mark that is almost the same but ever so slightly darker and fatter (Figure 2):

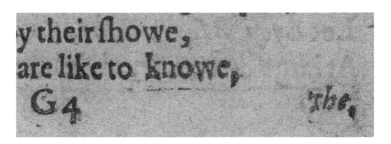

FIGURE 2   Detail from Q1 of *A Midsummer Night's Dream*, sig. G4r, copy MH, STC 22302, Houghton Library, Harvard University.

In the remaining three copies the mark looks different. The widely reproduced Huntington copy has a lumpen scalene triangle with its longest side set vertically to the left and a concentration of ink in the opposite corner (Figure 3):

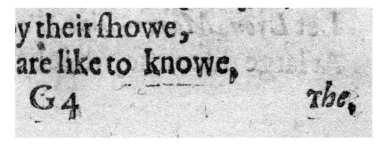

FIGURE 3   Detail from Q1 of *A Midsummer Night's Dream*, sig. G4r, copy CSmH, 69334, The Huntington Library, San Marino, California.

The Bodleian and Folger copies are similar to one another, but not to the other six. Each has something resembling a freshly pulled tooth or a root vegetable, with two fleshy tendrils hanging from a plump upper body, like so (Figure 4):

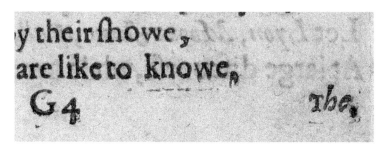

FIGURE 4   Detail from Q1 of *A Midsummer Night's Dream*, sig. G4r, copy DFo, STC 22302, by permission of the Folger Shakespeare Library.

The piece of type that made all these marks was probably either damaged or badly inked. In some copies there seems to be too much ink and in some copies too little—as though something had stuck to the face of the type and then come away part way through the print run, or as though the ink itself had congealed into a lump which later fell off (if ink ever does this).

Whatever its cause, the result is a typographical ambiguity—a mark that looks like a comma but might plausibly be a botched full stop. Opinion, in so far as it can be gauged, is divided. The second quarto of the play (a reprint of Q1) and the Folio text (set from a copy of Q2 but apparently with reference to an independent manuscript) both have a full stop, as does George Steevens' 1766 reprint, based on a collation of the two quartos.[2] The Griggs–Furnivall facsimile of 1880 has an unambiguous comma but has clearly been doctored (Figure 5):

[2] Q2 is *A Midsommer Nights Dreame* (London: William Jaggard for T. Pavier, 1619), sig. G4r. In the Folio the line is TLN 1915. *Twenty of the Plays of Shakespeare*, ed. by George Steevens, 4 vols (London: J. and R. Tonson et al.,1766), I, sig. D5v.

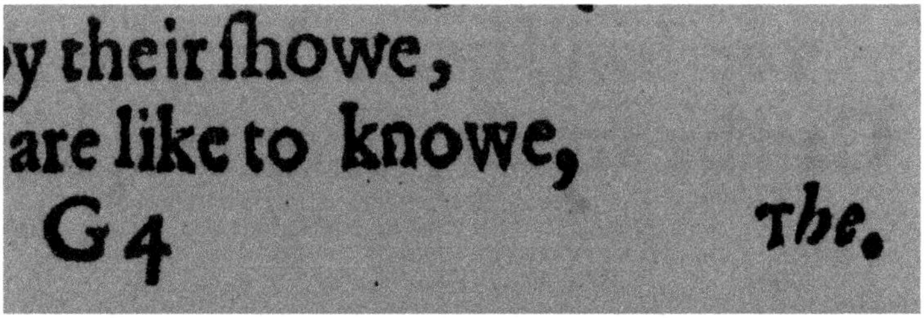

FIGURE 5   Detail from *Shakespeare's Midsummer Night's Dream: The First Quarto, 1600*, ed. by William Griggs (London: W. Griggs, 1880), p. 54, 11764.k.5., © British Library Board.

The fact that Griggs doctored it to look like a comma, however, at least tells us what he thought he saw in the quarto.[3] The available transcriptions are equally inconclusive. The *Oxford Text Archive* and the *Internet Shakespeare Editions* both have a comma but are based on the same transcription, originally made by T. H. Howard-Hill.[4] A separate transcription, made for the *Text Creation Partnership*, has an interpunct—used to indicate uncertainty over the punctuation in the source text.[5] In an otherwise circumspect chapter on dramatic punctuation, Antony Hammond transcribes the mark as a full stop without registering any uncertainty.[6]

It is fair to say, then, that the point is doubtful. It matters because it comes at the end of the only speech in Shakespeare that we can be confident was punctuated by the author:

[3] *Shakespeare's Midsummer Night's Dream: The First Quarto, 1600*, ed. by William Griggs (London: W. Griggs, 1880). On Griggs' unfortunate habit of tampering with his facsimiles, see G. S. McCaughey, 'A Midsommer Night's Mare, or What Was Griggs Up To?', *Humanities Association Bulletin* [Humanities Association of Canada], 26 (1975), 225–35.

[4] *A Midsummer Night's Dream (Quarto 1, 1600)*, ed. by Suzanne Westfall, Internet Shakespeare Editions (University of Victoria), http://internetshakespeare.uvic.ca/doc/MND_Q1/scene/5.1/ (accessed 16 November 2015).

[5] *A Midsommer Nights Dreame* (Richard Bradbrook for Thomas Fisher, 1600), ed. by Text Creation Partnership, Early English Books Online, http://gateway.proquest.com/openurl?ctx_ver=Z39.88-2003&res_id=xri:eebo&rft_id=xri:eebo:citation:99846577 (accessed 16 November 2015).

[6] Antony Hammond, 'The Noisy Comma: Searching for the Signal in Renaissance Dramatic Texts', in *Crisis in Editing: Texts of the English Renaissance*, ed. by Randall M Leod [sic] (New York: AMS Press, 1988), pp. 203–50 (p. 217).

Enter the Prologue.
Pro. If wee offend, it is with our good will.
That you should thinke, we come not to offend,
But with good will. To shew our simple skill,
That is the true beginning of our end.
Consider then, we come but in despight.
We doe not come, as minding to content you,
Our true intent is. All for your delight,
Wee are not here. That you should here repent you,
The Actors are at hand: and, by their showe,
You shall know all, that you are like to knowe[,]
    The. This fellow doth not stand vpon points.
    Lys. He hath rid his Prologue, like a rough Colte: hee
knowes not the stoppe.

                                        (G4r, 5.1.108–20)

Edward Capell was the first to point out that the pointing here is 'a
gentle rub' upon incompetent actors who mangle their lines by pausing
in the wrong places. Shakespeare, he concludes, must have 'taken some
pains' to ensure that his deliberately erroneous punctuation made it
through the press—if the compositor does not recognize the joke, there
is a danger he will remove it by repunctuating the speech correctly.[7]
Even Hammond, an arch-sceptic when it comes to Shakespearean
punctuation, is prepared to accept that the effect is authorial.[8] If the
disputed mark *is* a comma, in other words, that comma is likely to be
Shakespearean. So it is worth asking what it might be doing there.

An answer is not difficult to find. Having repeatedly made 'periods
in the middle of sentences', Peter Quince finishes by making a comma
at the end of one. The syntax says one thing and his voice says another.
The misplaced full stops suggest a delivery that completes, prosodically,
before it is grammatically appropriate to do so—an actor who thinks
the sentence is over when it still has further to run. The misplaced
comma suggests the opposite—an actor who thinks he is halfway
through a sentence when in fact he has come to the end. These two

[7] Edward Capell, *Notes and Various Readings to Shakespeare*, 3 vols (London: Henry
Hughs, 1779–80), II, sig. P4v (p. 115).
[8] Hammond, p. 217.

effects are complementary (two sides, in fact, of the same effect), and both are appropriate to the description provided by the onstage audience. Quince 'knows not the stop'. His voice runs out of words, like a rocket running out of fuel, before it has reached the end of its intonational arc. It is likely to be followed, in performance, by a moment of confusion in which the watching couples are expecting him to continue—an awkward silence broken by Theseus' observation that 'This fellow doth not stand upon points'.

The interest of such an effect for the student of turn-taking is clear. What the comma does is to suggest a way of hearing the lines that makes sense in context but is not otherwise obvious. Punctuation at the ends of speeches is uniquely valuable to the dramatist. It signals not just how one character speaks but how two characters interact. It has the potential, that is, to remove much of the ambiguity about the timing of transitions that is otherwise inherent to the dramatic text. If the mark is a comma, and if the comma is Shakespearean, then we have reason to look again at the dozens of other terminal commas in the early texts of the plays (commas that have traditionally been treated as misprints) and to ask what they are doing there. The purpose of this chapter is to follow that chain of conditionals and see how far it can take us. It will argue for renewed attention to terminal punctuation in Shakespeare's plays, particularly to the terminal comma. The first half of the chapter will revisit the evidence for how punctuation finds its way into an early modern play-text and review what little we know about Shakespeare's own punctuational habits. The second half will examine the use of terminal commas in Nicholas Okes' 1608 quarto of *King Lear*. The choice of this particular book may raise eyebrows. It is notorious, even amongst Shakespeare quartos, for its 'inadequate, erratic, and often insane' punctuation.[9] In spite of its eccentricities, however, the exhaustive bibliographical studies of Q1 carried out by W. W. Greg and Peter Blayney have made it possible to sift the punctuational evidence in this quarto with greater confidence than that in any other.

*　*　*

---

[9] Peter W. M. Blayney, *The Texts of* King Lear *and Their Origins, Volume I: Nicholas Okes and the First Quarto* (Cambridge: Cambridge University Press, 1982), p. 148.

The search for authorial punctuation in the early texts of Shakespeare's plays has long been considered a fool's errand. At first sight, the obstacles seem insurmountable. The closest thing we have to a contemporary account of printing-house practices—Joseph Moxon's *Mechanick Exercises*—makes two contradictory claims. On the one hand, the compositor is 'strictly to follow his *Copy*' in every respect. On the other hand,

> the carelessness of some good Authors, and the ignorance of other Authors, has forc'd *Printers* to introduce a Custom, which among them is look'd upon as a task and duty incumbent on the *Compositer*, viz. to discern and amend the bad *Spelling* and *Pointing*, &c. [of] his *Copy*.[10]

This double attitude is confirmed by the textual evidence. A painstaking comparison of Richard Field's 1591 edition of Sir John Harington's *Orlando Furioso* with the manuscript copy from which it was set led W. W. Greg to conclude both that 'Field evidently had no intention of following his copy' with respect to punctuation and that 'the influence of the copy on punctuation is restricted but clear'.[11] In other words, the punctuation we find in the printed texts of the period is unlikely either to be identical with, or to be independent from, the punctuation of the copy from which they were set. Nor is it possible to generalize with any confidence about how closely the two are related. Studies of compositorial habits in the First Folio have shown that compositors differ as to the extent to which they are prepared to alter the copy in front of them.[12] While punctuation was undoubtedly a compositorial prerogative in this period, it was not one that was exercised in a consistent or predictable way.

This uncertainty is compounded by the fact that we often do not know what kind of copy the compositor had in front of him. When a text is set from an earlier printed edition and the earlier edition is

---

[10] Joseph Moxon, *Mechanick Excercises, or, the Doctrine of Handy-works* (London: Joseph Moxon, 1677), sig. 2Ev.

[11] W. W. Greg, 'An Elizabethan Printer and His Copy', *The Library*, 4 (1923), 102–18 (pp. 115–16).

[12] See Charlton Hinman, *The Printing and Proof-Reading of the First Folio of Shakespeare*, 2 vols (Oxford: Clarendon Press, 1963); and D. F. McKenzie, 'Shakespearian Punctuation— A New Beginning', *The Review of English Studies*, 10 (1959), 361–70.

extant, it can usually be identified with confidence. When a text is set from a manuscript, however, and that manuscript is lost, things are a little more tricky. Like a compositor, a scribe would have considered it well within his rights to alter the punctuation of the copy he had in front of him. A manuscript which has not come directly from the author to the printing house is therefore likely to contain scribal as well as authorial punctuation. For much of the twentieth century, this was not considered a problem. The editorial community felt confident in its ability to identify the type of manuscript—and thus the nature of the copy—that lay behind the printed texts of Shakespeare's plays. W. W. Greg's pioneering work on theatrical documents provided a framework within which such judgements could be made. Greg identified authorial 'foul papers' and theatrical 'promptbooks' as the two most likely candidates and described the characteristics of each type of manuscript. All an editor need do was decide which description best fitted the text of the play she was editing and proceed accordingly. This confidence has now collapsed. In a detailed re-examination of the surviving documents, Paul Werstine has shown that Greg's distinction is not tenable. According to Werstine, 'when a play survives only in print, it is impossible for an editor intent on identifying printer's copy to know if the manuscript behind the printed text had already been copied out either in the theatre or elsewhere'.[13] There is no way of knowing, in other words, how many layers of repunctuation lie between the printed text and the holograph on which it is ultimately based. So even if we could be certain that a compositor was faithfully reproducing the punctuation of his copy, we still wouldn't be able to tell how much of that punctuation was Shakespearean.

Nor is that all. The uncertainty around Shakespearean punctuation is semiotic as well as bibliographic. The difficulty of knowing how the marks got into the text is further complicated by the difficulty of knowing what they mean. The history of punctuation since 1500 is often characterized as a shift from a 'rhetorical' or 'rhythmical' system to a 'logical' or 'grammatical' one—from a punctuation the main purpose of which is to indicate how the words should be read aloud to a punctuation the main purpose of which is to indicate how they

[13] Paul Werstine, *Early Modern Playhouse Manuscripts and the Editing of Shakespeare* (Cambridge: Cambridge University Press, 2013), p. 100.

relate syntactically. Percy Simpson locates this shift between Shakespeare and ourselves.[14] M. B. Parkes sets Shakespeare in the thick of it, describing the situation during his lifetime as 'a precarious balance between logical and rhetorical analysis'.[15] This would be easy enough to cope with if the conventions in use in early modern plays were merely different from our own. All we would need to do is learn the older system. What makes it a problem is that they were also less settled. Practice varied more widely between different writers, scribes, and compositors and was evolving more quickly.[16] A modern reader needs to be aware not only of a different set of conventions but of a wider range of possibilities—including the possibility of extremely idiosyncratic usages, brief punctuational fads, and deliberate attempts at innovation. As Parkes has it:

> The fundamental principle for interpreting punctuation is that the value and function of each symbol must be assessed in relation to the other symbols in the same immediate context, rather than in relation to a supposed absolute value and function for that symbol when considered in isolation.[17]

He does not specify quite how 'immediate' this context should be, but it will at least need to account for the fact that most plays are set by more than one compositor. Usage varies not just between texts but within them. And even within the work of a single compositor there can be variation—whether he chooses to use a dash or a comma at any given moment may depend on how much type he has left in his case and how soon he can expect a redistribution.

The final nail in the coffin of Shakespearean punctuation, as if one were still needed, is *The Booke of Sir Thomas Moore*—a manuscript play, in multiple hands, that never made it to performance. If we accept, as most scholars do, that Hand D belongs to Shakespeare, then this gives us an example of Shakespearean foul papers complete with authentic Shakespearean punctuation. What the manuscript suggests is that Shakespeare punctuated not just lightly but carelessly. It contains

---

[14] Percy Simpson, *Shakespearian Punctuation* (Oxford: Clarendon Press, 1911), p. 8.

[15] Parkes, *Pause and Effect*, p. 87.

[16] Hammond is particularly good on the diversity of dramatic punctuation in the period and the differences between plays in print and in manuscript.

[17] Parkes, p. 2.

no terminal commas and little terminal punctuation of any kind. If the additions to *Thomas Moore* are typical of his working practice, Shakespeare seems to have left the task of punctuating his dialogue to scribes and compositors.

It is little wonder, then, that editors and critics have felt entitled to disregard the punctuation of the early editions. For many years the standard position was that of Samuel Johnson:

> In restoring the authour's works to their integrity, I have considered the punctuation as wholly in my power; for what could be their care of colons and commas, who corrupted words and sentences? Whatever could be done by adjusting points is therefore silently performed, in some plays with much diligence, in others with less; it is hard to keep a busy eye steadily fixed upon evanescent atoms, or a discursive mind on evanescent truth.[18]

The rise of the New Bibliography in the first half of the twentieth century produced a change in editorial theory but not in editorial practice. W. W. Greg's famous relegation of punctuation to a place among the 'accidentals' of the text—those readings that affect only the 'formal presentation' of a book, as distinct from 'the author's meaning or the essence of his expression'—ensured that it remained wholly in the power of the editor.[19] Every now and then an overzealous critic pops up with a theory about the subtle artistry of Shakespearean punctuation, only to be shot down quickly (and gleefully) by a cranky bibliographer.[20] The best punctuation can offer us, it would seem, is a form of reader-response criticism—a record of how one early reader chose to interpret whatever manuscript he had in front of him.

*   *   *

Any argument for the significance of the terminal comma in these texts will therefore have to proceed with caution. But an argument can still be made. We might start by observing that the two best pieces of

[18] 'Preface', in *The Plays: Of William Shakespeare, in Eight Volumes*, ed. by Samuel Johnson, 8 vols (London: J. and R. Tonson et al., 1765), I, sigs E1r–v (no page numbers).
[19] W. W. Greg, 'The Rationale of the Copy-Text', *Studies in Bibliography*, 3 (1950), 19–36 (p. 21).
[20] Hammond describes such critics as 'well-meaning lunatics' and accuses them of 'rediscovering square wheels' (p. 207).

evidence for Shakespeare's own punctuational practice are contradictory. The mechanicals' prologue gives us an example of Shakespeare taking care over punctuation and making sure that a specific punctuational effect finds its way into print. *The Booke of Sir Thomas Moore*, on the other hand, suggests that he wrote the plays in much the same way as Johnson edited them—with little care for the 'evanescent atoms' with which they were dotted. The standard explanation for this discrepancy is that the additions in Hand D represent Shakespeare's usual practice, while the mechanicals' prologue is an anomaly. One half of this explanation is hard to disagree with—the prologue is undoubtedly a special case—while the other half is not.

The additions to *The Booke of Sir Thomas Moore* are themselves a special case—at least in the sense that they do not represent Shakespeare's usual way of working. Rather than writing alone, or with a single collaborator, he was one of a series of playwrights brought in to rework a play that was having difficulty getting past the censor (and that ultimately failed to do so). We do not know at what point he was called for, or quite what the status of the surviving manuscript is, but the assumption that a handwritten draft of one of Shakespeare's own plays—provided by his company for use as printer's copy—would be presented, chirographically, in the same form as this minor contribution to a doomed communal endeavour, is not safe.[21] Equally unsafe is the assumption that Shakespeare's approach to punctuation could not have evolved over the course of his career or that it would not have been adapted to the particular demands of the play or scene he was writing. The additions are simply too small a sample from which to generalize. They can tell us something about how Shakespeare may have punctuated his dialogue, but they do not establish a reliable norm against which we can check other texts.

They are still worth examining, however. At first glance the additions would appear to contain no terminal punctuation whatever—none of the speeches ends with a full stop, let alone a comma. With a couple of exceptions, however, they are separated by speech-rules—horizontal

[21] For a detailed account of the various theories, see *Shakespeare and Sir Thomas More: Essays on the Play and Its Shakespearian Interest*, ed. by T. H. Howard-Hill (Cambridge: Cambridge University Press, 1989); and Anthony Munday, et al., *Sir Thomas More*, ed. by John Jowett, The Arden Shakespeare (London: Arden Shakespeare, 2011).

lines on the left-hand side of the text that show at a glance where one turn ends and another begins. Shakespeare may have considered terminal punctuation as largely redundant when speech-rules are an option—in manuscript, that is, but not in print. This would not preclude the use of punctuation to identify those moments, even in manuscript, at which something out of the ordinary was happening, even if this particular manuscript does not contain an example. Something similar seems to be true for punctuation within turns, which is restricted almost entirely to commas marking mid-line pauses. Shakespeare seems to have considered it unnecessary to punctuate at the line end because, like a speech-rule, a line ending is itself a form of punctuation. So it may be that the additions are so lightly punctuated because the verse they contain is so consistently end-stopped. As Shakespeare's blank verse evolved to become increasingly fluid—and the play of line and phrase increasingly elastic—we might therefore expect his punctuation to evolve with it.

One further piece of evidence is worth mentioning before we turn to *King Lear*. Vivian Salmon has identified an odd usage of the comma that may well be Shakespearean:

> Also worth comment is the occasional use of a comma where later editors feel the need for a hyphen, e.g. *actiue, valiant* and *well, aimd* [*1H4*, TLN 2586, 593]. Shakespeare probably intended these to be understood as compounds: *actiue-valiant* and *well-aimd*. The use of commas in such cases may result from compositorial error [...] On the other hand, it seems to us more likely that Shakespeare himself in such cases used a comma as the equivalent of a hyphen: in *Hamlet* he wrote that peace should 'stand a Comma tweene their amities' [TLN 3310], in which most commentators understand 'Comma' to mean 'connecting link'.[22]

This kind of argument is more usually employed (not without some controversy) in the identification of Shakespearean spelling-forms. It rests on the sheer oddity of the practice it describes. If two texts, both written by Shakespeare, contain the same idiosyncratic spelling of a word, not otherwise characteristic of the compositors who set those texts, then

---

[22] *The Complete Works: Original-Spelling Edition*, ed. by Stanley Wells and Gary Taylor (Oxford: Clarendon, 1986), p. lv.

the assumption that the spelling is Shakespearean is reasonable (more so if it also occurs in the additions to *The Booke of Sir Thomas Moore*).[23] Salmon suggests that the same approach can be used to identify Shakespeare's punctuational habits—or at least to highlight his unusual relationship with the comma.

The remaining portion of this chapter will examine the use of terminal commas in the first quarto of *King Lear* and make the case that these too are plausibly Shakespearean. That case rests partly on the fact that Shakespeare seems to have used one in the mechanicals' prologue but mostly on the fact that they are deployed in Q1 with a purpose and subtlety that is hard—but not impossible—to attribute to a compositor.

* * *

There are thirty-one terminal commas in the first quarto of *King Lear*—more than any other Shakespeare quarto.[24] The number is large but not incontrovertible. It is still possible that all thirty-one of them are misprints. The first step, then, is to establish that at least one terminal comma in this quarto has been put there deliberately. Once that is established, all that remains is to haggle over the ratio of one type to the other—of terminal commas that are misprints to terminal commas that are not. And this step can be taken in the opening scene of the play. In the angry confrontation between Lear and Kent we find the following:

> *Lear.* Now by *Appollo*,
> *Kent.* Now by *Appollo* King thou swearest thy Gods
> (in vaine.
>
> (B2v, 1.143–4)

In 1619, a compositor of the second quarto—reprinted from the first—saw fit to replace the comma after '*Appollo*' with a dash. Four years later, when a third text of *Lear* was published as part of the First Folio, the comma was restored. The restoration is surprising, because

[23] See Salmon's introduction to the Oxford original-spelling *Works* for a comprehensive review of the evidence.
[24] Followed by George Eld's *Troilus and Cressida* with twenty-eight, and Nicholas Okes' other Shakespeare quarto, *Othello*, with seventeen. See, respectively, *M. William Shak-Speare: His True Chronicle Historie of the Life and Death of King Lear* (London: Nicholas Okes for Nathaniel Butter, 1608); *The Famous Historie of Troylus and Cresseid* (London: G. Eld for R. Bonian and H. Walley, 1609); and *The Tragoedy of Othello* (1622).

the Folio text is thought to have been printed without reference to Q1, from an independent manuscript of the play, but demonstrably relies on Q2 in the matter of punctuation.[25] The little pattern thus produced—comma becomes dash becomes comma—suggests two things. First, that the comma in Q1 is not a misprint. The chances of an identical misprint occurring at exactly the same moment in Q1 and in F are slim. Second, that the two marks—comma and dash—are at least partially equivalent.

Like the dash which replaced it, this comma is an example of what M. B. Parkes has called 'the sign of suspension'—an innovation of sixteenth-century printing houses that was yet to find a settled typographical form. According to Parkes, this first appears 'in editions of dramatic texts to indicate that a speech has been interrupted, or is incomplete'.[26] Anne Toner has identified Maurice Kyffin's translation of Terence's *Andria*, printed in 1588, as the first play in English to mark suspension, which she calls 'ellipsis'. Toner argues, very plausibly, that the innovation is an attempt to compensate for the absence, in the translated text of a classical play, of the learned commentary by which the Latin text was usually accompanied.

> It is almost as if we see a direct transformation of the rhetorical figure usually pointed out in Latin in the margin of the play into a modern graphic symbol incorporated into the body of the play.[27]

What the mark does first, then, is to signal an aposiopesis, but it quickly comes to be used for interruptions as well. The virtue of the term 'suspension', as we have seen, is that it accommodates both

[25] According to Peter Blayney, 'F could not have been punctuated without *constant* reference to a copy of Q2' by the compositor responsible for this passage (Compositor E). Blayney is quoted by Jay L. Halio in the introduction to his New Cambridge edition, *The Tragedy of King Lear* (Cambridge: Cambridge University Press, 1992), p. 67. It seems unlikely now that Blayney will publish the argument himself. See also Gary Taylor, 'The Folio Copy for *Hamlet, King Lear,* and *Othello*', *Shakespeare Quarterly*, 34 (1983), 44–61.

[26] Parkes, p. 56.

[27] *Ellipsis in English Literature: Signs of Omission* (Cambridge: Cambridge University Press, 2015), p. 32. For an earlier version of the same argument, see Anne Henry [Toner], '"Quid Ais Omnium?" Maurice Kyffin's 1588 "Andria" and the Emergence of Suspension Marks in Printed Drama', *Renaissance Drama*, 34 (2005), 47–67. Note that in the earlier article she is still using the term 'suspension' rather than 'ellipsis'.

possibilities—it tells us that the sentence is grammatically incomplete, without telling us why.

According to Parkes, the 'usual forms' of the sign of suspension are 'either a single dash, or three or more en-rules [i.e. hyphens] or points'.[28] That a comma can also be used in this way is more controversial, particularly in the first quarto of *King Lear*.[29] Despite recognizing that the terminal comma is 'probably sometimes used to mean the speaker breaks off', for example, W. W. Greg includes all thirty-one of them on a list of 'Misprints in the Original'.[30] According to Toner:

> There are eleven instances of ellipses in the first 1608 quarto of *King Lear*. They are all marked by a series of hyphens. In all cases they mark the interruption of one speaker by another, and capture urgency and anxiety as one character refuses to let another finish.[31]

This is true only if we rule out the possibility that any of the thirty-one terminal commas in Q1 is used to mark ellipsis. Likewise for Toner's larger claim that 'strikingly few of the quarto texts of Shakespeare's plays contain ellipsis marks'—according to her, only eight of thirty-three quartos she has examined are marked with ellipses.[32] She does not specify which quartos these are, but the twenty-two included in Muir and Allen's *Shakespeare Quartos in Facsimile* contain a total of 173 terminal commas, 92 terminal colons, and 5 terminal semi-colons. There are a further 53 occasions on which a speech ends without terminal punctuation. For Toner to be right, we would have to believe that none of these marks (or absences) is intended to signal an ellipsis.

---

[28] Parkes, p. 55.

[29] The suggestion has repeatedly been made but never seems to stick, primarily for the reasons outlined above. See, for example, Simpson, pp. 32–3; Anthony Graham-White, *Punctuation and Its Dramatic Value in Shakespearean Drama* (Newark: University of Delaware Press, 1995); Bernice K. Kliman, 'Explicit Stage Directions (Especially Graphics) in *Hamlet*', in *Stage Directions in* Hamlet: *New Essays and New Directions*, ed. by Hardin L. Aasand (Madison: Fairleigh Dickinson University Press, 2002), pp. 74–91; Evert Sprinchorn, *On Punctuation in Shakespeare's Plays* (Poughkeepsie, NY: Printer's Press, 2011); I. R. Burrows, '"The Peryod of My Blisse": Commas, Ends and Utterance in *Solyman and Perseda*', *Textual Cultures: Texts, Contexts, Interpretation*, 8 (2013), 95–120.

[30] W. W. Greg, *The Variants in the First Quarto of 'King Lear': A Bibliographical and Critical Inquiry*, Supplement to the Bibliographical Society's Publications 15 (London: BiblSoc, 1940), p. 66.

[31] Toner, *Signs of Omission*, pp. 40–1.   [32] Toner, *Signs of Omission*, p. 40.

She is not alone, however. A similar reluctance to recognize the possible significance of the terminal commas in Q1 is shared by the play's editors. Consider this one, for example:

> *Lear.* The bow is bent & drawen make from the shaft,
> *Kent.* Let it fall rather,
> Though the forke inuade the region of my heart
>
> (B3r, 1.127–9)

This comma occurs twenty lines earlier than the one after '*Appollo*', as part of the same exchange between the same two characters. It was replaced by a full stop in Q2, remained a full stop in F, and has been a full stop ever since.[33] Modern editors uniformly ignore it. Despite their proximity and apparent similarity, one comma is consistently accepted as meaningful and the other is consistently rejected as an error—one is treated as 'signal' and the other as 'noise'.[34] For an editor producing a conflated text of *King Lear*, the decision is understandable. They have chosen, rightly or wrongly, to prefer the Folio reading. An editor producing a text based on Q1, however, as an independent and earlier version of the play, might be expected to treat these two impostors just the same. Any such expectation would be disappointed. The modernized texts of Q1 edited by Wells and Taylor, René Weis, Jay L. Halio, and Stephen Orgel all agree in replacing one comma with a dash and the other with a full stop.[35] Even the original spelling edition of the Oxford *Complete Works*, which aims to emend rather than modernize the punctuation of Q1, treats the comma after 'shaft' as a misprint.[36]

---

[33] It is not unusual, as Percy Simpson has shown, for a full stop to coincide with what looks like an interruption in the Folio. This is, according to him, the 'commonest of the various forms of punctuation adopted in this case' (Simpson, p. 84). So we need not see a disagreement between the two texts here. Later editors who follow the Folio by placing a full stop after 'shaft', however, are ruling out the possibility that Lear's turn is suspended—a possibility suggested by Q1 and left open by F.

[34] Hammond, pp. 207–10.

[35] *King Lear: A Parallel Text Edition*, ed. by René Weis, Longman Annotated Texts (London: Longman, 1993); *The First Quarto of King Lear*, ed. by Jay L. Halio, The New Cambridge Shakespeare: The Early Quartos (Cambridge: Cambridge University Press, 1996); *King Lear: The 1608 Quarto and 1623 Folio Texts*, ed. by Stephen Orgel, The Pelican Shakespeare (New York: Penguin, 2000).

[36] The *Critical Reference Edition* of the New Oxford Shakespeare breaks new ground by printing a colon. This is possible but by no means clear. The type appears to have been damaged or over-inked, but previous transcriptions are unanimous in finding a comma.

The theoretical assumptions underpinning such decisions are rarely made explicit. The closest thing I can find to a discussion of the problem is in a footnote to Ronald B. McKerrow's *Prolegomena for the Oxford Shakespeare*:

> I have, however, allowed myself to emend the punctuation silently in one respect. There are very large numbers of cases in which there is either no punctuation at all, or a comma, at the end of a completed speech or of a stage direction, where a full point is undoubtedly required. This can only be due to carelessness, to the stop falling away in the course of printing, or to a shortage of type, and has no possible significance. I have therefore in all such cases supplied the stop without noting its absence (or the presence of a comma) in the original. This, of course, does not apply to speeches left incomplete either owing to the interruption of another speaker or by aposiopesis; in such cases any alteration is noted.[37]

McKerrow recognizes that some terminal commas are noise and others are signal but not that it can be difficult to tell the difference. The distinction rests, according to him, on whether the preceding speech is 'completed' or 'left incomplete'. If completed, the comma has 'no possible significance'. If incomplete, it will need to be modernized (presumably as a dash) and recorded in the collation. To edit in this way is to ignore the early punctuation whilst appearing to take account of it. McKerrow's logic is circular. A judgement is made—he does not specify how—about the status of the speech (complete or incomplete), and this determines whether or not the comma is significant. That the comma itself might provide evidence as to the status of the speech—might provide us with a reason, that is, for supposing it to be incomplete—is not admitted. Only when the punctuation confirms a conclusion that has already been reached on other grounds is it allowed to be meaningful. 'The bow is bent & drawn make from the shaft' is acceptable both as a complete sentence and as a complete line of verse. 'Now by *Appollo*' is not. This is why the two commas have been treated so differently—one confirms what the metre and syntax already seem to be telling us, the other tells us something we would not otherwise have known.

---

[37] Ronald B. McKerrow, *Prolegomena for the Oxford Shakespeare* (Oxford: Clarendon Press, 1939), p. 40n.

Lurking in McKerrow's explanation, and observable in the practice of Q1's editors, is a model of conversation that ignores precisely those ambiguities about when someone has finished speaking that are the subject of the second half of this book. McKerrow assumes that if a transition occurs at a transition-relevance place it cannot be an interruption. As I have been at pains to show, this is not true. 'The bow is bent & drawen make from the shaft' could easily be the opening of a longer turn, containing multiple sentences, or the opening of a longer sentence, containing multiple clauses. 'Now by *Appollo*', on the other hand, could just as easily be a complete turn (a pre-Christian equivalent of 'For God's sake!'). If we accept that a terminal comma can sometimes indicate suspension, and that suspension can occur even after what looks like a complete sentence, then we need to take seriously the possibility that the comma after 'shaft' is not noise but signal. This is not a judgement that can be made purely on the basis of syntax and metre. It is a judgement that rests instead on two kinds of context—the bibliographical context of the comma itself and the dramatic context of the speech it follows. I am going to examine both kinds, for this particular comma, in some detail—enough detail, at least, that the more impatient reader may find it difficult to bear with me. But rest assured that the bibliographical heavy lifting will (eventually) have a literary-critical pay-off. Having looked at one example in slow motion, we will accelerate.

* * *

Bibliographically, things do not look promising for our two commas. Most of the problems which afflict early modern play-texts in general afflict the first quarto of *King Lear* to an unusual degree.[38] It was the first play ever printed by Nicholas Okes, and thetypographical demands of the dramatic text seem to have placed considerable strain on both the competence of his compositors and his small stock of type. Worse still, Q1 was printed either side of Christmas 1607.[39] It would have been the last thing the compositors were working on as they looked forward to

---

[38] W. W. Greg, 'Bibliography in Literary Criticism Illustrated in the Text of *King Lear*', in *Collected Papers*, ed. J. C. Maxwell (Oxford: Oxford University Press, 1966), p. 284; Blayney, p. 181.

[39] Blayney, p. 148.

the holiday, and the first thing they faced when they dragged themselves back to the print-shop in January. According to Peter Blayney,
there were contemporary printers 'whose worst was worse' than
Nicholas Okes, but 'not very many, and not *much* worse'. Blayney
rejects the claim that Q1 is 'one of the worst books ever printed' but
concedes that 'beside some which have been so described it is in a class
of its own'.[40]

It is hardly surprising, then, that the punctuation of Q1 contains a
large number of errors. Blayney's description of it as 'inadequate,
erratic, and often insane', however, is too strong. When Edgar describes
his father as 'parti,eyd', for example, we have what looks like an obvious
misprint.[41] But, as Vivian Salmon has shown, this odd use of a comma
to do the job of a hyphen (parti-eyed) is not evidence of compositorial
insanity. It is evidence, if anything, that the compositor was working
from a Shakespearean holograph and that the author's idiosyncratic use
of commas has survived in the printed text. There is a logic, too, in Q1's
handling of turn-endings. Scott McMillin has mounted a spirited
defence of a later quarto by the same nefarious printer which can
help us to see how this works. Here is McMillin's description of the
punctuation in the first quarto of *Othello*:

> The key to the system operating in the Q1 punctuation is the
> withheld period—the period reserved for the end of the speech.
> Commas, semi-colons and colons are used for nearly all pauses and
> stops before the speech-endings, and this is what gives the punctu-
> ation its aura of haphazard abundance.[42]

The same is true of the first quarto of *Lear* with one important
difference. The compositors were working with a very limited set of
type. Colons, semicolons, exclamation marks, and question marks are
all used sparingly. The one thing they do seem to have possessed in
abundance, however, is commas. So the full stop is withheld to the end
of the speech, as in *Othello*, but most internal punctuation is performed
by commas. Two things make this disorientating for the reader.

---

[40] Blayney, p. 29.
[41] Q1, sig. H2r (15.7). Halio suggests that this is evidence for a Shakespearean
holograph as the copy for Q1. See *The First Quarto of King Lear*, p. 7.
[42] *The First Quarto of Othello*, ed. by Scott McMillin, The New Cambridge Shakespeare: The Early Quartos (Cambridge: Cambridge University Press, 2001), p. 17.

The first is that some of these commas are clearly misplaced (the punctuation is indeed 'erratic'). The second is that it damages the clarity with which the punctuation can carry out its 'grammatical' or 'logical' function. The words are grouped into grammatically coherent units, but the relations between those units cannot be indicated without the use of other marks. Instead of a structured hierarchy of sentences, clauses, and sub-clauses, we get a series of parallel phrases. The punctuation of Q1 is infuriating because it frequently leaves the reader syntactically at sea. It is certainly erratic, in other words, and it may well be inadequate, but it is not insane. What the two quartos have in common is that the unit of punctuation is the turn at talk rather than the sentence. They are based on a system of punctuation that is 'dramatic' in the sense that it prioritizes the dialogical over the grammatical. Within such a system, what the terminal comma denotes is not an incomplete sentence but an incomplete conversational turn—or, rather, a transition between two turns that is in some way fraught.

But why a comma rather than a triple hyphen? As Anne Toner has pointed out, there are eleven instances of ellipses in Q1 'marked by a series of hyphens' and all eleven of them 'mark the interruption of one speaker by another'.[43] If the commas in the exchange between Lear and Kent also mark interruptions, they too should be triple hyphens. Much as I might like to be able to draw a distinction between the use of the two marks—with the hyphens being used to mark strong interruptions, occurring at syntactically awkward moments, and the commas being used to mark those that are less brutal, occurring at moments when transition is relevant—no such distinction exists. There are several cases—and 'Now by *Appollo*' is one of them—at which the weaker mark is used when we would expect the stronger. The terminal comma has a wider range of uses in Q1 than the triple hyphen and is far more common, but the two marks are to some extent interchangeable. The most likely reason for this is (again) the poverty of type.

[43] Toner, *Signs of Omission*, pp. 40–1. These are (signature followed by line number, then, in parentheses, scene and line numbers from the NOS): D3v, 24 (6.26); D4r, 1 (6.40); F1r, 30 (7.314); G2v, 30 (11.113); G3v, 33 (13.17); H1r, 30 (14.31); H1v, 9 (14.49); H1v, 29 (14.69); H2v, 1 (15.11); H4r, 26 (16.67); I2r, 11 (19.22).

Despite being newly purchased, the type used to set Q1 contained no dashes and only a limited number of hyphens.[44] Since hyphens are also needed for hyphenated words and for turnovers, it makes sense to husband them carefully. So one way of reading the comma after '*Appollo*', and others like it, is as a typographical expedient. Keen to mark Kent's interruption but unwilling to lavish three hyphens on it, the compositor resorts to a comma to make up the shortfall. It is noticeable that all eleven triple hyphens occur in the work of compositor B—the more experienced of the two, who may have felt more confident about reckoning his type. There is some evidence, too, that they cluster around points in the text at which the type has been redistributed, as though B were more willing to use one when he knew his case was about to be replenished or to splash out in a moment of extravagance just after it had been.[45]

*   *   *

What the bibliographical context tells us, then, is that there is good reason to expect—at this point in the text—that a comma might be used to do the work of a triple hyphen. What the dramatic context tells us is that there is good reason to expect—at this point in the dialogue— that Kent may be interrupting Lear.

Notice, first, that the altercation between the two men is itself a form of interruption. The king is in the process of disowning his youngest daughter when Kent intervenes to plead on her behalf. In the twenty-two turns prior to Kent's intervention, no character has spoken without having been selected to do so by the king. Lear is the perfect orchestrator—demanding speech from each of his daughters in his turn and requiring them to perform before a silent and attentive audience of courtiers. Enraged by

---

[44] Blayney, p. 533. He finds no more than fifty-three hyphens, or 'en-rules', in use at any one time.

[45] The second of the two commas under consideration here (at B3r, 17) occurs ten pages before the first distribution of type (at C4r, 7) and seventeen pages before the first triple hyphen (at D3v, 24). Other distributions occur at D3v, 33 (nine lines after the first triple hyphen), at H1v, 29 (with three triple hyphens within a page), at H3r, 24 (two lines before a triple hyphen), and at I1v, 31 (fourteen lines before a triple hyphen). The line-number given for a distribution is that by which it *must* have occurred, owing to the recurrence of a recognizable piece of type, not that at which it necessarily did occur. For further details see Blayney, pp. 528–30.

Cordelia's refusal to play her part in this spectacle, he unleashes a tirade of abuse which ends with him declaring her his 'sometime daughter'. Before she can reply—or perhaps because she does not—Kent coughs up a vocative:

> *Kent.* Good my Liege.
> *Lear.* Peace *Kent*, come not between the Dragon &
> (his wrath,
> (B2v, 1.105–6)

What he says is not a complete sentence, so it is no surprise to find the play's editors adding a dash after 'Liege' to signal that Lear interrupts him. The full stop common to all three early texts does not rule this possibility out, but it is equally possible that 'Good my Liege' is a complete turn at talk. If so, it is the opening move in what a conversation analyst would call a 'pre-sequence'.[46] Kent is requesting permission to speak—he will go ahead only if Lear gives him the green light to do so. By testing the waters in this way, Kent is hoping to mitigate the rudeness of his intervention. As a trusted adviser, perhaps he feels he has earned the right to intervene, so long as he does so tactfully. Now, however, is not the time. Lear rejects his request and turns away, apostrophizing Kent to address, first, a servant, and then his two sons-in-law. Undeterred, Kent intervenes again:

> *Kent.* Royall *Lear*,
> Whom I haue euer honor'd as my King,
> Loued as my Father, as my maister followed,
> As my great patron thought on in my prayers.
> *Lear.* The bow is bent & drawen make from the shaft,
> (B2v, 1.123–7)

By doing so Kent progresses from speaking without having been spoken to—already a risky business—to speaking when he has been told not to. He attempts to mitigate the rudeness of his intervention, this time, with an elaborately courtly address—a form of words which simultaneously flatters the king and reminds him of Kent's loyalty,

---

[46] Schegloff, *Sequence Organization in Interaction*, pp. 28–57.

a loyalty which entitles him to an audience. The sentence has not yet reached its main verb when Lear issues him with a second warning to be quiet. It is at this moment that the disputed comma occurs. It marks the duke's third attempt to speak and the first time he has succeeded in getting past the preliminaries. It is followed by an eleven-line speech in which Kent makes explicit reference to his not having 'dread to speake' and describes his own behaviour as 'vnmannerly', in which he switches from addressing the king as 'Good my Liege' and 'Royall *Lear*' to addressing him as 'thou' and 'ould man', and in which he tells the king that his behaviour is 'folly'. Lear makes two further attempts to stop Kent before calling on the gods, at which point we get the second terminal comma (after '*Appollo*')—this one generally accepted as an interruption.

What we have, then, is an escalating series of interruptions. Kent progresses from speaking without licence to speaking when forbidden, from jumping in at a transition-relevance place to cutting the king off after only three words. The two terminal commas are an attempt to chart this progression—both of them marking transitions that are in some way interruptive. Not, however, in quite the same way, and it is this that causes problems for the play's editors. The contemporary dash is the typographical embodiment of the model of conversation outlined by McKerrow—a model which assumes a binary distinction between 'completed' speeches and those which are 'left incomplete'. To use one in place of the comma would be to produce a text that peaked, typographically, too early—that erased the dizzying sense of escalation crucial to this stand-off by going straight for the interruptional jugular. One solution would be to progress from a comma to a dash, and it might be that, with a larger set of type, this is what the compositor would have done. But one of the reasons the terminal comma can substitute for a triple hyphen is that it is a more flexible mark. It is partly because it is so flexible that editors pay it so little mind. The compositors of Q1 use the terminal comma in a wider variety of contexts than would be appropriate for a triple hyphen, even if they had all the type in the world. To demonstrate this I want to look at three more pairs of commas, each of which functions in a slightly different way.

*   *   *

Our second pair comes from an equally fraught but less adversarial exchange. This is Edmund, luring his father into the mistaken belief that his other son, Edgar, seeks his life:

> *Glost.* What paper were you reading?
> *Bast.* Nothing my Lord,
> *Glost.* No, what needes then that terrible dispatch of it into your pocket, the qualitie of nothing hath not such need to hide it selfe, lets see, come if it bee nothing I shall not neede spectacles.
>
> (C1v, 2.30–4)

Like the comma after 'shaft', this one tends to be ignored by the play's editors. But it still seems to be active here—to be signal rather than noise. It is possible, of course, that Edmund means to go on speaking and that Gloucester interrupts him. Such an interpretation is always possible, as we have seen, but it is not always probable. Edmund's answer is unsatisfactory from Gloucester's point of view but not obviously incomplete. What the comma seems to indicate has more to do with timing than suspension. It is not that Edmund has more to say but that his father comes in just a fraction of a second early. Harvey Sacks describes something very like what may be happening here in a lecture from the autumn of 1967:

> Now in the case of 'interrupting,' there seem to be parallel sorts of phenomena, such that if, for example, you want to show that something that somebody is saying really angers you, then placing your utterance by starting while they're still talking seems to be more effective than waiting and placing it after they've finished.[47]

One way of showing your impatience in the queue at the post office is to stand slightly closer than usual to the person in front of you. Your physical proximity expresses a sense of urgency that may succeed in hurrying them up (especially if it is part of a larger pantomime involving audible sighs and an ostentatious checking of your watch). But this is not the same thing as trying to usurp the turn of the customer ahead of you while they are still conducting their business at the counter. What Gloucester does is to snap at the heels of Edmund's turn in such a

---

[47] Sacks, *Lectures on Conversation*, I, p. 642.

way as to indicate impatience. This comma indicates overlap rather than interruption.

A few lines later it happens again:

> *Glost.* You know the Caractar to be your brothers?
> *Bast.* If the matter were good, my Lord I durst sweare it were his but in respect, of that I would faine thinke it were not,
> *Glost.* It is his?
> *Bast.* It is his hand my Lord, but I hope his heart is not in the contents.
>
> (C1v, 2.56–61)

Again the terminal comma seems to indicate some sort of urgency in the exchange of turns. Gloucester wants a yes-or-no answer to his question about the handwriting and quickly becomes impatient when he does not seem to be getting one. The transition occurs at a transition-relevance place, but that does not necessarily mean that Edmund has finished. The comma seems to be poised between two alternatives. Edmund may or may not have finished, and Gloucester may or not overlap with him in an attempt to speed things up. Or rather, these two things are not discrete. Edmund may be teasing his father with the possibility that he is about to finish without actually doing so—drawing his response out until the old man interrupts, not to stop his son from talking but to hurry him along. One reason the duke is taken in by these lies is that he mistakenly believes he has had to dig to uncover them. Edmund deliberately slows the pace of the conversion to encourage his father to press him, and by doing so he creates the impression that he has been forced to say more than he intended. Rather than the clash of competing voices, these commas suggest a skilfully staged defeat.

I want to add one further pair of examples before turning my attention to the tricky question of how likely any of these commas is to be authorial. Under instructions from their mistress to 'Put on what wearie negligence you please', Gonoril's servants begin to treat Lear with disrespect:

> *Lear.* Follow mee, thou shalt serue mee, if I like thee no worse after dinner, I will not part from thee yet, dinner, ho dinner, wher's my knaue, my foole, goe you and call my foole hether, you sirra,whers my daughter?

> *Enter Steward.*
> *Steward.* So please you,
> *Lear.* What say's the fellow there, call the clat-pole backe, whers my foole, ho I thinke the world's asleepe, how now, wher's that mungrel?
> *Kent.* He say's my Lord,your daughter is not well.
> *Lear.* Why came not the slaue backe to mee when I cal'd him?
> *seruant.* Sir, hee answered mee in the roundest maner, hee would not.
>
> (C3v–C4r, 4.34–44)

The 'steward' in this exchange is usually taken to be Oswald. The comma at the end of his line becomes a dash in Q2 (made up of five consecutive en-rules) and remains one in F. Most modern editors retain this dash and add the stage direction *Exit*. Rather than answering Lear's question, Oswald mutters the cryptic phrase 'So please you' and leaves the stage. It makes no sense to read this as an interruption, because Lear is waiting for an answer—so much so that he has difficulty comprehending the fact that he does not get one. His first assumption is that he must have misheard Oswald—a steward simply cannot have failed to supply him with the required information. More likely than an interruption, then, is that the comma signifies an aposiopesis of some sort. Oswald does not go so far as to refuse to acknowledge Lear, but what he says remains vague and non-committal, trailing off into nothing as he leaves the stage. Alternatively, the comma might mark the point at which Oswald becomes inaudible, both to Lear and to the audience, rather than the point at which he finishes speaking—and this may or may not be the moment at which his exit from the stage is complete. My point is that the comma seems to have a physical, rather than simply a verbal, significance. It signifies a turn that is in some way affected by action.[48]

Something similar happens once he has been called back in:

> *Lear.* Doe you bandie lookes with me you rascall?
> *Stew.* Ile not be struck my Lord,
> *Kent.* Nor tript neither, you base football player.
>
> (C4r, 4.68–70)

---

[48] Edmund's 'Nothing my Lord,' can also be interpreted in this way, with the comma seeming to signify the hurried dispatch of the letter into his pocket.

This comma becomes a full stop in Q2 and F2 and in most modern editions. Again, it is possible that Oswald means to go on talking and that what interrupts him is Kent's words. But it is equally possible that what interrupts him is physical—the kind of 'sudden occasion' described by Puttenham in his definition of aposiopesis (see p. 162). While it is clear that Kent trips the steward, it is not clear at exactly what point he does so—whether during Oswald's turn, during his own, or at the moment of transition. Once again, the comma seems to be an attempt to indicate action, and it may be that there is no interruption here at all. 'Ile not be struck my Lord' could be all that Oswald has to say, with the terminal comma functioning to indicate that he is tumbling backwards as he says it. As well as occurring at moments when speech becomes urgent, or stilted, terminal commas repeatedly occur at moments of interaction between the verbal and the physical.

In summary, then, the use of terminal commas in Q1 may be inconsistent, but it is not random. There are many occasions on which we might expect a comma that are marked instead with full stop.[49] When they do occur, however, they seem to have a purpose. As well as the various forms of interruption, a terminal comma can signify a snapped or surprised reply, a voice that is hushed or trailing off, or some sort of action disrupting what is said. What it signifies, in short, is a *marked* rather than an *unmarked* transition between two turns. In this respect it is both more flexible and more subtle than its modern equivalents, the dash and ellipsis marks.

*   *   *

This kind of evidence, however, is no more than suggestive. It suggests that Shakespeare may sometimes have employed terminal commas in manuscript and that some of his commas may have found their way into the text of Q1—along with others that are scribal or compositorial and others that are mistakes. In order to argue that any particular comma has a Shakespearean origin, we need to show that it is dramatically necessary, like the mispunctuation of the mechanicals' prologue in *A Midsummer Night's Dream*. We need to show that punctuation is an issue for the play as well as for the text. Anne Toner has laid the

---

[49] As, for example, at B2v, 34; B3r, 9; E1v, 17; E2r, 22; F2v, 4; H2v, 14.

groundwork for such an argument by suggesting that Gloucester's reference to 'late eclipses in the Sunne and Moone' has punctuational undertones:

> 'Eclipses' in the seventeenth century were grammatical and typographic as much as they were astronomical (and in all of these forms they were exactly homophonic). In contemporary guides to rhetoric, the word 'eclipsis' was more common than 'ellipsis' with which it was interchangeable.[50]

'Eclipsis', according to Puttenham, is a 'figure of defect' in which 'but one word or some little portion of speech be wanting'.[51] Gloucester's use of the word thus hints at the dialogical lacunae in the text—its stutterings and omissions and suspensions—including those, a few lines earlier, in the elliptical remarks of his own son. A second, more explicit, example of a punctuational metaphor, also cited by Toner, occurs at the end of act four, in a brief exchange between Kent and an unnamed gentleman:

> *Kent.* Report is changeable, tis time to looke about,
> The powers of the kingdome approach apace.
> *Gent.* The arbiterment is like to be bloudie,fare you well sir.
> *Kent.* My poynt and period will be throughly wrought,
> Or well, or ill, as this dayes battels fought.
>
> (K2v–K3r, 21.90–94)

Kent imagines his path through life as a lengthy sentence struggling to reach its 'poynt and period'. This is appropriate enough for a man (still in disguise) who has been the victim of a torturously convoluted narrative syntax since the moment he dared to interrupt his master. Now everything hangs, like a conditional clause, on the outcome of the final battle—or so Kent thinks.

Curiously, however, Toner does not cite the third and final occurrence of a punctuational metaphor in the play. This occurs in the last scene, as Edgar, Edmund, and Albany try to unravel the several strands of action that have led them to the current disaster. Edgar has just recounted how he met and nursed his blind father until 'some halfe hour passed' when

---

[50] Toner, *Signs of Omission*, p. 44.
[51] Puttenham, *The Arte of English Poesie*, sig. T2v.

the old man's heart 'Burst smillingly' at the revelation of his son's identity. This is how the other three characters respond:

> *Bast.* This speech of yours hath moued me,
> And shall perchance do good,but speake you on,
> You looke as you had something more to say,
>   *Alb.* If there be more, more wofull, hold it in,
> For I am almost ready to dissolue, hearing of this,
>   *Edg.* This would haue seemd a periode to such
> As loue not sorow,but another to amplifie too much,
> Would make much more, and top extreamitie
>
>   (L2v, 24.196–204)

Edgar's observation that this 'would haue seemd a periode' comes after two consecutive turns, each of which—despite seeming to require a full stop—has ended with a comma. Neither comma lends itself easily to modernization. Both are hardened into full stops by Halio, Weis, Wells and Taylor, and Orgel. But they are apt to this breathless exchange of news and consistent with the usage established in the rest of Q1. Overcome with emotion, and exhausted by the duel with Edmund, Edgar is momentarily unable to speak but ends his turn in such a way as to indicate he has more to say. An actor could play him choking back a sob and gesturing with a hand, for example. Alternatively, Edmund's sudden announcement that he has been 'moued' may signal an interruption—unable to contain himself at the story of his father's death, he breaks in on his brother's narrative only to withdraw self-consciously a moment later ('I'm so sorry—do go on. You look like you have something more to say'). Albany might be correcting Edmund in a further interruption or joining him, after a pause, in urging Edgar to go on. Albany's words simultaneously require a response from Edgar and express a reluctance to hear more. The commas seem to capture this painful ambiguity. They are signs, that is, not of suspension but of suspense.

The effect is more than local. The two commas usher in the final phase of the plot—a phase governed by the metaphor of the withheld period. From this point onwards the characters (and perhaps, at their suggestion, the audience) begin to look for the 'promist end'. Their breakings-off and gropings for closure are the dramatic counterpoint to the interruptions and rifts with which the play began. And they are alive in the same way in the commas that both divide and join their turns at talk. The terminal comma has become a perforated divide, a breaking dam, unable to keep one turn separate from another. Words slide across it, from one mouth to the next—'**more** to say, | *Alb.* If there be **more, more** wofull', 'hearing of **this**, *Edg.* | **This** would haue seemd'. Instead of cutting each other off before they can finish, the characters are urging each other on to a conclusion—as if following their words through to a period could somehow put a stop to what is happening. Edgar's metaphor suggests a kind of dramatic syntax at work in the unravelling of these events. The situation has become like a sentence that appears to be grammatically complete—that has reached a transition-relevance place—but to which the author keeps adding new clauses, each announcing a further disaster. It seems unlikely that this moment would just happen to coincide with two consecutive misprints, each of which enacts precisely the metaphor under discussion. Whoever placed these two commas here, the marks are not accidental. The only question is whether the compositor found them in his copy or had the happy inspiration to insert them himself. Given that they occur in the work of compositor C—generally thought to be an apprentice—I think the latter is unlikely.

One final objection, one final response, and then I'll rest. Unlike the mispunctuation of the mechanicals' prologue, these commas are unperformable. No one watching the play could be aware of the interplay between plot, metaphor, and punctuation which I have just described. This is true, but it need not constitute an objection. Shakespeare was a literary as well as a theatrical dramatist, and it is likely that the plays as they were originally performed may have differed from the printed texts we now have. It is likely, too, that some of these texts are closer to performance than others.[52] So it is worth noticing that this metaphor, which occurs twice in the closing scenes of the play—each time with striking dramatic prominence—is unique to Q1. Neither Kent's reference to his 'poynt and period' nor Edgar's reference to what 'would haue seemd a periode' appears in the Folio text. The strand of metaphor that seems to highlight the terminal commas in Q1—that makes the play itself a

---

[52] See Lukas Erne, *Shakespeare as Literary Dramatist*, 2nd edn (Cambridge: Cambridge University Press, 2013), especially the final chapter, 'Theatricality, literariness, and the texts of *Romeo and Juliet*, *Henry V*, and *Hamlet*', pp. 244–68.

struggle towards a withheld period—disappears from the text along with those commas.

* * *

If the argument I have just put forward appears as plausible to the reader as it does to me, I hope to have persuaded her of two things— that some of the commas in the first quarto of *King Lear* may be authorial, and that Shakespeare may have employed the terminal comma as part of his working practice. This is progress, I think, in our understanding of Shakespearean punctuation, but the victory may seem Pyrrhic. All I have succeeded in doing is to add one further example to a list that now consists of two special cases of authorial punctuation—the mechanicals' prologue in *A Midsummer Night's Dream* and the final scene of Q1 *King Lear*—and even this has only been possible off the back of the herculean bibliographical efforts of Peter Blayney. It remains the case, however much we might wish it were otherwise, that the punctuation of Shakespeare's plays is fundamentally inconsistent and unreliable. We can look to it for help, but the evidence it provides must always be treated with suspicion. If we want to know how transitions between turns at talk are timed in these plays, or when one person is interrupting another, we must look elsewhere.

| 8 |

The Play of Line and Turn

A fragment of Housman's 'Fragment of a Greek Tragedy':

> *Cho.* To learn your name would not displease me much.
> 15 *Alc.* Not all that men desire do they obtain.
> *Cho.* Might I then hear at what your presence shoots?
> *Alc.* A shepherd's questioned mouth informed me that—
> *Cho.* What? for I know not yet what you will say.
> *Alc.* Nor will you ever, if you interrupt.
> 20 *Cho.* Proceed, and I will hold my speechless tongue.
> *Alc.* —This house was Eriphyla's, no one's else.[1]

My interest here is the apparently self-defeating interruption in line 18. Having asked the stranger at what his presence 'shoots', the Chorus cuts him off halfway through the answer. It interrupts Alcmaeon to ask him what he is about to say—to ask him what he has been prevented from saying only by the fact it has interrupted. Three kinds of evidence support this reading. First, Alcmaeon makes sarcastic reference to the Chorus's habit of interrupting. Second, the transition is marked with a dash, which by the nineteenth century had long been established as the conventional mark for interruptions in a dramatic text. Third, the

---

[1] *The Poems of A. E. Housman*, ed. by Archie Burnett (Oxford: Clarendon Press, 1997), p. 245.

transition occurs at a syntactically awkward moment, between the introduction of reported speech and the speech itself. Notice, too, how the suspended syntax is picked up again in line 21, after a second dash. On the face of it, then, this is an unambiguous case. Syntax, punctuation, and an explicit reference within the dialogue all combine to make it clear that Alcmaeon has not finished speaking when the Chorus starts. Or so it would appear. What complicates matters is that the exchange is written in verse. More specifically, it is written in stichomythia, a dramatic convention in which a dialogical unit—the turn—and a metrical unit—the line—are temporarily fused. Alcmaeon has no choice but to stop speaking when he does, and the Chorus has no choice but to start, because in a stichomythic exchange every turn is exactly one line in length. The transition may be interactionally premature, but metrically it is right on time.

The result is a form of dramatic irony. The reader can see, and an audience could hear, the strict alternation of turns, but it seems to take the characters by surprise. Alcmaeon embarks on a two-line answer to the Chorus's question, apparently unaware of the one-line maximum in operation. He reaches the line end at full speed, as it were, like a dog reaching the end of its lead, and is choked to a halt by the metre. The Chorus, on the other hand, acts more like a drunk waking up in his chair—blurting out 'What?' before it quite knows what is happening and filling up the rest of the line with a feeble attempt to rationalize its own unnecessary exclamation. The joke lies less in the self-defeating nature of the interruption than in the inability of the two characters to comprehend the reasons for their own turn-taking behaviour. Or rather, the joke lies in the shifts to which Housman's fictional tragedian puts them in order to fulfil the requirements of the form. The answer Alcmaeon is required to give is too long for the turn into which it is required to fit, so the playwright snaps it in half. Since these two halves cannot sit next to each other, and their jagged edges must somehow be accounted for, he clumsily stuffs them with what looks like an interruption. It's the interactional equivalent of the expletives lampooned by Pope.[2] The unmotivated interjection lends its feeble aid to the dialogue

---

[2] *Poems of Alexander Pope, Volume 1: Pastoral Poetry and an Essay on Criticism*, ed. by E. Audra and Aubrey Williams, The Twickenham Edition of the Poems of Alexander Pope (London: Methuen, 1961), p. 278 (l. 346).

by padding it out with an extra turn at talk in much the same way as the extra syllable provided by a periphrastic *do* pads out a line of verse.

What the example shows is that the timing of a transition between speakers can be metrically loaded—that it can be made to sound early or late, or timely, depending on its position in the line. There is a 'play of line and turn' at work in Shakespeare's dialogue every bit as important as the celebrated 'play of phrase and line'.[3] At one end of the spectrum is stichomythia, in which the turn and line are one. At the other is the rangy, elastic, and occasionally inaudible blank verse of late Shakespeare, in which the 'sentences run increasingly from midline to midline' and transitions between turns often occur in a metrical no man's land of 'squinting' fragments that could just as easily be prose.[4] Rather than set the line and the turn flatly and comically at variance, as Housman does here, Shakespeare arranges for them to nudge and nag at one another in a variety of more subtle and suggestive ways.

This chapter will explore some of those suggestions in two short exchanges: one from *Antony and Cleopatra* and one from *Othello*. What the two examples have in common is that they each depict a conversation in which one character seems to dominate another. Metrically, however, they are handled quite differently, and, whether we realize it or not, these differences have implications for the ways in which we read the dialogue. Having been warned in Chapters 5–7 of the deep ambiguity of the Shakespearean text, with its lack of stage directions and its unreliable punctuation, the reader may be relieved, in this final chapter, to be given more hopeful news. On the page, dramatic dialogue lacks much of what we rely on in real conversation to help us time and interpret transitions between turns. When it is written in verse, however, it has at least one resource for indicating that a speaker has finished which real conversation lacks. Some of what is lost when we try to write conversation down can be put back in by the manipulation of metre—'prosody' in the literary sense can help to compensate for the absence, in written language, of the 'prosodic features' of speech. This is not to say that verse dialogue is inherently less ambiguous than dialogue written in prose. If anything, the extra consideration makes

---

[3] The phrase belongs to George T. Wright, *Shakespeare's Metrical Art* (Berkeley: University of California Press, 1988), pp. 207–28.

[4] Wright, pp. 120, 103.

things more complex. But we do at least have more information, and we can use that information to be a little more precise about the possibilities.

Before getting started, however, some light theoretical housekeeping is in order. It is necessary to consider how the turn-taking model of conversation might be adapted to account for the fact that characters sometimes speak verse. Understandably, this is not something that seems to have occurred to Sacks, Schegloff, and Jefferson. Less understandably, it does not seem to have to occurred, either, to Vimala Herman, Keir Elam, Mick Short, or any of the other literary linguists who engage, however fleetingly, with turn-taking in Shakespearean dialogue. More traditional literary critics have of course produced a large and diverse literature on Shakespeare's metrical art, and they do sometimes engage with questions of turn-timing and transition. But they do not conceive those questions in turn-taking terms. The kind of considerations that are central to my enquiry are incidental, or only fleetingly relevant, to theirs. One thing this chapter hopes to show is that these two approaches can be usefully combined.

The formal description of verse dialogue poses a unique set of problems. Approaching it as verse, we should be mindful of 'the play of phrase and line'. Approaching it as fictional conversation, we should be mindful of the relationship between turn-constructional units and transitions. Moreover, as the fragment from Housman shows, these two things are not independent. Fortunately, the two approaches are not difficult to synthesize. When George T. Wright describes the 'play of phrase and line' in Shakespeare's verse, he is using the word 'phrase' in an extended sense, to include clauses and sentences as well as shorter grammatical units. All we need do, therefore, is stretch the term a little further—to include anything a conversation analyst would describe as a 'turn-constructional unit'. In literary-critical terms, what we have in Shakespearean dialogue is thus 'the play of phrase and line *and turn*'—the interaction of three units rather than two. These can all coincide, as when a single turn is a whole number of lines in length and ends at what is obviously a transition-relevance place, or they can be at variance in a variety of ways—two against one, all three at odds, and so on. In linguistic terms, what we have is the addition of a new kind of turn-constructional unit—another basic set of building blocks (the line, the couplet, the stanza) that can make transition more or less relevant by being complete or incomplete. Whichever way round we choose to look at it, the two approaches dovetail neatly. Things only become complicated when we try to apply them to Shakespearean dialogue.

* * *

My first example is Antony's attempt, in 1.3 of *Antony and Cleopatra*, to inform Cleopatra that he will shortly be leaving for Rome.

> *Enter Antony*
> CHARMIAN [...]
>   But here comes Antony.
> CLEOPATRA   I am sick and sullen.
> ANTONY   I am sorry to give breathing to my purpose.
> 15 CLEOPATRA   Help me away, dear Charmian, I shall fall.
>   It cannot be thus long—the sides of nature
>   Will not sustain it.
> ANTONY   Now, my dearest queen.
> CLEOPATRA   Pray you, stand farther from me.
> ANTONY   What's the matter?
> CLEOPATRA   I know by that same eye there's some good news.
> 20   What says the married woman—you may go?
>   Would she had never given you leave to come!
>   Let her not say 'tis I that keep you here.
>   I have no power upon you; hers you are.
> ANTONY   The gods best know—
> CLEOPATRA   O, never was there queen
> 25   So mightily betrayed! Yet at the first
>   I saw the treasons planted.
> ANTONY   Cleopatra—
> CLEOPATRA   Why should I think you can be mine and true
>   Though you in swearing shake the thronèd gods—
>   Who have been false to Fulvia? Riotous madness,
> 30   To be entangled with those mouth-made vows
>   Which break themselves in swearing.
> ANTONY   Most sweet queen—
> CLEOPATRA   Nay, pray you, seek no colour for your going,
>   But bid farewell and go. When you sued staying,
>   Then was the time for words—no going then.

35   Eternity was in our lips and eyes,
      Bliss in our brow's bent; none our parts so poor
      But was a race of heaven. They are so still,
      Or thou, the greatest soldier of the world,
      Art turned the greatest liar.
ANTONY   How now, lady!
40 CLEOPATRA   I would I had thy inches. Thou shouldst know
      There were a heart in Egypt.
ANTONY   Hear me, Queen:
      The strong necessity of time commands
      Our services a while, but my full heart
      Remains in use with you.

                                        (3[1.3].13–44)

Between the moment at which Antony first mentions his 'purpose'
(l. 14) and the moment at which he succeeds in explaining it (l. 42)
are twenty-eight lines, or thirteen turns at talk. Like the reason for
Alcmaeon's arrival, the news is delayed—held in suspense by the
uncooperative behaviour of his interlocutor. Having guessed what
Antony is about to say—apparently from a look in his eye—Cleopatra
manages to prevent him from saying it until after she has shown him
what her reaction will be. In the spirit of Carwyn James, she gets her
retaliation in first. The question I want to examine in the first part of
this chapter is how she achieves this. The Cleopatra presented by most
modern editors is somewhat brutal in her approach. The New Oxford
edition repunctuates three of Antony's eight turns with dashes—to
indicate interruption—but five is not uncommon.[5] Cleopatra is able
to dominate the conversation, the logic seems to run, because she has
no regard for the rules by which conversation is usually conducted.
Every time Antony opens his mouth, she cuts him off. I want to suggest
that such a reading is unjust, both to the character and to the dramatist.
Cleopatra's ability to hold the floor has more to do with skill than
brutality. Rather than ignore the rules of conversation, she exploits

[5] See, for example, *Antony and Cleopatra*, ed. by David M. Bevington, The New
Cambridge Shakespeare (Cambridge: Cambridge University Press, 1990); *Antony and
Cleopatra*, ed. by John Wilders, The Arden Shakespeare: Third Series (London: Routledge,
1995); and the RSC *Works*.

them. The five transitions that editors harden into dashes are all of them fraught, but they are not all fraught in the same way. The Folio punctuation—five inscrutable full stops—is no more helpful here than its modern replacement. It is only by paying attention to the metrical and syntactical moment at which each transition occurs that we can differentiate between them. What follows will be a more or less chronological examination of the passage, taking each transition in turn and pausing only to fill in some necessary theoretical background.

Antony's first turn, 'I am sorry to give breathing to my purpose', is acceptable grammatically as a complete sentence. It is also acceptable as a complete line, if not a completely regular one. Phrase and line combine to suggest that he has finished speaking. But the referent of 'my purpose' is not yet clear—Antony has only just entered, and this is the first thing he says. His words look forwards rather than back. They project an explanation of what his 'purpose' is which is held in suspense until line 42.[6] Remove the intervening sequence and you get a rough idea of how Antony might have intended the conversation to go:

14   ANTONY   I am sorry to give breathing to my purpose [...]
42   The strong necessity of time commands
           Our services a while, but my full heart
           Remains in use with you.

Everything that happens in that ellipsis has somehow been inserted by Cleopatra. But even if this is what Antony had intended to say, both the syntax and the metre would have encouraged him to pause at the end of line 14. The line itself lingers, awkwardly padding its three unambiguous stresses with nine other syllables. With a little wrenching it will yield five beats—at least one of which would need to be realized by a semantically unmotivated stress on the preposition 'to'—but not six. This is (if anything) an inflated pentameter, not a hexameter line.

---

[6] Something similar has been observed by conversation analysts, specifically in relation to indexicals. According to Stephen E. Clayman, 'utterances that are referentially ambiguous—containing pronouns or other indexicals that cannot be retrieved from the extant context—project further talk to disambiguate what is being said'. These are known in the literature as *prospective indexicals* and 'are usually treated as in-progress or prefatory rather than as units to be responded to in their own right'. See 'Turn-Constructional Units and the Transition-Relevance Place', in Sidnell and Stivers, *The Handbook of Conversation Analysis*, pp. 155–66 (156).

It drags its feet towards the line end and is happy to rest when it gets there. Antony is reluctant to go on because he knows how Cleopatra is likely to react, and it is this reluctance that gives her the opportunity to speak. Yes, he has more to say, and, yes, he would probably have said it had she not interjected, but she is able to come in only because he leaves the door ajar. Notice, too, that when she does speak it is to Charmian rather than Antony—she 'blanks' her lover in the technical sense I have suggested for that word (see pp. 46–7). This move is characteristic of the queen, who uses Charmian in much the same way that Dora Spenlow uses Jip—repeatedly turning to her at opportune moments in order to delay, distract, or make an elaborate show of not listening to her interlocutor.[7] Like Jip, Charmian rarely replies—not because she is a dog, but because she understands her role as a conversational stooge. Despite timing her interruption with such precision, Cleopatra pretends not to have heard the turn she is interrupting. As well as preventing Antony from going on, she obliges him to start again.

Antony does so, but not from the beginning. His second attempt begins even earlier, with what a conversation analyst would call a *pre-sequence*: 'Now, my dearest queen'. More specifically, he begins with the kind of pre-sequence known as a 'summons'.[8] The function of a summons is to mitigate the vulnerability of the following turn to 'impaired uptake, hearing, or understanding' by securing the attention of the addressee before it starts.[9] It is precisely this vulnerability that allowed Cleopatra to wriggle off the hook first time around. She was able to exploit the ambiguity over whether or not she had heard Antony—whether or not they were yet in conversation at all—to derail his attempts to break the bad news. The problem with a summons, from Antony's point of view, is that it requires a response—at least in the sense that the addressee should demonstrate attentiveness to the speaker and a readiness to hear what follows. The kind of response Antony is looking for is minimal—a turn of the head or an exasperated 'yes'—but by insisting that Cleopatra give him her attention, he has again

---

[7] See, for example, David's first interview with Dora in the garden at Norwood, in Charles Dickens, *David Copperfield*, ed. by Jeremy Tambling (London: Penguin, 1996), pp. 366–8.

[8] Schegloff, *Sequence Organization in Interaction*, p. 28n.

[9] Schegloff, *Sequence Organization in Interaction*, p. 48.

given her the opportunity to speak. Instead of using that opportunity to confirm she is listening, she uses it to ask him to 'stand farther from' her. Two of Antony's subsequent turns (at lines 26 and 31) can be read in the same way—as attempted summons that effectively give the floor back to Cleopatra. Rather than interrupting him, she is refusing to orient herself to Antony as a speaker—withholding the 'go ahead, I'm listening' signal for which his vocatives repeatedly call—and exploiting the openings they provide to pursue her own conversational goals.

Once again, the timing of the transition is metrically loaded. Antony's turn is only five syllables long, but it follows a five-syllable line at the end of Cleopatra's previous speech. One way of hearing it, then, is as the second half of a shared line, ending exactly where we would expect it to. Taken together, these two half-lines fit snugly into the mould of an iambic pentameter ('Will not sustain it. Now, my dearest queen.') providing a brief moment of metrical regularity in the otherwise unpredictable verse of this play. To the extent that the metre can nudge us in one direction or another, it is nudging us towards hearing Antony's turn as complete. Dramatically too, the metrical cohesion makes sense. Antony is walking on eggshells, eager to break the news to Cleopatra as painlessly as possible. So he frames his turn to fit with hers—gives a rhythmical form to the physical posture and facial expression that might otherwise suggest conciliation. He fills in around Cleopatra rather than trying to make space for himself, the shared line a symptom of his sheepishness.

Shared lines are crucial to the exchange from this point onwards. Five of Antony's six subsequent turns can be heard as beginning, and the other one as ending, part way through a line. Modern editors overwhelmingly hear them this way and indent the second half of each shared line, as the New Oxford editors do here, to show that it is a continuation of the first:

15 CLEOPATRA   Help me away, dear Charmian, I shall fall.
        It cannot be thus long—the sides of nature
        Will not sustain it.
     ANTONY   Now, my dearest queen.

Even a sceptical editor, such as David Bevington, who believes that 'the editorial tradition has too complacently linked half-lines [. . .] to produce what seem to be whole lines of verse', does not see this particular exchange as controversial.[10] Antony and Cleopatra, so the logic runs, are speaking in iambic pentameter—when one of them stops part way through a line, the other has no choice but to complete it, just as Alcmaeon has no choice but to stop at the line end when speaking in stichomythia. I want to suggest that the situation is not quite this simple, but to do so I will need to digress, briefly, into the vexed question of 'white spaces' in Shakespeare.[11]

*   *   *

The introduction of white space into Shakespeare's text began with Edward Capell in 1768 and quickly gained acceptance—reaching its apogee twenty-five years later in George Steevens' variorum edition—since when it has been a 'standard feature' of Shakespearean typography.[12] The convention went without serious challenge until the twentieth century, when several scholars, most notably Paul Bertram, began to question its logic. Despite the title of Bertram's monograph, *White Spaces in Shakespeare*, his argument is as much about metre as typography, and a failure to distinguish these two things properly—related though they obviously are—has hampered the discussion ever since. Bertram had called for a return to the lineation of the Folio. Paul Werstine exploded his argument by conclusively showing that the Folio is riddled with examples of 'compositorial mislining'.

> To accept Bertram's argument that metrically linked speeches reflect eighteenth-century practice, not Shakespeare's, one must ignore the example of Ben Jonson and dismiss as lucky accidents the hundreds of cases in the early printed texts of Shakespeare's plays in which successive short lines can be linked together to form perfect pentameters.[13]

Both men confuse the practice of writing metrically linked speeches with the practice of presenting such speeches so that their metrical links are apparent on the page. The 'hundreds of cases' to which Werstine

[10] Bevington (ed.), *Antony and Cleopatra*, p. 72.
[11] The phrase belongs to Paul Bertram, *White Spaces in Shakespeare: The Development of the Modern Text* (Cleveland, Ohio: Bellflower Press, 1981).
[12] Lukas Erne, *Shakespeare's Modern Collaborators*, Shakespeare Now! (London: Continuum, 2008), p. 27.
[13] Paul Werstine, 'Line Division in Shakespeare's Dramatic Verse: An Editorial Problem', *Analytical and Enumerative Bibliography*, 8 (1984), 73–125 (p. 111).

refers are evidence that Shakespeare does indeed write shared lines. How we deal with those lines typographically is a separate question. That the example of Ben Jonson should weigh more heavily than the example of the early texts of Shakespeare's own plays is by no means obvious.[14] Nor does it follow from the fact that the lineation of the Folio is frequently erroneous that the conventions of lineation it employs should be discarded. The Folio convention is to set all speeches to the left-hand margin, regardless of their metrical status. 'On a purely visual level', as one recent scholar has remarked, the Folio arrangement suggests (at least to the modern reader) that successive short lines are prose. Indentation, on the other hand, 'has the considerable merit of making visible the metrical structure of divided lines'.[15] This is true, but it may be more true now, after two hundred years of indentation, than it was for Shakespeare's earliest readers. The semiotics of the dramatic text have changed since 1623, and the introduction of white space is both a result of this change and one of its causes. Where white space is expected, its absence means prose—but this is the product of the expectation rather than the writing. Where no white space is expected, the reader must listen—rather than look—for metrical links between turns. The advantage of indentation is that it saves him this trouble.

But the added clarity comes at a cost. It enforces a binary distinction between verse and prose, and between lines that are shared and lines that are not, which is not always true to Shakespeare's practice. The point is most obvious in cases of three consecutive short lines, the second of which can be combined with either of the other two. As David Bevington has suggested,

> the frequency (especially in the late plays) of such sequences of three half-lines suggests that Shakespeare may have regarded such versification as perfectly correct in its indeterminacy. [...] The editorial impulse to choose one of the two possibilities at the expense of the other may well misrepresent the author's intention.[16]

---

[14] Werstine repeats the claim a few lines later: 'In Jonson's practice, editors of Shakespeare can find good reason for arranging short lines to display metrical linking' ('Line Division in Shakespeare's Dramatic Verse', p. 118).

[15] Erne, *Shakespeare's Modern Collaborators*, p. 27.

[16] Bevington (ed.), *Antony and Cleopatra*, p. 266. He provides a range of interesting examples from the play.

But this is not just an 'impulse' that an editor could choose to resist—it is a constraint imposed on her by the white space convention. She does not have the option to leave the metrical relationship of the lines indeterminate because, unless she indents at least one of them, she signals that they are prose. To put it more sharply, the convention does not account for cases of metrical ambiguity, and such cases do exist in Shakespeare, often with good reason.

The only major edition of Shakespeare in recent memory to dispense with white space is Bate and Rasmussen's RSC *Complete Works*. It does so, however, on slightly different grounds. The editors chose to abandon the convention since 'the Folio does not use it, and nor did actors' cues in the Shakespearean theatre'.[17] The choice is owing, then, to the specific demands of an edition which aims to present 'the First Folio for modern readers' and to do so with a special emphasis on acting and performance.[18] Whatever the rationale, however, the RSC *Works* shows that it is not too late to change our minds about white space. One scene that might benefit from such a change is 1.3 of *Antony and Cleopatra*.

* * *

Here is Antony's third attempt to break the bad news:

CLEOPATRA   Pray you, stand farther from me.
ANTONY   What's the matter?
CLEOPATRA   I know by that same eye there's some good news.
20   What says the married woman—you may go?
     Would she had never given you leave to come!

The first two turns are again printed as one line, and the reasoning behind it is not hard to discern. They are sandwiched between the neatly metrical shared line already discussed and a longer speech which is unambiguously in verse. Together they constitute eleven syllables— not unusual for a line in late Shakespeare, especially with a feminine ending. So both the position of the potentially shared line and its length would suggest that what we have here is another pair of metrically linked turns. Rhythmically, however, the composite line is awkward.

[17] RSC *Works*, 'User's Guide', p. 58.
[18] RSC *Works*, p. 1.

Cleopatra's seven syllables are not easily resolved into iambs. The dominant stresses in her part of the line are on 'stand' and 'pray'. In classical terms, the first foot is either a trochee or a spondee, the second is a spondee, and the third can be made into an iamb only by stressing the preposition 'from'. Remove these seven syllables from their context and it is unlikely that anyone will recognize them as the first part of a blank verse line. Rather than hear her words as an act of metrical cooperation, then, it is possible to hear them as an act of metrical sabotage. Precisely in order to reject Antony's conciliatory completion of her previous line, Cleopatra drops into prose. As soon as he catches the melody of her speech, she changes her tune.

Cleopatra's half line can be made to fit the metre but only by someone who is determined to hear it that way. Someone like Antony, for example. The four syllables he adds are a perfectly shaped ending to an imperfectly shaped line. He rounds out the numbers and re-establishes the lost iambic pulse, recasting what might have been prose as a mere rhythmical glitch. Rather than abandon his policy of conciliation, he redoubles his effort. My point is not that we do not have a shared line here but that the characters seem to disagree about what they are doing metrically. They are quarrelling *over* metre as well as in it. The problem with the white space convention is that it forces us to side with one character or the other—to accept either Cleopatra's view of the situation or Antony's. The Folio convention lets us hear it both ways at once. Or rather, it lets us hear, in the tension between these two possibilities, the tension between the two characters at this moment in the dialogue.

I am conscious that this argument, while neat enough in its way, may seem far-fetched. So it may be worth providing a second, more obvious, example to show that arguing over metre is something that characters in Shakespeare do. Compare Hamlet and Gertrude:

> QUEEN   Good Hamlet, cast thy nighted colour off,
>   And let thine eye look like a friend on Denmark.
> 70   Do not for ever with thy veilèd lids
>   Seek for thy noble father in the dust.
>   Thou know'st 'tis common: all that lives must die,
>   Passing through nature to eternity.
> HAMLET   Ay, madam, it is common.

QUEEN   If it be,
75   Why seems it so particular with thee?
HAMLET   'Seems', madam? Nay, it is. I know not 'seems'.[19]
                                        (2[1.2].68–76)

The relation of the mother's turn to the son's is that of a balloon to a pin. Gertrude offers Hamlet a platitude in the form of a rhyming couplet—its neatness suggesting both the inevitability (to her) of its logic and the emptiness (to him) of its recitation—and, semantically at least, he seems to accept it. But the line in which he does so is short and not obviously iambic. It begins with two stressed syllables, followed by a slack, before pausing for a comma after 'madam'. Only a very eccentric actor would choose to stress the word 'it' over 'is'. On their own, these seven syllables do not sound like part of a blank verse line—they are pointedly prosaic (or common) in contrast to the glib and artificial chime of Gertrude's couplet. Hamlet's superficial acceptance of his mother's point is undercut, in other words, by a form of rhythmical sarcasm. Her response is to fill out his line in the same way that Antony fills out Cleopatra's. But Gertrude goes further—she envelops her son's words within a second, and even more jarringly insistent, couplet. How far this is a genuine attempt to comfort him, and how far it is an attempt to paper over the cracks in their relationship for the sake of the watching Danish court, is difficult to judge. What matters is that the conflict is played out, exactly as it is in *Antony and Cleopatra*, through the metrically ambiguous relation of one turn to another. Shakespeare frequently exploits this possibility to stage miniature dramas along the length of the line—to suggest voices which are in and out of tune with one another, finding, losing, offering, and rejecting metrical union. The two different ways of hearing each line are what make such moments dramatic.

*   *   *

Once the subject of Antony's departure has been broached—but before he has said a word on the matter himself—the conversation changes gear:

---

[19] The importance of the couplets in this exchange is the subject of an unpublished lecture by Eric Griffiths, to whom I am here indebted. The observations on metre, and the application of this example to the debate about white space, are my own.

CLEOPATRA   I know by that same eye there's some good news.
20   What says the married woman—you may go?
        Would she had never given you leave to come!
        Let her not say 'tis I that keep you here.
        I have no power upon you; hers you are.
ANTONY   The gods best know—
CLEOPATRA   O, never was there queen
25   So mightily betrayed! Yet at the first
        I saw the treasons planted.

Having forced Antony to abandon his attempts to break the awful news, at least temporarily, and to accept that her ill health should take priority, Cleopatra changes direction, launching a tirade, in verse, on precisely the subject she has prevented him from introducing. She claims to know already what Antony will say, she regrets that he ever came to Egypt, she replies to an imagined accusation from his wife, she disclaims her ability to influence him, she declares herself betrayed, and she admits that she saw it all coming. Most interestingly, from my point of view, she also asks him a question ('What says the married woman—you may go?'). If Antony is so keen to explain what has happened, why doesn't he answer it? It is not enough to say that the question is rhetorical because, as we have seen, whether or not a question is rhetorical is not entirely up to the speaker. Unlike Volumnia at the gates of Rome, Cleopatra is not addressing a reluctant interlocutor. Her question goes right to the heart of the subject at hand. She knows, and we know, that Antony is desperate to speak. Everything suggests that a transition should occur here, but somehow it does not.

Some editors have concluded that the text is corrupt. Troubled by the word 'may' where they would have expected the word 'must', they follow Rowe in bringing the question-mark forward to the midline ('What says the married woman? You may go!'). In this reading, Cleopatra harnesses the line's rhythmical impetus to get her safely past the transition-relevance place. She does so not by answering the question herself but by responding to what she assumes the answer will be. There is a phantom turn, as it were, between 'What says the married woman?' and 'You may go!'. This explanation has its logic, but the textual intervention is unnecessary. By phrasing the question in exactly the way she does, Cleopatra gives Antony two alternatives, neither of which he wants to take. 'Yes' means that Fulvia has said he can leave. To say this is to admit both that he wants to leave and that he needs his wife's permission to do so—to admit the charge of being henpecked. 'No' means that Fulvia has not said he can leave. To say this is to imply that he is not leaving—which, of course, he is. Finally, and most importantly, Fulvia is dead. She has not said anything at all. It is by placing Antony on the horns of this dilemma that Cleopatra manages to retain control of the floor. Research into response-times in a variety of languages has shown that speakers 'display inhibition in producing responses that in some way fail to conform with the terms of the question or with the questioner's agenda'.[20] People hesitate before giving a negative answer or refusing to give an answer in the expected form. Cleopatra seems to know this, and she exploits it here to prevent Antony from speaking while appearing to give him the chance to do so. A pair of actors might choose to draw the moment out, so that Antony stands with his mouth half open, visibly searching for a way to phrase his response, or they might choose for Cleopatra to maintain her blistering interactional pace—the tiniest flicker of a facial expression from Antony and she is off again, running. What matters is the contrast between her interactional reflexes and his. Cleopatra is able to take any opportunity he gives her to effect a transition—Antony hesitates even when one is dangled in front of him.

When Antony does manage to speak again, it is from the beginning of a fresh line—the first time since line 14 that he has had this opportunity. The basic pattern since then has been for him to make do with the space Cleopatra leaves him. She smokes three-quarters of a line before tossing him the dog-end and lighting up another. Metrically, then, line 24 is Antony's best chance to say what he has to say since the conversation began. He at least has his own line in which to do so. It is no surprise therefore that his first four words sound like the beginning of a suitably grand pronouncement in a suitably thumping verse.

ANTONY   The gods best know [...]

The strong emphasis on 'gods' in the second syllable and on 'know' in the fourth establishes a clear iambic beat, even in this rump of a line.

---

[20] Stivers, et al., 'Universals and Cultural Variation', p. 10588.

That's as far as Antony gets, however. It is possible, of course, that 'The gods best know' is all he had intended to say—that the phrase is an aphorism (a pious Roman alternative to 'Mother knows best'). Grammatically, the verb 'know' can be either transitive or intransitive, so his syntax is not necessarily suspended. The simpler explanation, however, is that Antony is about to explain what it is that the gods best know— 'The gods best know the power you have upon me', 'The gods best know you need not Fulvia fear', or some other such attempt to stem the tide of Cleopatra's reproaches. Line and phrase combine, on this occasion, to suggest that the turn is incomplete, that what we have is a full-blown interruption, and that the dash favoured by modern editors is justified. As in the exchange between Kent and Lear, however, full interruption is something towards which the dialogue builds—to see interruptions everywhere is to flatten out its interactional dynamic.

Antony's four remaining turns are two of them attempts at initiating a summons–response sequence (a feeble ruse against an interlocutor of Cleopatra's speed and skill) and one of them an expression of astonishment at having been called the world's greatest liar. The other, in which he finally succeeds in stopping Cleopatra, is a direct imperative:

ANTONY   Hear me, Queen
    The strong necessity of time commands
    Our services a while, but my full heart
    Remains in use with you.

This is, in a sense, another summons. It calls for attention, as a summons does, but assumes that this attention will be granted rather than asking for confirmation that it has been. 'Shut up and listen!' and 'Are you listening?' are pragmatically close, but it is easier to answer back to one of them than the other. Like all summons, however, Antony's imperative leaves an opening. It also occurs at the line end and is marked in the Folio by a colon. Metrically, syntactically, and typographically, a pause is suggested. That Cleopatra does not take this opportunity to speak—an opportunity no better than the previous seven she has taken—requires some explanation. The most obvious reading is that Antony loses patience at precisely this point and reinforces the imperative by shouting, a reading that is strengthened by the diminishing tenderness with which he addresses her—'my dearest queen', 'Cleopatra', 'Most sweet queen', 'How now, lady!', 'Hear me,

Queen'. This pause is a kind of check (in both senses) to see if Cleopatra is silent and whether she dare defy him. A second explanation, not mutually exclusive with the first, is that she has said what she wanted to say and is ready to hear the worst. Or perhaps her whole purpose has been to provoke Antony's rage, and, having succeeded, Cleopatra sits back to admire her handiwork. It remains moot, therefore, whether he finally succeeds in seizing the turn for which he has waited or whether she hands it to him.

A lesser dramatist, or even an earlier Shakespeare, would simply have written a speech here—guessing what Antony has come to tell her, Cleopatra would throw herself into a rhetorical set piece. Or he would have written the exchange as the editorial tradition is keen to read it, with Antony as a kind of bystander at the spectacle of Cleopatra's anger—putting his feeble oar in only to see it snapped off. What Shakespeare has written is a delicate game of cat and mouse, in which Cleopatra keeps Antony off guard by repeatedly switching tack—from verse to prose, from ignoring him to engaging with him, from refusing to talk about it to refusing to stop. She floats like a butterfly and stings like a bee, repeatedly seeming to invite Antony in—by asking him a question or leaving space for him at the end of a line—before gliding back out of range.

* * *

My second example is from 3.3 of *Othello*. Having worked Othello into a jealous rage, Iago tries, or pretends to try, to reason him out of it:

<pre>
OTHELLO   Ha, ha, false to me?
IAGO   Why, how now, general? No more of that.
OTHELLO   Avaunt, be gone. Thou hast set me on the rack.
330   I swear 'tis better to be much abused
           Than but to know't a little.
IAGO   How now, my lord?
OTHELLO   What sense had I in her stol'n hours of lust?
           I saw't not, thought it not; it harmed not me.
           I slept the next night well, fed well, was free and merry.
335   I found not Cassio's kisses on her lips.
           He that is robbed, not wanting what is stol'n,
           Let him not know't and he's not robbed at all.
</pre>

IAGO   I am sorry to hear this.

OTHELLO   I had been happy if the general camp,
340   Pioneers and all, had tasted her sweet body,
          So I had nothing known. O, now for ever
          Farewell the tranquil mind, farewell content,
          Farewell the plumèd troops and the big wars
          That makes ambition virtue! O, farewell,
345   Farewell the neighing steed and the shrill trump,
          The spirit-stirring drum, th'ear-piercing fife,
          The royal banner, and all quality,
          Pride, pomp, and circumstance of glorious war!
          And O, you mortal engines whose rude throats
350   Th'immortal Jove's dread clamours counterfeit,
          Farewell! Othello's occupation's gone.

IAGO   Is't possible, my lord?

OTHELLO   Villain, be sure thou prove my love a whore.
          Be sure of it. Give me the ocular proof,
355   Or, by the worth of mine eternal soul,
          Thou hadst been better have been born a dog
          Than answer my waked wrath.

IAGO   Is't come to this?

OTHELLO   Make me to see't, or at the least so prove it
          That the probation bear no hinge nor loop
360   To hang a doubt on, or woe upon thy life.

IAGO   My noble lord.

OTHELLO   If thou dost slander her and torture me,
          Never pray more; abandon all remorse,
          On horror's head horrors accumulate,
365   Do deeds to make heaven weep, all earth amazed,
          For nothing canst thou to damnation add
          Greater than that.

IAGO   O grace, O God forgive me!
          Are you a man? Have you a soul or sense?

                              (3.3.327–68)

The similarities between the two exchanges are obvious. Like Cleopatra, Othello suffers a fit of sexual jealousy. Like Cleopatra, he overwhelms his interlocutor with a torrent of speech—now talking past him, now straight at him—and barely gives him room to reply. Like Antony, Iago is both the object of Othello's rage and sidelined by it. Like Antony, he seems to be caught off guard by the change in mood, taking several turns to grasp the gravity of the situation. And like Antony, his concern and astonishment build to a climax at which he bursts back into the conversation. The two exchanges are of a similar length and have a similar shape, both interactionally and metrically. But there is also a sense in which they are dramaturgical opposites. Despite the violent emotions at work, neither outburst is unplanned. Cleopatra calmly discusses tactics with Charmian until the moment Antony enters, at which point she suddenly falls ill. Iago's whole scheme has been open to the audience from the beginning, and these lines are preceded by a brief monologue in which he exults at his own success. Both exchanges are engineered by one of the two characters. The difference is that, in the first case, it is the character who dominates the conversational floor, and in the second it is the character who is excluded from it. The role that Cleopatra artfully stages for herself—so overcome with rage and self-pity that she is unable to control her tongue—is here played in earnest by Othello. Antony's cautious handwringing is skilfully acted by Iago. If Cleopatra is a cat toying with a mouse, Iago is a Spaniard baiting a bull (many editors give physical form to the sense of menace in the dialogue by adding a stage direction to indicate that Othello takes him by the throat). And these differences are registered, I want to suggest, in the shifting relations of metre and syntax that shape the transitions between speaker and speaker. They are written, that is, into the structure of the dialogue.

We might start by observing that Othello's first turn is an ambiguity of address. He comes on stage speaking, but not, it would appear, to Iago. What he says is aside in the sense that it stands outside the boundaries of a ratified conversation, but this need not mean there is any attempt to conceal it. He may simply be too preoccupied to notice that he is not alone. It is unclear why Othello has returned to the stage, but it does not seem to be with the intention of speaking to Iago. It is the ensign who initiates the interaction, re-opening the subject of Desdemona's supposed infidelity by pretending to close it (just as he had originally introduced it by pretending to be reticent). Othello's reaction is to shun all contact with Iago, as a child might shun a dog by which she has been bitten.

OTHELLO   Avaunt, be gone. Thou hast set me on the rack.
330   I swear 'tis better to be much abused
    Than but to know't a little.
    IAGO   How now, my lord?

His turn ends at a transition-relevance place and with an aphoristic neatness that makes it sound complete. But it does not reach the line end. Othello may not want a reply, but he does leave space for one. Iago tactfully fills that space, treading carefully around the general's words but without overstepping the bounds of the metre.

It is at this point that the pattern of the two exchanges diverges. Othello's next two turns can be heard as a single utterance that Iago fails to interrupt. Here are the relevant lines with Iago removed:

    He that is robbed, not wanting what is stol'n,
337   Let him not know't and he's not robbed at all.
339   I had been happy if the general camp,
    Pioneers and all, had tasted her sweet body,
    So I had nothing known.

It is the coincidence of the line ending with a transition-relevance place at line 337 that suggests to Iago that he may be able to get a word in. But Othello shows no sign of having heard him. What he says is not addressed to Iago, either before or after the attempted transition. Join the two turns and you have a single coherent speech following a single train of thought. It seems clear, then, that Othello ignores Iago—or that he does not hear him—so intent is he on working through the conse-quences of Desdemona's infidelity. But the shape of lines suggests more than this. Iago's seven syllables are metrically superfluous. They fail to register in the rhythm of Othello's language, just as his words fail to register in Othello's train of thought. The general leaves no space, in any of his lines, for Iago to fill, and he shows no awareness of the space that Iago leaves him. Metrically speaking, he ignores his interlocutor. Had Shakespeare used another shared line here, it would have sug-gested that Othello was at least aware of Iago, that there was at least a brief pause in his morbid ruminations while Iago speaks. Instead he shows us a man too distracted for such coordinated action—a man whose pre-occupation with his wife's chastity causes him to violate the most fundamental rule of conversation. Rather than speaking one at a time, the two characters speak simultaneously. Shakespeare uses the fact that he is writing in verse to escape the most basic typographical limitation of the dramatic text.

I am conscious, once again, that this claim may seem more convenient than probable, so I want to bolster it with a second example. This is Hamlet, in the second quarto, recounting the somewhat implausible story of his pirate-adventure to Horatio:

> *Ham.* Sir in my hart there was a kind of fighting
> 5   That would not let me sleepe, m[e] thought I lay
>   Worse then the mutines in the bilbo, rashly,
>   And praysd be rashnes for it: let vs knowe,
>   Our indiscretion sometime serues vs well
>   When our deepe plots doe fall, & that should learne vs
> 10   Ther's a diuinity that shapes our ends,
>   Rough hew them how we will.
>   *Hora.* That is most certaine.
>   *Ham.* Vp from my Cabin,
>   My sea-gowne scarft about me in the darke
> 15   Gropt I to find out them [...]
>
>   (1Nr, 19[5.2].4–15)

On the face of it, this looks like another one of George Wright's 'squinting' lines. Hamlet's first turn ends with a half line and his second turn begins with one. In between is a half line spoken by Horatio. An editor can choose to fill out one turn or the other—to make Horatio's half line a completion of the one before or to complete it with the one that follows. Whichever way round he does it, however, there will be a half line left over. This matters because a short line is often taken to indicate a pause. According to Coleridge, 'Shakespeare never introduces a catalectic line without intending an equivalent to the foot omitted, in the pauses, or the dwelling emphasis, or the diffused retardation'.[21] This is a fine remark, but it could have been improved by the substitution of the word 'rarely' for 'never'. Coleridge's theory of the short line, shorn of its subtlety, becomes dogma in the hands of Peter Hall, founder of the RSC:

---

[21] *Coleridge on Shakespeare*, ed. by Terence Hawkes (London: Penguin, 1969) p. 164.

> Horatio can come in to complete Hamlet's line or he can pause, allowing the thought of the divinity that shapes our ends, to give a moment of reflection. Or Hamlet can pause after Horatio's line to let the moment sink in before beginning his malevolent tale of revenge. What is certain is that we have three incomplete lines that make up one complete line, a pause and a half line. How the passage is phrased is up to the actors and the director. But it is mandatory to have a pause somewhere. Shakespeare wrote it.[22]

The option taken by editors of the play is usually to print Horatio's turn as a completion of the line left unfinished by Hamlet. Metrically this is the neater fit, and, as Hall suggests, a pause in either place can make dramatic sense. But Hall is wrong to insist that a pause is mandatory. As E. A. Abbott had pointed out more than a century earlier, there is another explanation. For Abbott these lines are an example of an 'interruption that [is] not allowed to interfere with the speaker's verse'.[23] Like Othello, Hamlet picks up metrically exactly where he left off. If one of the half lines is redundant, it is the one belonging to Horatio. This technique is appropriate, according to Abbott, to those moments at which 'a man is bent on continuing what he has to say'.[24] Abigail Rokison has credited Abbott with suggesting that 'the central line of a three consecutive short-line structure might constitute an overlap'.[25] This is not quite what he says—Abbot's point is about the shape of the verse, not how it might be delivered—but the suggestion is a good one. And the impression is reinforced by the syntax of Hamlet's lines. Despite printing Horatio's words as a metrical completion of Hamlet's turn, editors tend to punctuate the transition with a dash. They do so because, syntactically, what Hamlet says is suspended—he is halfway through an unfinished sentence when the change of speakers occurs. And despite the aphoristic finality of his reflections about divinity shaping our ends, those reflections are housed, syntactically, within a parenthesis. Horatio may have forgotten it, and Peter Hall too,

[22] Peter Hall, *Shakespeare's Advice to the Players* (London: Oberon, 2003), p. 39.
[23] E. A. Abbott, *A Shakespearian Grammar*, 2nd edn (London: Macmilan, 1870), p. 427.
[24] Abbott, p. 427. He provides further examples from *Merchant*, *Julius Caesar*, and *Richard III*.
[25] Abigail Rokison, *Shakespearean Verse Speaking* (Cambridge: Cambridge University Press, 2009), p. 105.

but Hamlet has not yet told us what it is that he did 'rashly'. This adverb turns out to govern 'gropt' despite being separated from it by eight lines of text ('rashly, | And praysd be rashnes for it: [. . .] Gropt I to find out them'). Horatio tries to speak at what sounds like a transition-relevance place, and after the kind of remark for which Hamlet usually invites applause, but the main verb of this torturous sentence has not yet arrived. Syntactically as well as metrically, there is reason to hear Hamlet hurrying on—either without a pause or with a pause of insufficient length for Horatio's five syllables. We might prefer to hear these turns as overlapping rather than simultaneous, but their similarity to the example from *Othello* is clear. In both cases the 'interruption [is] not allowed to interfere with the speaker's verse' because 'a man is bent on continuing what he has to say'.

Iago's next turn comes closer to re-establishing a two-way conversation. It succeeds in attracting Othello's attention but fails to weaken his grip on the speakership.

> OTHELLO [. . .]
>   And O, you mortal engines whose rude throats
>   Th'immortal Jove's dread clamours counterfeit,
>   Farewell! Othello's occupation's gone.
> IAGO   Is't possible, my lord?
> OTHELLO   Villain, be sure thou prove my love a whore.
>   Be sure of it. Give me the ocular proof,
> 355   Or, by the worth of mine eternal soul,
>   Thou hadst been better have been born a dog
>   Than answer my waked wrath.

Like Horatio, Iago speaks at what sounds like an auspicious moment. Through a series of six 'farewells' to various aspects of a soldier's life, Othello has arrived at the declaration that his occupation is 'gone'. Metrically, syntactically, and rhetorically, his turn has reached an endpoint when Iago tries to speak. But again his words are metrically superfluous, excluded from the structure of the verse by the self-sufficiency of Othello's lines. Although rhythmically identical to Iago's previous turn, interactionally this one is different. Othello does seem to recognize that Iago has spoken, because he comes out of his reverie to address him. The shape of the dialogue suggests one thing, its content another. The implication, I think, is that Iago carves at least some space for himself in the smooth front of Othello's speech. There is a pause after 'gone' but not a pause long enough for Iago to reply. What we have is aggressive overlap rather than oblivious simultaneity.

This pattern—of progress towards the restitution of turn-taking normality—is continued in Iago's next turn, when he finally gains a foothold in a shared line.

> OTHELLO [...]
>   Thou hadst been better have been born a dog
>   Than answer my waked wrath.
> IAGO   Is't come to this?
> OTHELLO   Make me to see't, or at the least so prove it
>   That the probation bear no hinge nor loop
> 360   To hang a doubt on, or woe upon thy life.
> IAGO   My noble lord.
> OTHELLO   If thou dost slander her and torture me,
>   Never pray more [...]

Iago's question is at least partly rhetorical. It is not clear what sort of reply he is expecting, nor whether he is addressing Othello or himself. So it is hardly surprising that the general does not answer it directly. But he does at least give Iago the space in which to ask a question. By allowing Iago's turn to stand, metrically, Othello seems to ratify Iago's words as a turn— as a recognized contribution to the conversation. The trouble is not over, however. Othello embarks, at line 358, on a further series of threats to which Iago's summons, 'My noble lord', can gain no admittance. Othello's syntax in line 360 is curiously double-jointed—seeming both to be complete and to span the line end. Another brief dip into conversation analytic theory can help to explain what may be going on here:

> Besides compressing an emerging transition space, speakers can also work to obscure the space by building a linguistic bridge to further talk. Consider the phenomenon known as a turn-constructional *pivot*—an item of talk that can be seen as both the end of one grammatical unit and the beginning of the next unit [...] the pivot can be read in retrospect as a unit-bridging and boundary-obscuring item of talk.[26]

[26] Clayman, p. 161.

An example taken from real conversation is 'that's what I'd like to have is a fresh one', in which the speaker avoids making transition relevant at the end of the phrase 'that's what I'd like to have' by also making it the beginning of the phrase 'what I'd like to have is'. My suggestion is that something similar may be going on with Othello's use of 'woe vpon thy life'. It is possible to hear this as both 'Make me to see't [...] or woe upon thy life' and 'woe upon thy life | If thou dost slander her'. The implication, I think, is that Othello recognizes in advance that Iago will try to effect a transition and uses the pivot to head off the danger. We might want to distinguish, therefore, between his aggression here and his insensibility earlier in the exchange. One seems deliberate, the other instinctive.

Iago finally manages to speak to Othello only when he pretends no longer to be trying. So implacable is his interlocutor that he turns instead to address the heavens:

> OTHELLO [...]
> 366   For nothing canst thou to damnation add
>   Greater than that.
> IAGO   O grace, O God forgive me!
>   Are you a man? Have you a soul or sense?

Whether he actually succeeds in stopping Othello or Othello stops of his own accord is moot. The general's final turn ends mid-line, but with a rhetorical snap that suggests rather that he is aiming for a Coleridgean pause or 'dwelling emphasis' than that Iago has succeeded in interrupting him. It is Othello, rather than Iago, who can nothing 'to damnation add', having called down every curse at his disposal. The moment Othello subsides, however, Iago seizes the opportunity to privilege his own high despair. Having caught Othello's attention with an apostrophe, he turns his voice back in the direction of his interlocutor and finally succeeds in engaging him.

*   *   *

If we compare the exchange to Antony and Cleopatra, the most obvious difference is that the two lovers remain within the shared framework of their blank verse—with the possible exception of line 18 ('Pray you, stand farther from me') which I have suggested can be heard as Cleopatra dropping into prose. Unlike Iago's, none of Antony's turns is extrametrical. However heated the exchange becomes, it stays within the bounds of the metre. There are several ways in which we might interpret this difference. Perhaps the lovers stay rhythmically in tune because, at bottom, that's what they are. Their fatal compatibility is present in the writing even when they are most at odds. Perhaps, in the presence of Charmian, Alexas, and Iras, they are struggling to maintain at least some decorum. Or perhaps the distinction between Othello's rage and Cleopatra's is that his is genuine and hers is at least partly calculated. Othello temporarily loses the ability to hear his interlocutor and to respect the rules of conversation. Cleopatra never loses either of these things—she is always alert to the situation. She repeatedly encourages Antony to lunge for the ball precisely so that she can leave him on his backside. Like Lionel Messi, part of her skill lies in giving the impression that a tackle can be made. Othello, on the other hand, talks over Iago like a steamroller running over a frog, oblivious to its feeble croaking. Taken together, the two examples show the subtlety with which Shakespeare can differentiate between broadly analogous dramatic situations and work those differences out through the minutiae of his writing. The shape of the verse into which these exchanges are arranged is acutely sensitive to the dramatic demands of the scene— it is, in Eric Griffiths' fine phrase, 'the intricate wake left by steering through choppy, interpersonal waters'.[27]

[27] 'On Lines and Grooves from Shakespeare to Tennyson', in *Tennyson Among the Poets*, ed. by Robert Douglas-Fairhurst and Seamus Perry (Oxford: Oxford University Press, 2009), pp. 132–59 (149).

Conclusion

I want to end with a question that has been lurking in the wings since the beginning. Throughout this book, I have been treating Shakespeare's plays primarily as works of literature—as texts for reading—with only occasional glances at how they might have been performed. Even when discussing how transitions between turns are timed, I have tended to treat those transitions as belonging to a fictional world—as occurring between characters rather than actors. I make no apology for this. Shakespeare was a literary as well as a theatrical dramatist, even during his lifetime.[1] But plays are still plays, and their life on the stage matters. I cannot end, then, without some consideration of what my argument might mean for our understanding of original performance practices. I have relegated the question to a place just outside the main body of the work because my answers to it are no more than provisional. A conclusion, it seems to me, is the right place to be inconclusive.

As I hope this book has shown, Shakespearean dialogue is full of subtle effects of timing and sequence that would seem to call for careful rehearsal and a detailed knowledge of the script. Everything we know about early modern theatre, on the other hand, suggests that it was performed with minimal rehearsal by actors who had never

---

[1] See Erne, *Shakespeare as Literary Dramatist*, for the definitive statement of the case.

seen a complete text of the play. They worked instead from 'parts'— handwritten scrolls containing 'all the words the actor was going to speak, but nothing that would be said to or about him'.[2] Nothing, that is, save for a short cue-phrase preceding each speech. The actor's job was to memorize both his speeches and his cues and to speak one when he heard the other. Since the company would perform a different play each day and an unsuccessful play would never be repeated, he was expected to have 'upwards of forty roles in [his] head or to hand, and might regularly be asked to learn new plays while performing an endless series of old ones'.[3] There was little time for rehearsal as we now understand it, although exactly how little is unclear.[4] The actor would rely instead on his part, which 'had to provide enough information to determine [his] entire performance'.[5] In practice this meant that he was unlikely to know, at any given moment, either where his next cue was coming from or when it was likely to arrive. The apparent mismatch between the demands of the dialogue and the circumstances under which it was performed I call 'the performability gap'. The question is how it can be bridged.

The explanation provided by Simon Palfrey and Tiffany Stern in their celebrated monograph, *Shakespeare in Parts*, is nothing if not ingenious. Their basic claim is that Shakespeare exploits the lack of foreknowledge inherent to the part-based system to produce, spontaneously, in his actors, precisely the behaviour he wants his characters to display. When he wants a character to stumble—dialogically speaking—he trips the actor up. Palfrey and Stern are thus able to account for features of the plays that would otherwise seem to cause problems—the large number of 'repeated cues', for example.[6] Hearing what he thinks is his cue, the actor will begin to speak his lines. Then, realizing that his colleague has not finished, he will withdraw. The result is an abortive attempt to speak, a 'battle for the cue space' that

---

[2] Simon Palfrey and Tiffany Stern, *Shakespeare in Parts* (Oxford: Oxford University Press, 2010), p. 1.

[3] *Shakespeare in Parts*, p. 74.

[4] This question is discussed at greater length in Stern's *Rehearsal from Shakespeare to Sheridan* (Oxford: Oxford University Press, 2000), pp. 52–79. The answer would seem to be that more than one group rehearsal was unusual and sometimes even this was considered superfluous.

[5] *Shakespeare in Parts*, p. 65.   [6] *Shakespeare in Parts*, pp. 157–64.

mimics the appearance of a genuine argument.[7] Acting in parts can make such moments seem more real because, not knowing when or from whom their next cue will arrive, the actors are discovering the dialogue as they perform it, like real people improvising a conversation. In this way, Palfrey and Stern explain how 'complete ignorance of any context is no bar to organizing genuinely coherent playing'.[8] If anything, it is an advantage. Without the 'meta-performative surprises' inherent to acting in parts, Shakespearean dialogue would be as flat in performance as it is on the page:

> When a speech is clearly scripted, each actor must wait for his cue, pause until the other ceases speaking, and then say his piece: the play performed is as linear as the play written. But what if Shakespeare does not want linear performance? Played from cues, each actor speaks not after but around, or inside, the other. When Shakespeare wants to create parallel or mutually oblivious lines of thinking, with one character in one 'mental space' and the rest somewhere quite different, repeated cues can obviate the need for what can be produced typographically only by parallel columns.[9]

Two things make me uneasy about this line of argument. The first is that it is happy to condemn the written texts of the plays to a turgid linearity from which they can only escape in performance. This seems to me at odds with the experience of reading them, in which the characters do very much more than simply 'say their piece' one after another. Even on the page, Shakespearean dialogue is not linear—at least, it is no more linear than the canvas of an oil painting is flat. To describe it as such, while technically correct, is to miss the point entirely. My second reservation is that, even in performance, Palfrey and Stern recognize only two dialogical gears. The onstage interaction is either linear, resulting in a mechanically regular *cue-pause-speak* delivery, or it descends into the mutual obliviousness of parallel thoughts and words. Once again, this is at odds with the agility of Shakespeare's writing and the kind of performance it seems to demand.

In their analyses of specific scenes and passages, Palfrey and Stern are less dogmatic than these comments would suggest, but their examples

---

[7] *Shakespeare in Parts*, p. 208.   [8] *Shakespeare in Parts*, p. 31.
[9] *Shakespeare in Parts*, p. 163.

do all tend to point in the same direction. They have an awful lot to say about 'cross-purposes, lateral recognitions, and meta-performative surprises'—about moments at which the dialogue heats up and the voices of the characters clash—but relatively little about the opposite sort of effect, those moments at which turn-exchange stalls, the characters pause or hesitate, and there is a palpable reluctance to speak.[10] The obvious explanation for this lopsidedness is that surprise and confusion are the two effects which the lack of foreknowledge inherent to the part-based acting system can most easily produce. When these are appropriate to the dramatic moment, Palfrey and Stern are persuasive—the plays do sometimes seem to be shaped in such a way as to make artistic capital of their own under-rehearsal. But when something else is called for—not conflict and interruption but silence and reticence—it becomes more difficult to see how the dialogue could have been performed in the way they describe.

Consider, for example, the stage direction that follows Volumnia's great speech, in which Coriolanus '*Holds her by the hand silent*' (TLN 3539, 5.3.183). As Raphael Lyne has pointed out:

> The single person who would benefit most from this direction would be the prompter: if that individual were to mistake the silence onstage for a forgotten line, and then tried to help out, the dramatic moment would be destroyed.[11]

The same can be true even when there is no stage direction (at the moment of Hotspur's death, for example). It can be true, in fact, whenever the dialogue calls for a pause. If the actors have no knowledge of one another's parts, there is always a risk that this will be misinterpreted as a forgotten line or a missed cue. And the consequence of trying to correct such a mistake is to destroy the pregnancy of a carefully scripted silence. Consider Helena, the heroine of *All's Well that Ends Well*, a character all but defined by her interactional

---

[10] *Shakespeare in Parts*, p. 118. To see this we need only glance at the structure of the book. What Palfrey and Stern call a 'false cue'—something very like what I would call a failed transition—is mentioned on four occasions (pp. 181–3, 211–12, 243, and 246). The repeated cue, on the other hand, is the subject of one of the book's four main parts and explored in great detail over the course of 152 pages (155–307).

[11] Raphael Lyne, 'The Shakespearean Grasp', *The Cambridge Quarterly*, 42 (2013), 38–61 (p. 42).

reticence. Helena pursues her conversational aims in the same way she pursues her beloved Bertram, with patient urgency and a shy insistence. How is such a character to be played, by a teenage boy, in 'complete ignorance' of the context of his lines? To do any sort of justice to Shakespeare's dialogue, the actors sometimes need to be late with their lines (as well as sometimes being early). They need to know when not to panic if the next line does not arrive immediately. They need to know more, in other words, than the isolated study of their own parts can tell them.

My point is not that Palfrey and Stern are wrong but that, even if they are right, their account is incomplete. A recognition that some consequences of part-based acting may sometimes have been desirable—that Shakespeare had the wit to make a virtue of theatrical necessity—can help us to narrow the performability gap but not to close it. More is needed if we are to bring the two sides within touching distance. But what? I see five possibilities, each of which may have been a factor, even if their relative importance is difficult to gauge. Rather than try to provide a single answer, I will lay these possibilities out. My aim is not to offer a new and competing model of early modern performance but to put the ball back into the theatre historians' court.

The first possibility is that I may be overestimating the subtlety of Shakespeare's dialogue with regard to the timing and sequencing of turns. If the plays are cruder in this respect than I imagine, they are also easier to perform. It may be that the detailed analyses of dialogical effects on which this book is built are more the result of my own ingenuity than Shakespeare's genius. I don't think so, obviously, but it is in my interests not to think so. You, dear reader, can decide for yourself.

The second possibility is that Shakespeare's company did not prepare in quite the way that Palfrey and Stern describe. It is an unfortunate accident that most of our evidence for how a professional acting company functioned in this period relates not to Shakespeare's own troupe but to their rivals, the Admiral's Men. Much of what we know about the performance of his plays is underpinned by the assumption that theatrical practice was uniform across London and throughout Shakespeare's career. This assumption may be necessary—without it we would be able to say very little—but it remains an assumption. It is not the case that all groups of actors rehearse in the same way now, and it is unlikely to have been the case then. Moreover, as Bart van Es has recently argued, Shakespeare's company was uniquely successful, and his position within that company—as both a sharer and the principal dramatist—was unique. According to van Es, this professional 'singularity' enabled Shakespeare to develop a new kind of drama, distinct from that of his contemporaries:

> Marlowe's anti-heroes [...] have a stand-alone quality: they are extractable as independent entities, little damaged by the removal of their interlocutors. This is not the case with the characters that Shakespeare introduced in his position as a sharer from 1594 onwards: these figures emerge through their interaction with other speakers on the stage. [...] Having a literary playwright at the centre of commissioning, casting, rehearsing, and performing plays was transformative. Shakespeare knew the players for whom he was writing and he must have been instrumental in the way the drama was rehearsed.[12]

If Shakespeare was a uniquely influential playwright writing a uniquely interactional style of drama—writing dialogue, that is, which was uniquely difficult to perform—then it would not be surprising if his company rehearsed that dialogue in a way that differed from their competitors. At least, this is not a possibility we can safely rule out. Most obviously, as van Es points out, Shakespeare would have been in a position to spend more time with the actors, instructing them on how the lines were to be delivered—not just as individual speeches but as carefully timed exchanges of turns.

The third possibility is linked to the second. If Shakespeare's company prepared differently, perhaps they prepared from documents that were themselves different. Perhaps they prepared, that is, from parts that contained more than just their own lines and cues. It would not have been difficult for an actor to annotate his part in such a way as to record, for example, who spoke each cue, to whom he should address his lines, and where to expect an interruption or a pause. Even quite a simple system of annotation would have made complex turn-taking easier to perform. We know that parts were 'busy' documents 'alive with scribbles and emendations', some of them made by the actors

---

[12] Bart van Es, *Shakespeare in Company* (Oxford: Oxford University Press, 2013), p. 93, 120.

themselves.[13] So why *wouldn't* they scribble on them in such a way as to make performance easier? The answer, according to Palfrey and Stern, is that they did not see the need. But the logic behind that answer looks suspiciously circular. It rests on the fact that the only surviving part from the professional theatre of Shakespeare's time (the part of Orlando from Robert Greene's *Orlando Furioso*) contains little more than cue-phrases and speeches. A lot depends, therefore, on how typical we take this part to be. Palfrey and Stern are confident that it 'almost certainly' reflects what a Shakespearean part would have looked like.[14] W. W. Greg, on the other hand, concludes that it is 'impossible to say'.[15] There are reasons to be sceptical, as Palfrey and Stern admit:

> It has been conjectured that the [Orlando] part—improved by correction, but still not perfect—is itself a rejected text. For our purposes the question is immaterial: used or unused, the part is written to the formula adopted at a public theatre.[16]

The question of whether an early modern actor ever performed Orlando from this document is not immaterial. It is very material indeed when we are trying to determine how typical the part is of the documents from which early modern actors performed. If it was never used then the process of preparing from it is likely to have been unfinished. And if, as Palfrey and Stern insist, parts were 'alive with scribbles and emendations'—if preparing from a part meant writing on it—then an unused part is also an incomplete one. To put it more bluntly, some of the information absent from the Orlando part may be absent because it had not yet been added when the part was discarded. We cannot dismiss this possibility on the grounds that the part is 'written to the formula adopted at a public theatre' when the part is our best piece of evidence for what that formula was during Shakespeare's lifetime.

And even if the Orlando part is typical, the parts used by Shakespeare's own company may not have been. As Greg suggests, professional parts may have 'differed somewhat' between 'different companies and at different dates'.[17] We know, for example, that the parts used by amateur

---

[13] *Shakespeare in Parts*, p. 20.   [14] *Shakespeare in Parts*, p. 22.
[15] W. W. Greg, *Dramatic Documents from the Elizabethan Playhouses*, 2 vols (Oxford: The Clarendon Press, 1931), I, p. 181.
[16] *Shakespeare in Parts*, p. 20.   [17] Greg, *Dramatic Documents*, I, p. 181.

actors often included more information than is found on the part used (or not used) by Edward Alleyn to play Orlando. As Palfrey and Stern point out, 'from the middle of the sixteenth century onwards, various parts across Europe name the speaker of the cue' and 'performers readying a miracle play seem to have regularly been told to whom their speeches were addressed'.[18] The parts used by student actors at Oxford in the early seventeenth century have longer cue-phrases than the Orlando part and speech-headings to identify who delivers each cue. They also use dashes to indicate shared lines of verse and numbers to indicate repeated cues.[19] So if Shakespeare's company did choose to deviate from standard professional practice, they would not have been doing something without parallel or precedent. Other actors in other contexts had already found it useful to include more information on their parts.

The fourth possibility is that the turn-taking subtleties we find in Shakespeare's printed plays did not make it onto the stage. The very idea of a performability gap rests on the assumption that the company's aim would have been the faithful reproduction of the play as Shakespeare had written it—that one measure of how good a performance is (albeit not the only one) is how closely it sticks to the written text. This assumption may be anachronistic. We know that clowns had licence to improvise on the early modern stage, and there is some evidence that, at least some of the time, other actors did too.[20] They may have used the script more in the way that a jazz musician makes use of a fake book than a classical musician makes use of a score. The whole performance may have been more chaotic, improvisatory, and unpredictable than the carefully scripted turn-taking of the printed texts suggests. Or rather, it may have been more chaotic than the best of the printed texts suggests. The so-called 'bad' quartos of Shakespeare's plays have a haphazard, freewheeling character that has often been explained as the result of memorial reconstruction. It is possible, in other words, that the early performances of *Hamlet* more closely resembled Q1 than Q2—not only in their structure and length

---

[18] *Shakespeare in Parts*, p. 19.   [19] *Shakespeare in Parts*, pp. 24–8.
[20] See Tiffany Stern, *Documents of Performance in Early Modern England* (Cambridge: Cambridge University Press, 2009), pp. 245–50.

but also in their willingness to approximate what Shakespeare had written.[21]

It is also possible that early modern actors had different priorities from actors today: more focused on the delivery of their own lines than the coherence of the play as a whole, more concerned with dramatic recitation than interactional verisimilitude. Palfrey and Stern are ambivalent about this. On the one hand, they explicitly reject the possibility, insisting that 'the players knew that the one thing they must at all costs avoid is the appearance of "reciting" the words'.[22] On the other hand, they repeatedly hint at a style of performance in which the actors do just that:

> The part was more important to the production than the group interaction [...] actors who were anyway concentrating on solo performance simply did not have the same concern to practise together [...] not being told who would speak the next cue on the part, it might be easier to address the audience than risk speaking to the wrong person on a busy stage [...] the closing line of a speech [might] have received a more emphatic, 'teeing-up' delivery.[23]

Needless to say, the existence of a convention whereby each speech ended with an audible 'teeing-up' of the next speaker would remove any ambiguity about whether a character had finished speaking. Similarly, actors who spent much of the play addressing the audience because they did not know to which character they ought to be speaking would make it impossible to follow the delicate game of tag through which sequences of turns are built. It is difficult to reconcile this style of acting with the exquisitely calibrated interactivity of Shakespeare's plays, but that difficulty may be a trick of historical perspective. The past is a foreign country, after all. We should not be surprised if they act things differently there.

Finally, the plays in performance may have differed from the plays in print, not because the process of performance had in some way altered them but because the texts from which they were performed were

[21] Respectively, *The Tragicall Historie of Hamlet Prince of Denmarke* [Q1] (London: Valentine Simmes for Nicholas Ling and John Trundell, 1603); and *The Tragicall Historie of Hamlet, Prince of Denmarke* [Q2] (London: James Roberts for Nicholas Ling, 1604).
[22] *Shakespeare in Parts*, p. 151.
[23] *Shakespeare in Parts*, pp. 62, 71, 75, 145.

already different. In the absence of any surviving theatrical documents from Shakespeare's own company, we have no way of making the comparison. Even the Orlando part is of little help here, as Palfrey and Stern point out:

> The problem is that the version of the play reflected in the part seems to be the one given a performance at the Rose in 1591/2, while the Quarto records a different version of the play, perhaps the result of the fact that Greene sold *Orlando* twice, to two different companies, the Admiral's Men and the Queen's Players.[24]

The discrepancies between the part and the quarto do at least illustrate the danger of working backwards from a printed play to a lost theatrical document. They should perhaps give us pause when it comes to trying to reconstruct the parts used by Shakespeare's own company from the printed texts of his plays. We are not completely in the dark, however. If we accept—as most scholars now do—that Shakespeare wrote for the page as well as the stage, then it is likely that a text used in performance was at least partially shaped to meet the needs of the performers. It is equally likely that a text printed in a playbook was at least partially shaped to meet the needs of its readers. Exactly how much the theatrical and literary versions of the same play differed is difficult to say, and the answer will no doubt vary from play to play and text to text—but it is still possible to sketch some of those differences in outline.

Lukas Erne has shown that many of the printed texts of Shakespeare's plays are simply too long to have been performed in the time available.[25] Either they must have been cut for performance or extra material must have been added later. To the reader ensconced in her study, on the other hand, or the bookseller hawking his wares, the extra length is not a problem. In fact, it is something of a selling point. This is why early modern playbooks sometimes advertise themselves as containing 'more than hath been publickely spoken or acted'.[26] And, as Erne has also shown, the longer and more literary texts of the plays tend to handle stage action differently from their shorter and more theatrical

---

[24] *Shakespeare in Parts*, p. 20–1.   [25] Erne, *Literary Dramatist*, pp. 155–97.
[26] Ben Jonson, *The Comicall Satyre of Euery Man out of His Humor* (London: Adam Islip for William Holme, 1600), sig. A2r.

counterparts—often making clear through a character's speech what an audience would be able to see without being told.[27]

So the final possibility is that something similar is happening with dialogue. Like excessive length, highly intricate turn-taking may be a marker of literariness rather than theatricality—at least in so far as it would have caused problems for actors performing in 'complete ignorance of any context'. Like length, performability ceases to be a concern in a text that is printed to be read. If Shakespeare was a literary as well as a theatrical dramatist then it is likely that he was aware of what worked best in each medium and ready, when the opportunity arose, to tailor his dialogue accordingly. This is not to suggest that either medium should take priority over the other, only that the dialogical requirements of the players differed from (and were potentially at odds with) those of the play-reading public. We might even see the deftly scripted turn-taking of the printed plays as an attempt to compensate for the absence of the actors. Deprived of the opportunity to play the kind of tricks described by Palfrey and Stern, Shakespeare finds a more literary equivalent for them. Or we might see the printed dialogue as a record of things that had happened first in the theatre—mistakes or improvisations that struck the author as worth preserving in a more permanent form. Perhaps, perhaps, perhaps. Having reached such a pinnacle of inconclusiveness, I think I had better conclude.

*   *   *

This book has been a success if it sends the reader back to Shakespeare with a heightened sensitivity to dramatic dialogue—more alert to the interactional shape of his writing and better able to describe it. My aim has been to establish the viability of a new approach to Shakespearean dialogue, not to say everything worth saying with it. I have not attempted to 'do' turn-taking in Shakespeare but to show how much there is to be done. The next moves are obvious. By paying the same kind of attention to a wider range of material, we can begin to chart the development of dramatic dialogue across the period and to draw comparisons between the turn-taking styles of different playwrights. What I suspect this would show is that the two great well-springs of

---

[27] Erne, *Literary Dramatist*, pp. 245–9.

early modern drama, Seneca and Terence, are also the two great poles of dialogical style—one stately and the other nimble, one tragic and the other comic. T. S. Eliot has remarked of Seneca that his characters exchange speeches 'like members of a minstrel troupe sitting in a semicircle, rising in turn each to do his "number"'.[28] And it was to cope with Terence's more agile dialogue, we recall, that Maurice Kyffin found it necessary to invent the sign of suspension.[29] If Dryden is right that the development of tragi-comedy is a distinctively English achievement, then a part of that achievement may be the fusion of these two dialogical styles.[30] But these are questions for another book and, perhaps, another writer. This turn, at last, is over. Whether or not I take another one will depend on what comes back by way of reply.

[28] T. S. Eliot, *Selected Essays*, 3rd edn (London: Faber & Faber, 1951), p. 69.

[29] Anne Henry [Toner], '"Quid Ais Omnium?" Maurice Kyffin's 1588 "Andria" and the Emergence of Suspension Marks in Printed Drama', *Renaissance Drama*, 34 (2005), 47–67.

[30] *Of Dramatick Poesie, an Essay by John Dryden* (London: Henry Herringman, 1668), sig. F4r (p. 39). Such, at least, is Neander's position. Lisideius agrees that tragi-comedy is distinctively English but not that it is an achievement. See sig. E2v (p. 28).

BIBLIOGRAPHY

Abbott, E. A., *A Shakespearian Grammar*, 2nd edn (London: Macmillan, 1870).

Adamczyk, Magdalena, 'Shakespeare's Wordplay Gender-Wise: Punning as a Marker of Male-Female Relationships', in *Topics in Shakespeare's English*, ed. by Piotr Kakietek and Joanna Nykiel (Czestochowa: Wydawnictwo Wyzszej Szkoly Lingwistycznej, 2010), pp. 185–200.

Adamson, Sylvia, 'Literary Language', in *The Cambridge History of the English Language*, ed. by Roger Lass, 6 vols (Cambridge: Cambridge University Press, 2000), III, 539–653.

Adamson, Sylvia, Gavin Alexander, and Katrin Ettenhuber, eds., *Renaissance Figures of Speech* (Cambridge: Cambridge University Press, 2007).

Adelman, Janet, *Suffocating Mothers: Fantasies of Maternal Origin in Shakespeare's Plays*, Hamlet *to* The Tempest (London: Routledge, 1991).

Albert, Ethel M., ' "Rhetoric," "Logic," and "Poetics" in Burundi: Culture Patterning of Speech Behavior', *American Anthropologist*, 66 (1964), 35–54.

Arnold, M. L., *The Soliloquies of Shakespeare*, Columbia University Studies in English (New York: Columbia University Press, 1911).

Aubignac, François Hédelin, abbé d', *La pratique du théâtre* (Paris: Antoine de Sommaville, 1657).

Aubignac, François Hédelin, abbé d', *The Whole Art of the Stage*, translator unknown (London: Printed for the author, 1684).

Austen, Jane, *Pride and Prejudice*, ed. by Pat Rogers, The Cambridge Edition of the Works of Jane Austen (Cambridge: Cambridge University Press, 2006).

Bakhtin, Mikhail Mikhailovich, 'The Problem of Speech Genres', in *Speech Genres and Other Late Essays*, ed. by Michael Holquist and Caryl Emerson, trans. by Vern W. McGee (Austin: University of Texas Press, 1986), pp. 60–102.

Baldwin, T. W., *William Shakspere's Small Latine & Lesse Greeke*, 2 vols (Urbana: University of Illinois Press, 1944).

Barker, Irena, 'Don't Ask Students to Quit Mucking about—Tell Them', *TES*, 2 January 2015, https://www.tes.com/news/dont-ask-students-quit-mucking-about-tell-them (accessed 21 January 2019).

Bartlett, Henrietta C., and Alfred W. Pollard, *A Census of Shakespeare's Plays in Quarto, 1594–1709*, rev. edn (New Haven: Yale University Press, 1939).

Beckett, Samuel, *Endgame*, trans. by Samuel Beckett (London: Faber & Faber, 1958).

Beckett, Samuel, 'Happy Days', in *The Complete Dramatic Works* (London: Faber & Faber, 1986), pp. 135–68.

Bertram, Paul, *White Spaces in Shakespeare: The Development of the Modern Text* (Cleveland, Ohio: Bellflower Press, 1981).

Blake, N. F., *A Grammar of Shakespeare's Language* (Basingstoke: Palgrave, 2002).

Blayney, Peter W. M., *The Texts of* King Lear *and Their Origins, Volume I: Nicholas Okes and the First Quarto* (Cambridge: Cambridge University Press, 1982).

Bliss, Lee, 'Scribes, Compositors, and Annotators: The Nature of the Copy for the First Folio Text of *Coriolanus*', *Studies in Bibliography*, 50 (1997), 224–61.

Boccaccio, Giovanni, *The Decameron Containing an Hundred Pleasant Nouels*, translator unknown (London: Isaac Jaggard, 1620).

Bourdieu, Pierre, 'L'économie des échanges linguistiques', *Langue française*, 34 (1977), 17–34.

Bourdieu, Pierre, 'The Economics of Linguistic Exchanges', trans. by Richard Nice, *Social Science Information*, 16 (1977), 645–68.

Brown, Roger, and Albert Gilman, 'The Pronouns of Power and Solidarity', in *Style in Language*, ed. by Thomas A. Sebeok (London: John Wiley & Sons, 1960).

Brown, Roger, and Albert Gilman, 'Politeness Theory and Shakespeare's Four Major Tragedies', *Language in Society*, 18 (1989), 159–212.

Bryson, Anna, *From Civility to Courtesy: Changing Codes of Conduct in Early Modern England*, Oxford Studies in Social History (Oxford: Clarendon Press, 1998).

Bullough, Geoffrey, ed., *Narrative and Dramatic Sources of Shakespeare*, 8 vols (London: Routledge and Kegan Paul, 1957–75).

Burrow, Colin, 'Shakespeare and Humanistic Culture', in *Shakespeare and the Classics*, ed. by Charles Martindale and A. B. Taylor (Cambridge: Cambridge University Press, 2004), pp. 9–27.

Burrow, Colin, *Shakespeare and Classical Antiquity*, Oxford Shakespeare Topics (Oxford: Oxford University Press, 2013).

Burrow, Colin, '"Rare Accidents" in *1 Henry IV* and the *Ad Herennium*', *Notes and Queries*, 62 (2015), 107–9.

Burrow, Colin, 'Shakespeare's Authorities', in *Shakespeare and Authority*, ed. by Katie Halsey and Angus Vine (London: Palgrave Macmillan, 2018), pp. 31–53.

Burrows, I. R., '"The Peryod of My Blisse": Commas, Ends and Utterance in *Solyman and Perseda*', *Textual Cultures: Texts, Contexts, Interpretation*, 8 (2013), 95–120.

Busse, Beatrix, *Vocative Constructions in the Language of Shakespeare* (Amsterdam: John Benjamins, 2006).

Calvo, Clara, 'Pronouns of Address and Social Negotiation in *As You Like It*', *Language and Literature*, 1 (1992), 5–27.

Capell, Edward, ed., *Prolusions; or, Select Pieces of Antient Poetry* (London: J. and R. Tonson, 1760).

Capell, Edward, *Notes and Various Readings to Shakespeare*, 3 vols (London: Henry Hughs, 1779).

Cave, Terence, *Montaigne*, How to Read (London: Granta, 2007).

Chapple, Eliot D., 'The Interaction Chronograph: Its Evolution and Present Application', *Personnel*, 25 (1949), 295–307.

Chapple, Eliot D., 'The Standard Experimental (Stress) Interview as Used in Interaction Chronograph Investigations', *Human Organization*, 12 (1953), 23–32.

Chaucer, Geoffrey, *The Riverside Chaucer*, ed. by Larry D. Benson, 3rd edn (Oxford: Oxford University Press, 1987).

Cixous, Hélène, in conversation with Nicholas Royle, 'Rites of Tenderness, Killing the Dead, Living On: Thoughts for the Times on Shakespeare and Death', *Oxford Literary Review*, 38 (2016), 279–88.

Clayman, Stephen E., 'Turn-Constructional Units and the Transition-Relevance Place', in *The Handbook of Conversation Analysis*, ed. by Jack Sidnell and Tanya Stivers (Chichester: Wiley-Blackwell, 2013), pp. 150–66.

Coleridge, Samuel Taylor, *Coleridge on Shakespeare: A Selection of the Essays, Notes and Lectures of Samuel Taylor Coleridge on the Poems and Plays of Shakespeare*, ed. by Terence Hawkes, Penguin Shakespeare Library (Harmondsworth: Penguin, 1969).

Congreve, William, *The Double-Dealer* (London: Jacob Tonson, 1694).

Cooper, Marilyn M., 'Implicature, Convention, and *The Taming of the Shrew*', *Poetics*, 10 (1981), 1–14.

Cowley, Stephen J., 'Of Timing, Turn-Taking, and Conversations', *Journal of Psycholinguistic Research*, 27 (1998), 541–71.

Culpeper, Jonathan, *Language and Characterisation in Plays and Texts: People in Plays and Other Texts*, Textual Explorations (Harlow: Longman, 2001).

Cummings, Brian, *Mortal Thoughts: Religion, Secularity, and Identity in Shakespeare and Early Modern Culture* (Oxford: Oxford University Press, 2013).

Curry, Julian, *Shakespeare on Stage: Thirteen Leading Actors on Thirteen Key Roles* (London: Nick Hern, 2010).

Daniel, Michael, 'Understanding Inclusives', in *Clusivity: Typology and Case Studies of Inclusive-Exclusive Distinction*, ed. by Elena Filimonova, Typological Studies in Language, 63 (Amsterdam: John Benjamins, 2005), pp. 3–48.

Day, Angel, *The English Secretorie* (London: Richard Jones, 1592).

De Grazia, Margreta, 'Soliloquies and Wages in the Age of Emergent Consciousness', *Textual Practice*, 9 (1995), 67–92.

Della Casa, Giovanni, *Galateo of Maister Iohn Della Casa*, trans. by Robert Peterson (London: Henry Middleton, 1576).

Della Casa, Giovanni, *Galateo*, ed. by Claudio Milanini (Milan: Rizzoli, 2008).

Dessen, Alan C., *Recovering Shakespeare's Theatrical Vocabulary* (Cambridge: Cambridge University Press, 1995).

Dessen, Alan C., and Leslie Thomson, eds., *A Dictionary of Stage Directions in English Drama, 1580–1642* (Cambridge: Cambridge University Press, 1999).

Dickens, Charles, *Sketches by 'Boz': Illustrative of Every-Day Life and Every-Day People*, 2 vols (London: John Macrone, 1836).

Dickens, Charles, *David Copperfield*, ed. by Jeremy Tambling, Penguin Classics (London: Penguin, 1996).

Dingwall, Robert, 'Orchestrated Encounters: An Essay in the Comparative Analysis of Speech-Exchange Systems', *Sociology of Health & Illness*, 2 (1980), 151–73.

Dodd, William, review of *Shakespeare and Social Dialogue: Dramatic Language and Elizabethan Letters* by Lynne Magnusson, *Shakespeare Quarterly*, 52 (2001), 154–7.

Drummond, Kent, and Robert Hopper, 'Back Channels Revisited: Acknowledgment Tokens and Speakership Incipiency', *Research on Language and Social Interaction*, 26 (1993), 157–77.

Dryden, John, *Of Dramatick Poesie, an Essay by John Dryden* (London: Henry Herringman, 1668).

Dryden, John, and William Davenant, *The Tempest, or The Enchanted Island* (London: Henry Herringman, 1670).

Duncan Jr, Starkey, 'Some Signals and Rules for Taking Speaking Turns in Conversations', *Journal of Personality and Social Psychology*, 23 (1972), 283–92.

Duncan Jr, Starkey, and Donald W. Fiske, *Face-to-Face Interaction: Research, Methods, and Theory* (Hillsdale, NJ: L. Erlbaum, 1977).

Edelsky, Carole, 'Who's Got the Floor?', *Language in Society*, 10 (1981), 383–421.

Elam, Keir, *Shakespeare's Universe of Discourse: Language-Games in the Comedies* (Cambridge: Cambridge University Press, 1984).

Eliot, T. S., *Selected Essays*, 3rd edn (London: Faber & Faber, 1951).

Ellis-Fermor, Una, *The Frontiers of Drama*, 2nd edn (London: Methuen, 1946).

Elton, G. R., ed., *The Tudor Constitution: Documents and Commentary* (Cambridge: Cambridge University Press, 1960).

Empson, William, 'The Structure of Complex Words', *The Sewanee Review*, 56 (1948), 230–50.

Erasmus, Desiderius, *De Civilitate Morun* [Sic] *Puerilium* [*Lytell Booke of Good Maners for Chyldren*], trans. by Robert Whittington (London: Wynkyn de Worde, 1532).

Erne, Lukas, *Shakespeare's Modern Collaborators*, Shakespeare Now! (London: Continuum, 2008).

Erne, Lukas, *Shakespeare as Literary Dramatist*, 2nd edn (Cambridge: Cambridge University Press, 2013).

Fenton, Doris, *The Extra-Dramatic Moment in Elizabethan Plays* (Philadelphia: Westbrook, 1930).

Fish, Stanley E., 'How to Do Things with Austin and Searle: Speech Act Theory and Literary Criticism', *MLN*, 91 (1976), 983–1025.

Fletcher, Janet, 'The Prosody of Speech: Timing and Rhythm', in *The Handbook of Phonetic Sciences*, ed. by William J. Hardcastle, John Laver, and Fiona E. Gibbon, Blackwell Handbooks in Linguistics, 2nd edn (Chichester: Wiley-Blackwell, 2010), pp. 523–602.

France, Abraham, *The Arcadian Rhetorike* (London: Thomas Orwin, 1588).

George, David, ed., *Coriolanus*, Shakespeare: The Critical Tradition (Bristol: Thoemmes Continuum, 2004).

Gilbert, A. J., *Shakespeare's Dramatic Speech: Studies in Renaissance Literature* (Lewiston, N.Y.: Edwin Mellen Press, 1997).

Goffman, Erving, 'On Face-Work: An Analysis of Ritual Elements in Social Interaction', *Psychiatry: Journal for the Study of Interpersonal Processes*, 18 (1955), 213–31.

Goffman, Erving, 'The Neglected Situation', *American Anthropologist*, 66 (1964), 133–6.

Goffman, Erving, *Interaction Ritual: Essays on Face-to-Face Behaviour* (New York: Anchor, 1967).

Goffman, Erving, *Relations in Public: Microstudies of the Social Order* (New York: Basic Books, 1971).

Goffman, Erving, *Forms of Talk* (Oxford: Blackwell, 1981).

Goffman, Erving, 'The Interaction Order', *American Sociological Review*, 48 (1983), 1–17.

Graham-White, Anthony, *Punctuation and Its Dramatic Value in Shakespearean Drama* (Newark: University of Delaware Press, 1995).

Gratier, Maya, Emmanuel Devouche, Bahia Guellai, Rubia Infanti, Ebru Yilmaz, and Erika Parlato, 'Early Development of Turn-Taking in Vocal Interaction between Mothers and Infants', *Language Sciences*, 6 (2015), art. no. 1167.

Greg, W. W., 'An Elizabethan Printer and His Copy', *The Library*, 4 (1923), 102–18.

Greg, W. W., *Dramatic Documents from the Elizabethan Playhouses*, 2 vols (Oxford: Clarendon Press, 1931).

Greg, W. W., *The Variants in the First Quarto of 'King Lear': A Bibliographical and Critical Inquiry*, Supplement to the Bibliographical Society's Publications 15 (London: BiblSoc, 1940).

Greg, W. W., 'The Rationale of the Copy-Text', *Studies in Bibliography*, 3 (1950), 19–36.

Greg, W. W., *Collected Papers*, ed. by J. C. Maxwell (Oxford: Clarendon Press, 1966).

Griffiths, Eric, *The Printed Voice of Victorian Poetry* (Oxford: Clarendon Press, 1989).

Griffiths, Eric, 'On Lines and Grooves from Shakespeare to Tennyson', in *Tennyson among the Poets: Bicentenary Essays*, ed. by Robert Douglas-Fairhurst and Seamus Perry (Oxford: Oxford University Press, 2009), pp. 132–59.

Gurr, Andrew, *The Shakespearean Stage, 1574–1642*, 3rd edn (Cambridge: Cambridge University Press, 1992).

Haddon, John, 'Talk in Life and *Othello*', *Use of English*, 56 (2005), 202–21.

Hall, Peter, *Shakespeare's Advice to the Players* (London: Oberon, 2003).

Hammond, Anthony, 'The Noisy Comma: Searching for the Signal in Renaissance Dramatic Texts', in *Crisis in Editing: Texts of the English Renaissance*, ed. by Randall M Leod [sic] (New York: AMS Press, 1988), pp. 203–50.

Happé, Peter (ed.), *English Mystery Plays*, Penguin Classics (London: Penguin, 1985).

Hardcastle, William J., John Laver, and Fiona E. Gibbon, eds., *The Handbook of Phonetic Sciences*, Blackwell Handbooks in Linguistics, 2nd edn (Chichester: Wiley-Blackwell, 2010).

Harris, Roy, 'The Speech-Communication Model in Twentieth Century Linguistics and Its Sources', in *The Foundations of Linguistic Theory: Selected Writings of Roy Harris*, ed. by Nigel Love (Routledge, 1990), pp. 151–7.

Hasbro, 'Hungry Hungry Hippos Commercial', https://www.youtube.com/watch?v=8HPI_HT6yjo (accessed 27 March 2016).

Heath, Christian, 'The Analysis of Activities in Face to Face Interaction Using Video', in *Qualitative Research: Theory, Method and Practice*, ed. by David Silverman (London: SAGE, 1997), pp. 183–200.

Henry [Toner], Anne C., '"Quid Ais Omnium?" Maurice Kyffin's 1588 "Andria" and the Emergence of Suspension Marks in Printed Drama', *Renaissance Drama*, 34 (2005), 47–67.

Herman, Vimala, 'Dramatic Dialogue and the Systematics of Turn-Taking', *Semiotica*, 83 (1991), 97–122.

Herman, Vimala, *Dramatic Discourse: Dialogue as Interaction in Plays* (London: Routledge, 1995).

Hilbrink, Elma E., Merideth Gattis, and Stephen C. Levinson, 'Early Developmental Changes in the Timing of Turn-Taking: A Longitudinal Study of Mother–Infant Interaction', *Frontiers in Psychology*, 6 (2015), art. no. 1492.

Hinman, Charlton, *The Printing and Proof-Reading of the First Folio of Shakespeare*, 2 vols (Oxford: Clarendon Press, 1963).

Hirsh, James, *The Structure of Shakespearean Scenes* (New Haven: Yale University Press, 1981).

Hirsh, James, *Shakespeare and the History of Soliloquies* (Madison, NJ: Fairleigh Dickinson University Press, 2003).

Hirsh, James, 'The "To Be, or Not to Be" Speech: Evidence, Conventional Wisdom, and the Editing of *Hamlet*', *Medieval and Renaissance Drama In England*, 23 (2010), 34–62.

Hirsh, James, 'Guarded, Unguarded, and Unguardable Speech in Late Renaissance Drama', in *Who Hears in Shakespeare? Auditory Worlds on Stage and Screen*, ed. by Laury Magnus and Walter W. Cannon (Madison: Fairleigh Dickinson University Press, 2012), pp. 17–40.

Holinshed, Raphael, *Chronicles*, 3 vols (London: Henry Denham, 1587).

Honigmann, E. A. J., 'Re-Enter the Stage Direction: Shakespeare and Some Contemporaries', *Shakespeare Survey*, 29 (1976), 117–26.

Hooper, David, and Kenneth Whyld, eds., *The Oxford Companion to Chess*, 2nd ed (Oxford: Oxford University Press, 1992).

Hostettler, John, *Fighting for Justice: The History and Origins of Adversary Trial* (Winchester: Waterside Press, 2006).

Housman, A. E., 'On Soph. Electr. 564, and Eur. I. T. 15 and 35', *The Classical Review*, 1 (1887), 240–1.

Housman, A. E., *The Poems of A. E. Housman*, ed. by Archie Burnett (Oxford: Clarendon Press, 1997).

Howard-Hill, T. H., ed., *Shakespeare and Sir Thomas More: Essays on the Play and Its Shakespearian Interest* (Cambridge: Cambridge University Press, 1989).

Howard-Hill, T. H., 'The Evolution of the Form of Plays in English During the Renaissance', *Renaissance Quarterly*, 43 (1990), 112–45.

Ives, E. W., 'Tudor Dynastic Problems Revisited', *Historical Research*, 81 (2008), 255–79.

Jefferson, Gail, 'Glossary of Transcription Symbols with an Introduction', in *Conversation Analysis: Studies from the First Generation*, ed. by Gene H. Lerner, Pragmatics & Beyond New Series 125 (Amsterdam: John Benjamins, 2004).

Jones, Emrys, *Scenic Form in Shakespeare* (Oxford: Clarendon Press, 1971).

Jones, Emrys, *The Origins of Shakespeare* (Oxford: Clarendon Press, 1977).

Jonson, Ben, *The Comicall Satyre of Euery Man out of His Humor* (London: Adam Islip for William Holme, 1600).

Joseph, Brian D., 'The Editor's Department: Reviewing Our Contents', *Language*, 79 (2003), 461–3.

Kehoe, Alice Beck, and Jim Weil, 'Eliot Chapple's Long and Lonely Road', in *Expanding American Anthropology, 1945–1980: A Generation Reflects*, ed. by Paul L. Doughty, Nancy K. Peske, and Alice Beck Kehoe (Tuscaloosa: University of Alabama Press, 2012), pp. 94–103.

Kliman, Bernice W., ed., *The Enfolded Hamlet*, 1996, http://triggs.djvu.or g/global-language.com/ENFOLDED/ (accessed 3 March 2015).

Kliman, Bernice W., 'Explicit Stage Directions (Especially Graphics) in *Hamlet*', in *Stage Directions in* Hamlet: *New Essays and New Directions*, ed. by Hardin L. Aasand (London: Associated University Presses, 2003), pp. 74–91.

Lamb, Charles, *Charles Lamb on Shakespeare*, ed. by Joan Coldwell (Gerrards Cross: Smythe, 1978).

Lambrou, Marina, 'Stylistics, Conversation Analysis and the Cooperative Principle', in *The Routledge Handbook of Stylistics*, ed. by Michael Burke, Routledge Handbooks in English Language Studies (London: Routledge, 2014), pp. 137–54.

Langbein, John H., *The Origins of Adversary Criminal Trial*, Oxford Studies in Modern Legal History (Oxford: Oxford University Press, 2002).

Lanham, Richard A., *A Handlist of Rhetorical Terms*, 2nd edn (Berkeley: University of California Press, 1991).

Lerner, Gene H., 'Turn-Sharing: The Choral Co-Production of Talk In Interaction', in *The Language of Turn and Sequence*, ed. by Cecilia E. Ford, Barbara A. Fox, and Sandra A. Thompson, Oxford Studies in Sociolinguistics (Oxford: Oxford University Press, 2002), pp. 225–56.

Lerner, Gene H., 'Collaborative Turn Sequences', in *Conversation Analysis: Studies from the First Generation*, ed. by Gene H. Lerner (Amsterdam: John Benjamins, 2004), pp. 225–56.

Lerner, Richard M., ed., *Handbook of Child Psychology and Developmental Science*, 7th edn, 4 vols (Chichester: Wiley, 2015).

Levinson, Stephen C., *Pragmatics*, Cambridge Textbooks in Linguistics (Cambridge: Cambridge University Press, 1983).

Levinson, Stephen C., 'Turn-Taking in Human Communication—Origins and Implications for Language Processing', *Trends in Cognitive Sciences*, 20 (2016), 6–14.

Löfqvist, Anders, 'Theories and Models of Speech Production', in *The Handbook of Phonetic Sciences*, ed. by William J. Hardcastle, John Laver, and

Fiona E. Gibbon, Blackwell Handbooks in Linguistics, 2nd edn (Chichester: Wiley-Blackwell, 2010), pp. 353–77.

Lyne, Raphael, *Shakespeare's Late Work*, Oxford Shakespeare Topics (Oxford: Oxford University Press, 2007).

Lyne, Raphael, 'The Shakespearean Grasp', *The Cambridge Quarterly*, 42 (2013), 38–61.

Magnusson, Lynne, '"Voice Potential": Language and Symbolic Capital in *Othello*', *Shakespeare Survey*, 50 (1997), 91–9.

Magnusson, Lynne, *Shakespeare and Social Dialogue: Dramatic Language and Elizabethan Letters* (Cambridge: Cambridge University Press, 1999).

Magnusson, Lynne, 'Dialogue', in *Reading Shakespeare's Dramatic Language*, ed. by Sylvia Adamson, Lynette Hunter, Katie Wales, Anne Thomson, and Lynne Magnusson, The Arden Shakespeare (London: Thomson Learning, 2001), pp. 130–43.

Magyari, Lilla, Marcel C. M. Bastiaansen, Jan P. de Ruiter, and Stephen C. Levinson, 'Early Anticipation Lies behind the Speed of Response in Conversation', *Journal of Cognitive Neuroscience*, 26 (2014), 2530–9.

Marcus, Leah S., 'Editing Shakespeare in a Postmodern Age', in *A Concise Companion to Shakespeare and the Text*, ed. by Andrew Murphy (Oxford: Blackwell, 2007), pp. 128–44.

McCaughey, 'A Midsommer Night's Mare or What Was Griggs up To?', *Humanities Association Bulletin*, 26 (1975), 225–35.

McKenzie, D. F., 'Shakespearian Punctuation—A New Beginning', *The Review of English Studies*, 10 (1959), 361–70.

McKerrow, Ronald B., *Prolegomena for the Oxford Shakespeare* (Oxford: Clarendon Press, 1939).

Montaigne, Michel de, *The Essayes or Morall, Politike and Millitarie Discourses of Lo: Michaell de Montaigne*, trans. by John Florio (London: Valentine Sims for Edward Blount, 1603).

Moxon, Joseph, *Mechanick Excercises, or, the Doctrine of Handy-Works* (London: Joseph Moxon, 1677).

Munday, Anthony, et al., *Sir Thomas More*, ed. by John Jowett, The Arden Shakespeare (London: Arden Shakespeare, 2011).

Neill, Michael, *Issues of Death: Mortality and Identity in English Renaissance Tragedy* (Oxford: Clarendon Press, 1998).

Nordlund, Marcus, *The Shakespearean Inside: A Study of the Complete Soliloquies and Solo Asides* (Edinburgh: Edinburgh University Press, 2017).

Nuttall, A. D., '*Henry IV*: Prince Hal and Falstaff', in *Modern Critical Interpretations: William Shakespeare's* Henry IV, Part 1, ed. by Harold Bloom (New York: Chelsea House, 1987), pp. 115–34.

O'Connell, Daniel C., Sabine Kowal, and Erika Kaltenbacher, 'Turn-Taking: A Critical Analysis of the Research Tradition', *Journal of Psycholinguistic Research*, 19 (1990), 345–73.

Orgel, Stephen, 'What Is a Character?', *Text*, 8 (1995), 101–8.

Palfrey, Simon, and Tiffany Stern, *Shakespeare in Parts* (Oxford: Oxford University Press, 2010).

Parkes, M. B., *Pause and Effect: An Introduction to the History of Punctuation in the West* (Aldershot: Scolar Press, 1992).

Peacham, Henry, *The Garden of Eloquence*, rev. edn (London: Richard Field for H. Jackson, 1593).

Plutarch, *The Lives of the Noble Grecians and Romanes*, trans. by Thomas North (London: Thomas Vautroullier and John Wight, 1579).

Pope, Alexander, *Poems of Alexander Pope, Volume 1: Pastoral Poetry and an Essay on Criticism*, ed. by E. Audra and Aubrey Williams, The Twickenham Edition of the Poems of Alexander Pope (London: Methuen, 1961).

Puttenham, George, *The Arte of English Poesie* (London: Richard Field, 1589).

Quintilian, *The Orator's Education*, Loeb Classical Library 124–8, 5 vols (Cambridge, MA: Harvard University Press, 2001).

Rackin, Phyllis, 'The Role of the Audience in Shakespeare's *Richard II*', *Shakespeare Quarterly*, 36 (1985), 262–81.

Rackin, Phyllis, *Stages of History: Shakespeare's English Chronicles* (Ithaca, NY: Cornell University Press, 1990).

Replogle, Carol, 'Shakespeare's Salutations: A Study in Stylistic Etiquette', *Studies in Philology*, 70 (1973), 172–86, repr. in *A Reader in the Language of Shakespearean Drama*, ed. by Vivian Salmon and Edwina Burness (Amsterdam: John Benjamins, 1987), pp. 101–15.

Rhetorica Ad Herennium, trans. by Harry Caplan, The Loeb Classical Library 403 (Cambridge, MA: Harvard University Press, 1954).

Rhodes, Neil, *The Power of Eloquence and English Renaissance Literature* (London: Harvester Wheatsheaf, 1991).

Righter [Barton], Anne, *Shakespeare and the Idea of the Play* (London: Chatto & Windus, 1962).

Rokison, Abigail, *Shakespearean Verse Speaking: Text and Theatre Practice* (Cambridge: Cambridge University Press, 2009).

Rokison, Abigail, 'Laurence Olivier', in *Gielgud, Olivier, Ashcroft, Dench*, ed. by Russell Jackson, Great Shakespeareans 16 (London: Bloomsbury, 2013), 61–109.

Sacks, Harvey, *Lectures on Conversation*, ed. by Gail Jefferson, 2 vols (Oxford: Blackwell, 1992).

Sacks, Harvey, Emanuel A. Schegloff, and Gail Jefferson, 'A Simplest Systematics for the Organization of Turn-Taking for Conversation', *Language*, 50 (1974), 696–735.

Sacks, Harvey, Emanuel A. Schegloff, and Gail Jefferson, 'L'organizzazione Della Presa Di Turno Nella Conversazione', in *Linguaggio e Contesto Sociale*, ed. by R. Giglioli and G Fele (Bologna: Il Mulino, 2000), pp. 97–135.

Saul, Nigel, 'Richard II and the Vocabulary of Kingship', *The English Historical Review*, 110 (1995), 854–77.

Saussure, Ferdinand de, *Saussure's Third Course of Lectures on General Linguistics (1910–11): From the Notebooks of Emile Constantin*, ed. by Eisuke Komatsu, trans. by Roy Harris (Oxford: Pergamon Press, 1993).

Schegloff, Emanuel A., 'Goffman and the Analysis of Conversation', in *Erving Goffman: Exploring the Interaction Order*, ed. by Paul Drew and Anthony J. Wootton (Cambridge: Polity Press, 1988), pp. 89–135.

Schegloff, Emanuel A., 'On the Organization of Sequences as a Source of "Coherence" in Talk-in-Interaction', in *Conversational Organization and Its Development*, ed. by Bruce Dorval (Norwood, NJ: Ablex, 1990), pp. 51–77.

Schegloff, Emanuel A., 'Overlapping Talk and the Organization of Turn-Taking for Conversation', *Language in Society*, 29 (2000), 1–63.

Schegloff, Emanuel A., *A Primer in Conversation Analysis, Volume 1: Sequence Organization in Interaction* (Cambridge: Cambridge University Press, 2007).

Schegloff, Emanuel A., 'Conversational Interaction: The Embodiment of Human Sociality', in *The Handbook of Discourse Analysis*, ed. by Deborah Tannen, Heidi E. Hamilton, and Deborah Schiffrin, Blackwell Handbooks in Linguistics, 2nd edn (Chichester: Wiley-Blackwell, 2015).

Schegloff, Emanuel A., and Harvey Sacks, 'Opening up Closings', *Semiotica*, 8 (2009), 289–327.

Shakespeare, William, *A Midsommer Nights Dreame* [Q1] (Richard Bradbrook for Thomas Fisher, 1600).

Shakespeare, William, *A Midsommer nights dreame*, ed. by Text Creation Partnership, Early English Books Online, Q1 edn (Richard Bradbrook for Thomas Fisher, 1600), http://gateway.proquest.com/openurl?ctx_ver=Z39.88-2003&res_id=xri:eebo&rft_id=xri:eebo:citation:99846577 (accessed 16 November 2015).

Shakespeare, William, *The Tragicall Historie of Hamlet Prince of Denmarke* [Q1] (London: Valentine Simmes for Nicholas Ling and John Trundell, 1603).

Shakespeare, William, *The Tragicall Historie of Hamlet, Prince of Denmarke* [Q2] (London: James Roberts for Nicholas Ling, 1604).

Shakespeare, William, *M. William Shak-Speare: His True Chronicle Historie of the Life and Death of King Lear* [Q1] (London: Nicholas Okes for Nathaniel Butter, 1608).

Shakespeare, William, *The Famous Historie of Troylus and Cresseid* [Q] (London: G. Eld for R. Bonian and H. Walley, 1609).

Shakespeare, William, *M. VVilliam Shake-Speare, His True Chronicle History of the Life and Death of King Lear* [Q2] (London: William Jaggard for Nathaniel Butter, 1619).

Shakespeare, William, *A Midsommer Nights Dreame* [Q2] (London: William Jaggard for T. Pavier, 1619).

Shakespeare, William, *The Tragoedy of Othello, the Moore of Venice* (London: Nicholas Okes for Thomas Walkley, 1622).

Shakespeare, William, *Mr. VVilliam Shakespeares Comedies, Histories, & Tragedies* [F1, Folio] (London: Isaac Iaggard and Ed. Blount, 1623).

Shakespeare, William, *The Works of Mr. William Shakespear*, ed. by Nicholas Rowe, 6 vols (London: Jacob Tonson, 1709).

Shakespeare, William, *The Works of Shakespear*, ed. by Alexander Pope, 6 vols (London: Jacob Tonson, 1725).

Shakespeare, William, *The Works of Shakespeare*, ed. by Lewis Theobald, 8 vols (London: A. Bettesworth, et al., 1733).

Shakespeare, William, *The Works of Shakespeare*, ed. by Lewis Theobald, 2nd edn, 8 vols (London: H. Lintott et al., 1740).

Shakespeare, William, *The Plays: Of William Shakespeare, in Eight Volumes*, ed. by Samuel Johnson, 8 vols (London: J. and R. Tonson et al., 1765).

Shakespeare, William, *Twenty of the plays of Shakespeare*, ed. by George Steevens (London: J. & R. Tonson et al., 1766).

Shakespeare, William, *Mr William Shakespeare His Comedies, Histories, and Tragedies*, ed. by Edward Capell, 10 vols (London: Dryden Leach for J. and R. Tonson, 1768).

Shakespeare, William, *The Plays of Shakespeare*, ed. by Howard Staunton, 3 vols (London: Routledge, 1858).

Shakespeare, William, *The Plays of Shakespeare*, ed. by Charles and Mary Cowden Clarke, Cassell's Illustrated Shakespeare, 3 vols (London: Cassell, Petter, & Galpin, 1864–8).

Shakespeare, William, *Shakespeare's Midsummer Night's Dream. The first quarto, 1600*, ed. by William Griggs (London: W. Griggs, 1880).

Shakespeare, William, *The Tempest*, ed. by H. H. Furness, A New Variorum Edition of Shakespeare (Philadelphia: J. B. Lippincott, 1892).

Shakespeare, William, *The Works of Shakespeare*, ed. by Arthur Quiller-Couch and John Dover Wilson, 39 vols (Cambridge: Cambridge University Press, 1921–66).

Shakespeare, William, *The Tempest*, ed. by G. L. Kittredge, The Kittredge Shakespeares (Boston: Ginn & Co, 1939).

Shakespeare, William, *The Tempest*, ed. by Frank Kermode, The Arden Shakespeare: Second Series (London: Methuen, 1954).

Shakespeare, William, *The Tragedy of Coriolanus*, ed. by John Dover Wilson, The Cambridge Shakespeare (Cambridge: Cambridge University Press, 1960).

Shakespeare, William, *Coriolanus*, ed. by Philip Brockbank, The Arden Shakespeare: Second Series (London: Methuen, 1976).

Shakespeare, William, *Shakespeare's Plays in Quarto: A Facsimile Edition of Copies Primarily from the Henry E. Huntington Library*, ed. by Michael J. B Allen and Kenneth Muir (Berkeley: University of California Press, 1981).

Shakespeare, William, *The Complete Works: Original-Spelling Edition*, ed. by Stanley Wells and Gary Taylor (Oxford: Clarendon, 1986).

Shakespeare, William, *The Tempest*, ed. by Stephen Orgel, The Oxford Shakespeare (Oxford: Oxford University Press, 1986).

Shakespeare, William, *Henry IV, Part One*, ed. by David Bevington, The Oxford Shakespeare (Oxford: Oxford University Press, 1987).

Shakespeare, William, *Antony and Cleopatra*, ed. by David M. Bevington, The New Cambridge Shakespeare (Cambridge: Cambridge University Press, 1990).

Shakespeare, William, *The Tragedy of King Lear*, The New Cambridge Shakespeare (Cambridge: Cambridge University Press, 1992).

Shakespeare, William, *King Lear: A Parallel Text Edition*, ed. by René Weis, Longman Annotated Texts (London: Longman, 1993).

Shakespeare, William, *Antony and Cleopatra*, ed. by John Wilders, The Arden Shakespeare: Third Series (London: Routledge, 1995).

Shakespeare, William, *The First Folio of Shakespeare: The Norton Facsimile*, ed. by Charlton Hinman, 2nd edn (New York: Norton, 1996).

Shakespeare, William, *The Tempest*, ed. by Virginia Mason Vaughan and Alden T. Vaughan, The Arden Shakespeare: Third Series (London: Thomson Learning, 1999).

Shakespeare, William, *The First Quarto of King Lear*, ed. by Jay L. Halio, The New Cambridge Shakespeare: The Early Quartos (Cambridge: Cambridge University Press, 1996).

Shakespeare, William, *King Lear: The 1608 Quarto and 1623 Folio Texts*, ed. by Stephen Orgel, The Pelican Shakespeare (New York: Penguin, 2000).

Shakespeare, William, *The Tempest*, ed. by Christine Dymkowski, Shakespeare in Production (Cambridge: Cambridge University Press, 2000).

Shakespeare, William, *The First Quarto of Othello*, ed. by Scott McMillin (Cambridge University Press, 2001).

Shakespeare, William, *King Henry IV, Part One*, ed. by David Scott Kastan, The Arden Shakespeare: Third Series (London: Thomson Learning, 2002).

Shakespeare, William, *The Complete Works*, ed. by Stanley Wells and Gary Taylor, The Oxford Shakespeare, 2nd edn (Oxford: Oxford University Press, 2005).

Shakespeare, William, *Complete Works*, ed. by Jonathan Bate and Eric Rasmussen, The RSC Shakespeare (Basingstoke: Macmillan, 2007).

Shakespeare, William, *Richard II*, ed. by Anthony B. Dawson and Paul Yachnin, The Oxford Shakespeare (Oxford: Oxford University Press, 2011).

Shakespeare, William, *A Midsummer Night's Dream (Quarto 1, 1600)*, ed. by Suzanne Westfall, Internet Shakespeare Editions (University of Victoria), http://internetshakespeare.uvic.ca/doc/MND_Q1/scene/5.1/ (accessed 16 November 2015).

Shakespeare, William, *The Complete Works: Critical Reference Edition*, ed. by Gary Taylor, Gabriel Egan, John Jowett, and Terri Bourus, The New Oxford Shakespeare, 2 vols (Oxford: Oxford University Press, 2017).

Shakespeare, William, *The Complete Works: Modern Critical Edition*, ed. by Gary Taylor, Gabriel Egan, John Jowett, and Terri Bourus, The New Oxford Shakespeare (Oxford: Oxford University Press, 2017).

Sherry, Richard, *A Treatise of the Figures of Grammer and Rhetorike* (London: Robert Caly[?] for Richard Tottel, 1555).

Short, Mick, *Exploring the Language of Poems, Plays, and Prose*, Learning about Language (London: Longman, 1996).

Sidnell, Jack, and Tanya Stivers, eds., *The Handbook of Conversation Analysis* (Chichester: Wiley-Blackwell, 2013).

Simpson, Percy, *Shakespearian Punctuation* (Oxford: Clarendon Press, 1911).

Skinner, Quentin, *Forensic Shakespeare* (Oxford: Oxford University Press, 2014).

Smith, Thomas, *De Republica Anglorum* (London: Henry Middleton for Gregory Seton, 1583).

Sprinchorn, Evert, *On Punctuation in Shakespeare's Plays* (Poughkeepsie, NY: Printer's Press, 2011).

Stanford, William, *An Exposicion of the Kinges Prerogatiue* (London: Richard Tottel, 1567).

Stern, Tiffany, *Rehearsal from Shakespeare to Sheridan* (Oxford: Oxford University Press, 2000).

Stern, Tiffany, *Documents of Performance in Early Modern England* (Cambridge: Cambridge University Press, 2009).

Stivers, Tanya, N. J. Enfield, Penelope Brown, Christina Englert, Makoto Hayashi, Trine Heinemann, et al., 'Universals and Cultural Variation in Turn-Taking in Conversation', *Proceedings of the National Academy of Sciences*, 106 (2009), 10587–92.

Tannen, Deborah, 'The Relativity of Linguistic Strategies: Rethinking Power and Solidarity in Gender and Dominance', in *Gender and Conversational Interaction*, ed. by Deborah Tannen (Oxford: Oxford University Press, 1993), pp. 165–88.

Taylor, Gary, 'The Folio Copy for *Hamlet, King Lear*, and *Othello*', *Shakespeare Quarterly*, 34 (1983), 44–61.

Taylor, Gary, and Gabriel Egan, eds., *Authorship Companion*, The New Oxford Shakespeare (Oxford: Oxford University Press, 2017).

Taylor, Talbot J., and Deborah Cameron, *Analysing Conversation: Rules and Units in the Structure of Talk*, Language & Communication Library (Oxford: Pergamon, 1987).

Tillyard, E. M. W., *Shakespeare's History Plays* (London: Chatto & Windus, 1944).

Toner, Anne, *Ellipsis in English Literature: Signs of Omission* (Cambridge: Cambridge University Press, 2015).

Van Es, Bart, *Shakespeare in Company* (Oxford: Oxford University Press, 2013).

Vickers, Brian, *In Defence of Rhetoric* (Oxford: Clarendon Press, 1988).

Vickers, Brian, 'Incomplete Shakespeare: Or, Denying Coauthorship in *1 Henry VI*', *Shakespeare Quarterly*, 58 (2007), 311–52.

Vine, Angus, '"A Trim Reckoning": Accountability and Authority in *1* and *2 Henry IV*', in *Shakespeare and Authority*, ed. by Katie Halsey and Angus Vine (London: Palgrave Macmillan, 2018), pp. 157–78.

Vygotsky, Lev, *Thought and Language*, trans. by Alex Kozulin, rev. edn (Cambridge, Mass.: The MIT Press, 1986).

Wales, Kathleen M., 'Thou and You in Early Modern English: Brown and Gilman Re-Appraised', *Studia Linguistica*, 37 (1983), 107–25.

Werstine, Paul, 'Line Division in Shakespeare's Dramatic Verse: An Editorial Problem', *Analytical and Enumerative Bibliography*, 8 (1984), 73–125.

Werstine, Paul, *Early Modern Playhouse Manuscripts and the Editing of Shakespeare* (Cambridge: Cambridge University Press, 2013).

Wilson, Thomas, *The Arte of Rhetorique* (London: Richard Grafton, 1553).

Wilson, Thomas P., John M. Wiemann, and Don H. Zimmerman, 'Models of Turn Taking in Conversational Interaction', *Journal of Language and Social Psychology*, 3 (1984), 159–83.

Wright, George T., *Shakespeare's Metrical Art* (Berkeley: University of California Press, 1988).

Zimmerman, Don H., and Candace West, 'Sex Roles, Interruptions and Silences in Conversation', in *Language and Sex: Difference and Dominance*, ed. by Barrie Thorne and Nancy Henley (Rowley, MA: Newbury House, 1975), pp. 105–29.

INDEX

Abbott, E. A. 243–4
Adamson, Sylvia 161, *see also* Adamson, Alexander, and Ettenhuber
Adamson, Alexander, and Ettenhuber, *Renaissance Figures of Speech* 161, 166–9
addition (figure of dialogue) 175, 177–8, 181–3
address
  as means of selecting next speaker 31–42 *see also* selection
  terms of 13, 81–2, 87
  see also addressivity
addressivity 51–3, 88–90, 114–15, 117–21, 240
adjacency pair 24, 32–4, 237–8 *see also* summons-response
allocation (of turns at talk)
  local 28–9, 31–5
  pre- 28–31
  see also sequence, selection, orchestration
altercation (legal term) 80, 93–4, 98, 209–10
aposiopesis 160–6, 168–71, 173–7, 187, 202–3, 214–15 *see also* suspension, interruption
apostrophe (figure of dialogue) 47–9, 51, 75, 178, 187, 246
aside (dramatic convention) 52–3, 103, 240
  addressivity 114–23
  audibility 103–4, 106–15
  as representation of unspoken thought 123–31
  editorial history 76, 104–5, 111–12
  liminality 115, 240
  in medieval drama 116, 123
  monological versus dialogical 106–7
  relation to turns at talk 105–6, 115–16, 131–2

d'Aubignac, abbé (François Hédelin) 106–7, 127–8
audibility 52–3, 214 *see also* asides
Austen, Jane, *Pride and Prejudice* 40–2

Bakhtin, Mikhail 52–3, 59, 138–9, 142–3
Baldwin, T. W. 162
Bate, Jonathan and Eric Rasmussen (editors) 105, 232
Barton, Anne 116
Beckett, Samuel
  Endgame 103–7
  Happy Days 105
Bevington, David 229–32
Bertram, Paul 230–1
blanking (figure of dialogue) 46–9, 57–9, 91, 109–10, 114–15, 178, 227–8
Blayney, Peter W. M. 194, 202n.25, 206–7, 209n.45, 219
Bliss, Lee 156
Boccaccio, Giovanni, *Decameron* 22, 28
Book of Common Prayer 30–1, 101
Booth, Stephen 90–1
Bourdieu, Pierre 59–60, 63, 65–6
Burrow, Colin 155–6

Capell, Edward 76–8, 82, 85–6, 88–90, 193, 230
Castiglione, Baldassare, *The Book of the Courtier* 22
Chapple, Eliot D. 135–41, 148, 152, 155–7, 178–9
Chaucer, Geoffrey, *The Canterbury Tales* 4n.5, 21–3, 28, 32
Cisoux, Hélène 188
Clayman, Stephen E. 227n.6, 245
clusivity 52–3, 81–2, 89–90 *see also* addressivity, plural of majesty
cognition 37–8, 141–2
Coleridge, Samuel Taylor 242, 246